Benjamin Jenks, Charles Simeon

Prayers and offices of devotion

For families and for particular persons

Benjamin Jenks, Charles Simeon

Prayers and offices of devotion

For families and for particular persons

ISBN/EAN: 9783337278403

Printed in Europe, USA, Canada, Australia, Japan

Cover: Foto ©Lupo / pixelio.de

More available books at **www.hansebooks.com**

PRAYERS

AND

OFFICES OF DEVOTION;

FOR FAMILES, AND FOR PARTICULAR PERSONS,
UPON MOST OCCASIONS.

By BENJAMIN JENKS.

A NEW EDITION, ALTERED AND IMPROVED

BY THE

REV. CHARLES SIMEON.

LONDON:
T. NELSON AND SONS, PATERNOSTER ROW;
EDINBURGH; AND NEW YORK.

MDCCCLXI.

CONTENTS.

STATED PRAYERS.

MORNING.

	Page		Page
First	9	Fifth	19
Second	12	Sixth	22
Third	14	Seventh	26
Fourth	17		

EVENING.

First	28	Fifth	44
Second	32	Sixth	48
Third	35	Seventh	53
Fourth	39		

SABBATH MORNING.

First	57	Mid-day	63
Second	59		

EVENING.

First	66	Second	69

PUBLIC AND GENERAL OCCASIONS.

BEFORE RECEIVING THE SACRAMENT.

A Confession from the Commandments	74	A Prayer	81

AT THE SACRAMENT.

Ejaculations before receiving	86	Ejaculations after receiving	89

AFTER THE SACRAMENT.

A Prayer	92	A Dedication	95

CONTENTS.

FAST DAYS.

(SEE PAGE 74.)

	Page		Page
Morning	97	Evening	103

HOLY SEASONS.

The Incarnation of Christ......109
The Death of Christ...............111
The Resurrection of Christ.....114
The Ascension of Christ.........116
The Descent of the Holy Ghost......117
The Commemoration of any Saint......119

PRIVATE AND PARTICULAR OCCASIONS

UNDER AFFLICTIVE CIRCUMSTANCES—OF A TEMPORAL NATURE.

Abuses and Provocations......121
Infamy and Disgrace............124
Crosses and Disappointments..126
Difficulties and Perplexities...127
Losses and Damages.............128
Imminent Dangers................129
Bodily Accidents..................131
Confinement and Loss of Liberty......133
Death of Neighbours............135
Death of dear Friends..........136

OF A SPIRITUAL NATURE.

A Review of Past Sins.........138
Conviction of Sin................139
A Dread of God's Wrath.......144
Doubts and Fears................146
Temptations......................148
Backslidings.....................150
Relapse into gross Sin.........152

UNDER PROSPEROUS CIRCUMSTANCES.

For Temporal Blessings.........156
In a State of Prosperity.........157
In Prospect of Marriage.........159
On undertaking any great Enterprise......161
When going from Home.......163

FOR PARTICULAR GRACES AND BLESSINGS.

Illumination and Knowledge..164
Faith 167
Prayer for Power to live upon the Promises......168
Repentance......................174
Humility..........................176
Tenderness of Heart............178

CONTENTS.

OBEDIENCE.

	Page		Page
Fear of God	180	Meekness	190
Love of God	182	Patience	192
Hope in God	185	Mortification of Sin	194
Love to Man	187	Sincerity	196
Chastity	188		

INCREASING SANCTIFICATION.

Increase of Grace	199	Constancy in the profession of Religion	220
Quickening Grace	201	Zeal in the practice of it	222
Assisting Grace	202	Delight in God's Service	225
Before hearing the Word	204	Wisdom to fill up our station	226
After hearing the Word	205	Wisdom to conduct ourselves aright	228
Mindfulness of God's presence	207		
A devout Frame	209	Wisdom to use our speech aright	231
Communion with God	210		
Comfort	213	Persevering Grace	233
Heavenly-Mindedness	215	Preparation for Death	235
Earnestness in the pursuit of Religion	217		

PRAYERS FOR THE USE OF PARTICULAR PERSONS.

A Minister	237	The Rich	253
A Magistrate	240	The Poor	256
A Husband	243	A Master	258
A Wife	245	A Servant	260
A Widow	246	A Soldier	263
An Orphan	248	A Sailor	266
An Aged Person	249	A condemned Malefactor	268
A Child	251		

INTERCESSIONS.

GENERAL.

The Prosperity of the Church of Christ	272	The Queen and all our Rulers	280
Reformed Churches abroad	274	The Bishops and Ministers	283
Our own Church	276	Societies for the Reformation of Manners	285
Unity among Christians	279		

CONTENTS.

PRAYERS FOR THE NATION AT LARGE.

	Page		Page
War	288	Friends, that are pious	301
Public Commotions	290	Friends, that appear unconverted	302
Infection	292		
Drought	293	Children	305
Excessive Rains	294	Parents	306
Famine	295	Enemies	307
Thunder or Tempests	296	The Unconverted	309
Calamities of any kind	298	Hardened Sinners	313
Benefactors	300	All that desire our Prayers	315

PARTICULAR INTERCESSIONS.

A woman in Travail	317	One in Great Pain	330
A Sick Child	318	One under Lingering Sickness	332
One Melancholy and dejected	319		
One in Trouble of Soul	321	One under Dangerous Sickness	333
One Lunatic and distracted	323		
One Stupified or Light-headed	325	One Dying	336
One Blind	327		

THANKSGIVINGS.

GENERAL.

Temporal Blessings	338	Victory over our Enemies	341
Rain	339	Peace	342
Fair Weather	ib.	On a Public Thanksgiving Day	343
Infection Removed	ib.		
Plenty Restored	340		

PARTICULAR TEMPORAL BLESSINGS.

A safe and good Journey	346	Deliverance from Travail	351
Deliverance from Dangers and Troubles	348	Recovery from Sickness	352

PARTICULAR SPIRITUAL BLESSINGS.

Conversion	355	A Prayer in the Order of the Lord's Prayer	361
Recovery from Backsliding	358		
Spiritual Victory	360	A Soliloquy, by way of Paraphrase on the Creed	367

PRAYERS

AND

OFFICES OF DEVOTION.

FIRST MORNING PRAYER FOR A FAMILY.

O LORD, thou God of our salvation! Thou art the hope of all the ends of the earth; upon thee the eyes of all do wait: for thou givest unto all life, and breath, and all things. In thee we ever live, and move, and are; and upon thee we continually depend for all the good that we either have, or hope for. Still thou watchest over us for good, and takest care of us in our sleep, when we are incapable of caring for ourselves: daily thou renewest to us thy tender mercies: every morning affords us fresh occasions for praise and thanksgiving. And thou hast assured us by thy word, that, if we commit our affairs to thee, and acknowledge thee in all our ways, thou wilt establish our thoughts, and direct our path. We desire therefore, O Lord, still to put ourselves under thy gracious conduct, and thy fatherly protection: and we beg the guidance, and blessing, and assistance of thy good Spirit, to choose our inheritance for us; and to dispose of us, and of all that concerns us, to the glory of thy name.

O Lord, withdraw not thy tender mercies from us; take not away the comforts of thy presence, or the assistance of thy Spirit, on account of our manifold abuses of thy grace and goodness. Never punish our past sins, by giving us over to the love and power of our sins: but give us truly penitent hearts, and grant us thy merciful discharge from all the guilt that lies upon us. And grant us, O good God, the comfortable sense of thine acceptance of us in the Son of thy love, that our souls may bless thee, and all that is within us may praise thy holy name.

And O that we may find the joy of the Lord to be our strength; that we may be strengthened by it against all our sins; especially the sins to which we are most addicted, and whereof we are most in danger: make us also more ready to every good work, and better disposed for all the duties which we owe to Thee, our neighbour and ourselves; that herein we may exercise ourselves, to have always a conscience void of offence, towards God, and towards men.

O help us to walk circumspectly, not as fools, but as wise; carefully redeeming the time that we have lost, and conscientiously improving all those seasons of grace which thou art pleased to put into our hands. And while we are upon earth, O give us all things needful and convenient for our present pilgrimage: sanctify to us all our enjoyments, and all our occupations in the world: let our crosses also, and our comforts, and all events that now befall us, be improved to thy glory; till, through the merits of thy Son, and the multitude of thy mercies, we are conducted safely to be ever with the Lord. Amidst all our other affairs in this world, O let us never forget or neglect the *one thing needful;* but may it be our principal care so to demean ourselves every day, that we may give up our account with joy in the great day of thine appearing.

O gracious Father! keep us, we beseech thee, this day in thy fear and favour; and help us to live to thine honour and glory. If thou guide us not, we shall run into errors; if thou preserve us not, we shall fall into dangers. O let thy good Providence be our defence and security: and let thy Holy Spirit be our guide and counsellor in all our ways. And grant that we may do those things which are agreeable to thy will, and acceptable in thy sight, through Jesus Christ; in whose sacred name and words, we close our imperfect petitions. *Our Father,* &c.

Let thy grace, O Lord Jesus Christ; thy love, O heavenly Father; thy comfortable fellowship, O holy blessed Spirit, be with us, and with all the Israel of God, this day, and for evermore. *Amen.*

A SECOND MORNING PRAYER FOR A FAMILY.

O LORD, thou art the God, whose we are and whom we ought to serve, with all the abilities wherewith thou hast blessed us. We are bound by all the obligations of thy laws, and by all the endearments of thy love, to be faithful in the covenant of our God, and to abound in the work of the Lord. But we desire to humble ourselves before thee, that our lives have been so unserviceable to thee, and so full of provocation against thee: that the dishonour which we have done thee, O Lord, has so far exceeded all our services; that we have lived to ourselves, rather than to thee; and have served our own lusts and pleasures, more than thy holy blessed will. O how have we disbelieved thy truths, disobeyed thy commands, disregarded thy promises and threats! How have we resisted and defeated all the gracious methods, which thou hast used to reclaim us from our evil ways, and to bring us over to thyself.

We have sinned against thee our God, and done infinite wrong and damage to our own souls: by our sins we have spoiled and destroyed ourselves. But it is not in us, O Lord, to recover and save ourselves: in thee, O heavenly Father, in thee alone, is all our help. Yea, thou hast laid help upon One that is mighty, and that is able to save to the uttermost all that come to Thee through him: through him thou hast encouraged us to come boldly to the throne of grace, that we may obtain mercy, and find grace to help in every time of need. In him, therefore, we beg, O Lord, that thou wilt be reconciled to us, and make thyself known to us as a Father of mercies, and a God of all consolation.

For his sake, enable us also (we beseech thee) to demean ourselves as becomes the children of God, and the members and followers of Christ. O put such principles of grace and holiness into our hearts, as may make us to hate all iniquity, and to abhor every false way. Put thy Spirit within us, causing us to walk in thy statutes, and to keep thy judgments, and to do them. Do not merely lay thy commands upon us; but be pleased, O Lord, to enable us for the performance of them. And so quicken us by thy grace, that we may make it our meat and drink to do thy will; and may run the way of thy commandments with enlarged hearts. O make our *services acceptable* to thee while we live; and our *souls ready* for thee when we die. And as long as we are in this world, keep us, O Lord our God, from the evil of it, and from the snares and dangers to which thou knowest we are continually exposed. O make our passage safe through all the changes, troubles, and temptations of this mortal life, and bring us finally to the unchangeable glories and felicities of the eternal world.

Be merciful to us, good Lord, and bless us, and keep us this day, in all our ways. Let us take nothing in hand which is not warranted by thy word. O let us be in the fear of the Lord all the day long: let thy fear be ever before our eyes to restrain us from the things which are displeasing to thee, and destructive to our own souls. And let thy love abound in our hearts, and sweetly and powerfully constrain us to perform whatever is acceptable in thy sight, through him that hath loved and redeemed us, even the Lord our righteousness: in whose blessed name and words we continue praying, *Our Father,* &c.

The blessing of God Almighty, Father, Son, and Holy Ghost, be with us, and with all that belong to us, this day, and for evermore. *Amen.*

A THIRD MORNING PRAYER.

O LORD God, merciful and gracious, long-suffering, and abundant in goodness and truth! thou keepest mercy for thousands; thou pardonest iniquity, transgression, and sin; thou retainest not thine anger for ever, because thou delightest in mercy; how excellent is thy loving-kindness, O God! therefore do the sons of men put their trust under the shadow of thy wings; and therefore do we desire still to look up to that bountiful hand of thine, from whence we have received all our good things. O Lord our God! be thou pleased to look down mercifully upon us, and be gracious and favourable to us, as thou usest to be unto those that love thy name. O look not upon the sin of our nature, nor the sins of our hearts and lives, which are more than we can remember, and greater than we can express; behold, we are vile; we are exceeding guilty; we acknowledge that it is of thy mercies we are not consumed, even because thy compassions fail not. But look upon us in mercy, through the merits and mediation of thy Son our Saviour; pity us for his sake who did no sin, and was manifested to take away our sins: by him let us have access to thy Majesty; and for his sake bestow upon us the blessings which we so greatly need. Thou hast treasured up in Him an infinite fulness of all that we can ever want or wish: O that we may all receive out of his fulness grace sufficient for us! Let us receive from him those gifts which He is now empowered and commissioned to bestow; those gifts which are the purchase of his blood, and the necessary means of our salvation. Pour down upon us the abundance of thy grace. Accept and justify our persons; renew and sanctify our souls; and so transform us into thy blessed image, that we may be meet to be partakers of the inheritance of thy saints in light.

Teach us, O Lord our God, to use this world without abusing it, and to enjoy the things of it, without suffering them to engross our affections. Whatever we have of the world, O let it be sanctified to us by the word of God, and prayer. And whatsoever we want of the things of this life, O Lord our heavenly Father, leave us not destitute of those things that accompany salvation: but do thou adorn our souls with all the graces of thy Holy Spirit, that we may glorify thee in all things, and that our conversation may be such as becometh the Gospel of Christ.

Help us, O gracious Lord, in the whole of our duty to thee our God; and also in the discharge of all relative duties which we owe to men, whether superiors, equals, or inferiors; enable us to walk wisely toward them which are without, and kindly toward them that are within. Let us never cast a stumbling-block in the way of others, or cause thy holy name to be blasphemed through our misconduct: but let us pass the time of our sojourning here in fear; that, having glorified thee on earth, we may be glorified by thee in the great day of our Lord Jesus Christ.

And now that thou hast renewed thy mercies to us this morning, help us gracious God, to renew our desires and endeavours to serve and honour thee. O restrain us from the evils and follies into which we are prone to fall; and quicken us to the offices and duties which we are averse to perform. And grant that we may think, and speak, and act as becometh saints; ever remembering that we are bought with the precious blood of Christ, and ever striving to live unto him, who died for us and rose again; to whom, with the Father and the Holy Ghost, be glory and honour world without end. *Amen. Our Father,* &c.

A FOURTH MORNING PRAYER.

O LORD GOD, that hearest prayer, and art nigh to all that call upon thee in truth, we are moved by our own necessities, and encouraged by thy daily mercies, to renew our supplications at the throne of thy grace. And we beg of thee, who fashionest all the hearts of the sons of men, to prepare our hearts, that we may now come into thy holy presence, and call upon thy blessed name in a due and acceptable manner. O! pour upon us the spirit of grace and of supplication; let thy good Spirit help our infirmities; and teach us to ask such things, and in such a way, as shall be most agreeable to thy will, and most advantageous to our souls.

Behold! we, who are but poor worms, and sinful dust and ashes, have taken upon us now to speak unto thee, the sovereign Majesty of heaven and earth: we have too just cause to be afraid lest our great and manifold sins should have provoked thee to hide thy face from us, and to shut up thy loving-kindness in displeasure. We know that we have done wickedly, in not hearkening to the calls of thy word, or yielding to the motions of thy Spirit. Our iniquities are increased over our heads; our trespass is grown up even unto heaven; and our sins are a sore burden, too heavy for us to bear. If thou, O Lord, shouldst enter into judgment with us for our actions, we could not answer thee for one of a thousand; we must lay our hands upon our mouths, and plead guilty before thee, and place our whole dependence upon thy mercy.

O God, be merciful to us, miserable sinners: for the sake of Him, whom thou hast exalted to be a Prince and a Saviour, to give repentance to thy people, and forgiveness of sins, be merciful to us, we pray thee; and heal our souls, that have greatly sinned against thee. O heal our backslidings, renew us to repentance, and establish our goings in thy holy ways: let us not be so wavering, and bent to backslide; let us not so revolt from thee, and return to folly after thou hast spoken peace unto us; but may we go on conquering and to conquer all the enemies of our souls; till every obstacle to our salvation be surmounted, and Satan himself be bruised under our feet.

O thou God of all grace! bring such thoughts to our minds, and lay such considerations upon our hearts, as thou knowest will effectually keep us from our iniquity, and prevail with us to do thy will: put thy fear in our hearts, that we may not any more depart from thee; and preserve us holy and unblameable unto the coming of our Lord Jesus Christ. In the mean time sanctify to us all the dispensations of thy Providence, and bless us in every condition and relation of life. Make us humble in an high estate, or contented in a low one; nor let us ever forget, that the care of our souls is the *one thing needful.* O make us mindful of this, that we may follow incessantly those things which shall bring us peace at the last.

Dispose of us, we beseech, and of all that concerns us, to the glory of thy name. O keep us at all times, and in all places and companies, from the evil of sin, and from all other evils to which the greatness of our sins has made us liable. And take thou, O heavenly Father, the gracious charge and government of us this day; and so guide us by thy counsel, that hereafter thou mayest receive us to glory. All this we ask through thy tender mercies, and our Saviour's abundant merits; in whose own words, we beg all things needful for ourselves and others, at thy hands. *Our Father,* &c.

A FIFTH MORNING PRAYER.

O LORD our God! thy name is most excellent in all the earth: thou hast set up thy glory above the heavens, and thou art worthy to be celebrated with everlasting praises of men and angels: for thou hast created all things, and for thy pleasure they are, and were created. Thy hands, O Lord, have made us and fashioned us; and thou hast breathed into our nostrils the breath of life; yea, still thou holdest our souls in life, and givest us every good thing that makes our life a blessing and comfort to us. Thou hast formed us for thyself that we should show forth thy praise, and that we should live to thy glory, as we do live continually upon thy bounty.

But, O Lord our God! we have in no respect glorified thee as we ought: yea, rather, how greatly have we dishonoured thee in the whole course of our lives! Time after time have we forgotten thee, the gracious giver of all our good things, who art never unmindful of us. O how soon have we been weary of doing thee service, who art never weary of doing us good! We have not only neglected thy word, but have been disobedient to thy word, and have walked after our own foolish and hurtful lusts, which might long since have drowned us in destruction and perdition.

For these things we desire to pour out our hearts, and to humble our sinful selves here before thee; and for the sake of that mercy of thine in Christ Jesus, which has moved thee to spare us so long, and to do so much for us already, we intreat thee to pity us. Give us repentance and pardon for all that is past, wherein we have offended thee; whether in omitting our duty, or failing in it, or doing contrary to it. Howsoever we have transgressed, O humble us duly under the sense of it; and, for thy dear Son's sake, absolve us thoroughly from the guilt of it.

And strengthen us, good Lord, with might by thy Spirit in the inner man; that we may be more watchful against temptation, and more victorious over our corruptions. O destroy in us every vicious inclination, every evil habit, every rebellious motion, that exalts itself against the knowledge of God, and of Christ Jesus our Lord. And increase and confirm in us, still more and more, the graces of thy Holy Spirit, especially those which thou knowest to be most wanting in us, and most necessary for us. Fill us with the knowledge of thy will, with faith in thy promises, and with the fear and love of thy holy name. Give us whatsoever shall make our lives more comfortable to ourselves, more profitable to others, and more honourable to thee our God. And, whatever be our condition as to the concerns of this present time, may we still be found in the way of our duty, fearing God and working righteousness: may we secure our interest in the great Saviour of the world, that when all earthly help shall fail us, thou mayest take us up, and be the strength of our hearts, and our portion for ever.

Day by day we magnify thee, O Lord, who art making every day a further addition to thy mercies. We bless thee for our last night's preservation and protection, and for the rest and refreshment which thou hast given us therein. O cause us to hear thy loving-kindness in the morning, for in thee do we trust; cause us to know the way wherein we shall go, for we lift up our souls to thee. Cast us not away from thy presence; take not thy Holy Spirit from us: but direct all our ways to please thee our God, that thou mayest crown us with blessing and good success. Help us to see thy power, to own thy presence, to admire thy wisdom, and to love thy goodness in all thy creatures. And by all the comforts of creatures, draw us still nearer to thyself, the blessed Creator of every comfort; and let our meditations of God be sweet as well as frequent, that delighting ourselves in the Lord, we may obtain the desire of our hearts. Such thy mercy and grace we beg for ourselves, and all ours, and thine, every where, in our great Mediator's form of prayer, *Our Father*, &c.

A SIXTH MORNING PRAYER.

WE do here present ourselves this morning before thy glorious Majesty, most blessed Lord God, desiring to pay unto thee that tribute of homage and service, of prayer and praise, which is so justly due. We desire to approach thee in such a manner, that thou mayest mercifully accept both us and our services, at the hands of Jesus Christ. In his great name we come to thee at thy command, and worship at thy footstool: in his name we implore thy pardon; we intreat thee to give us an increase of thy grace, and fresh tokens of thy love. We are not worthy indeed that thou shouldst take notice of us, or be intreated by us: but worthy is the Lamb, that was slain to take away the sins of the world; worthy is the Lamb, that thou shouldst for his sake do more for us than we can ask or even think: for he has fulfilled those holy laws which we have broken, and perfectly satisfied thy justice for all our transgressions of them. In him thou art a God gracious and merciful, slow to anger and of great kindness even to the chief of sinners: in him thou art reconciled to those who deserve nothing but to be forsaken and abhorred by thee. We acknowledge that to us belong shame and confusion of face: our sins have been so multiplied, that we might well expect thy judgment and fiery indignation: and if thou shouldst be extreme to mark what is done amiss, we could not escape the curses of thy holy law.

But, O gracious Father, regard not what we have done against thy Majesty; but rather regard what our blessed Saviour has done for our souls: consider not what we have made ourselves, but what he is made of thee our God unto us. And O that Christ may be to every one of us (what he is to all thy faithful people) wisdom and righteousness, and sanctification and redemption! Let his precious blood cleanse us from all our sins; and let the grace of thy Holy Spirit renew and sanctify our souls. Righteous Father, subdue, we pray thee, our iniquities, and mortify our lusts; quicken us to all the duties of thy holy service, and enable us to perform them with profit and delight. O let not sin reign in our mortal bodies, that we should obey it in the lusts thereof. Let there be no sin in us which is not felt and hated, bewailed and resisted by us: let us approve our very hearts to thee, the searcher of them; and let all our ways be pleasing in thy sight.

O teach us to know thee our God; and enable us to do thy will, as we ought to do. Give us hearts to fear thee, and to love thee: cause us to trust in thee, and to adhere with faithfulness unto thee. Let no temptations draw us, nor any tribulations drive us, from thee: but let all thy dispensations to us be received as messengers of thy love to our souls; and let all thy dealings with us bring us nearer to thy blessed self, and make us fitter for thy heavenly kingdom. Quicken us, O Lord, in our dulness; that, instead of dishonouring thee by our lifeless and listless services, we may abound in thy work, and be fervent in spirit, serving the Lord. Make us also faithful in all our intercourse with our neighbours. Make us ready to do good, and to bear evil: make us just and kind, merciful and meek, peaceable and patient, sober and temperate, humble and self-denying, inoffensive and exemplary in our conduct; that so glorifying thee here upon earth, we may, at our departure hence, be received into the joy of our Lord, and be for ever glorified in thy heavenly kingdom.

O thou that hast kept us alive to this day, and hast refreshed us during the night season, renew thy mercy to us together with this morning light. Thou that makest the outgoings of the morning and evening to rejoice, lift up the light of thy countenance upon us, and make us glad with the tokens of thy love: and as thou art ever present with us, O make us ever sensible of thy presence, that we may duly remember thee in all our ways, and wisely demean ourselves in all our affairs. Be with us, good Lord, at our going out, and our coming in: and let thy grace follow us this day, and all the days of our life. O never leave us, never, never forsake us; but be our guide unto death, in death our comfort, and after death our everlasting portion. O hear us from heaven, thy dwelling-place; and, when thou hearest, have mercy; forgive the sins of our persons, and the sins of our prayers: and do more for us, than we are worthy to expect at thy hands; for his sake, who alone is worthy: in whose comprehensive words we sum up all our desires, *Our Father,* &c.

A SEVENTH MORNING PRAYER.

O LORD God Almighty, thou art the sovereign Majesty of heaven and earth, against whom all our sins have been committed, and by whom alone they can be pardoned! there is none but thee, by whom our iniquities can be subdued, our souls be sanctified, or our necessities supplied. But thou art able, and also ready to hear and help, to bless and save, thy people that call upon thee; thou delightest to show mercy, and lovest the occasions of glorifying thy compassion. We come to thee therefore, O Lord, begging that mercy, which thou knowest we extremely want, and grace to help us in this time of our need. We beg the same for the sake of thine infinitely beloved Son, who alone is worthy, and in whose precious blood is all our trust.

We are unclean, Lord, we are unclean; and thou mayest well abhor our guilty souls: but O look upon us in the Son of thy love; and prepare us for the mercies which thou hast treasured up for us in him. Make us to feel the burden and the bitterness of our sins; nor let us ever attempt to cover and conceal them, lest they find us out at the last, and overwhelm us with shame and misery. Holy Father! carry on with power thy great work, even the work of faith, and the sanctification of our souls. Quicken us, O Lord our God, and stir us up to thy work; and assist us in the performance of all our duties, which of ourselves thou knowest we are unable to perform. Work in us to will and to do, of thy good pleasure; establish the things, O God, which thou hast already wrought for us; and go on to work mightily upon our hearts by thy grace, till our souls are fitted for the enjoyment of thy glory.

Gracious Lord, thy mercies are fresh and new to us every morning. We have laid us down and slept, and awaked again; for thou hast sustained us: thou hast kept us from the terrors of the night, and from all evil accidents; so that we are once more risen in peace and safety. Glory be to thee, O God of our salvation, who art still so mindful of us, so merciful unto us. Go on, we pray thee, to be good to us this day, and teach us how to demean ourselves aright, and to order our affairs to thy glory. O direct our undertakings, and prosper our endeavours. Rule our hearts in thy fear and love, and keep us living to thy praise and honour. Behold, we commit ourselves to thee, and shelter ourselves under the shadow of thy wings: O keep us from evil, and help us to do that which is good and pleasing to our God, through Jesus Christ. Give us, Lord, all that we have asked as we should; forgive us all that we have asked amiss; and bestow on us all things needful, which we should have asked; and which we continue to ask, in the comprehensive words of thy dear Son—*Our Father*, &c.

FIRST EVENING PRAYER FOR A FAMILY

O LORD our God! thou art infinitely great, and infinitely good. Thy glory is above all our thoughts, and thy mercies are more than can be numbered. O what cause have we to admire, and bless, and praise thee, for making us the objects of thy love, and the living monuments of thy goodness! When we survey thy glorious perfections, especially as they shine forth in the person of Jesus Christ, we are encouraged to come unto thee, we are emboldened to call thee Father. And though we have great and many sins to confess, yet do we look up with confidence, trusting that thou wilt pardon them, and give us power from on high to mortify and subdue them.

[Thou didst create us, O Lord, after thine own blessed image, in a holy and happy estate: but we have made ourselves vile and miserable; we are no longer upright, but have sought out many inventions: we are become averse to good, and prone to evil; yea, so full are we of all iniquity, that we are a mystery to ourselves; we wonder at the depravity of our own hearts, and are astonished that thou hast not long since cut us off in anger, and shut us up under final despair of mercy. But thou hast declared thy willingness to be reconciled even to thine enemies; yea, thou hast sent thine only Son into the world for this very end: thou hast sent him, that all might believe in him; and that whosoever believeth in him, should not perish but have everlasting life. O Lord, we believe, help our unbelief: and give us true repentance towards God, and right faith in our Lord Jesus Christ; that we may be of the number of those who repent and believe to the saving of their souls.

And save us, O good Lord, from the love and course of this present evil world, and from every self-destroying way which we are tempted to follow. Make us a way to escape out of all the snares of temptation, wherewith we have been entangled; and let us so experience the bitterness of sin and the excellence of thy ways, that we may never regard either the allurements or discouragements of this sinful world. Establish, strengthen, settle us, O Lord: that going forth in thy strength, we may do thy will to all well-pleasing, and continue in thy fear to our lives' end.]

While we supplicate thy mercy for ourselves, we would humbly implore thy blessing, O Lord, on all those whom we ought to remember in our prayers. O bring nigh unto thee all those that are yet afar off! and make manifest the savour of thy knowledge in every place: let such as yet sit in darkness and the shadow of death, behold the light of thy truth, and the joy of thy salvation. O that all who name the name of Christ may depart from iniquity, and so live up to their profession, as to give no just occasion for thine enemies to blaspheme! Let it be the ambition of all thy people to adorn the doctrine of God our Saviour in all things, and to put to silence the ignorance of foolish men by well doing.

Be gracious and favourable, O Lord, to thy church, and especially to that part of it which thou hast planted in this nation. Arise, O God, and plead thine own cause, and maintain thy holy religion, which thou hast so long established amongst us. O let not the enemies of thy church ever have cause to say, that they have prevailed against thy people; but let those that espouse thy cause, and stand up for the defence of thy truth, go on and prosper; and ever have cause to say, *The Lord be magnified who hath pleasure in the prosperity of his servants.*

Bless, with the choicest of thy blessings, the *Queen*, whom thou hast put in authority over us. Protect her person, direct her councils, and prosper all her endeavours for the peace and welfare of her dominions. Give to all *magistrates* wisdom and courage to defend thy truth, and to do right to all. Make all *ministers* to be ensamples to the flock, in all righteousness and holiness of living. And establish *all of us* to be an holy people to thyself; granting us one heart, and one way, that we may fear thee for ever, for the good of us and of our children after us.

Comfort all who want the comforts which we

FOR A FAMILY.

enjoy; and relieve the necessities of all thine afflicted people throughout the world. Remember all our friends and benefactors, our kindred after the flesh, and all who are near and dear unto us; remember them with the favour which thou bearest to thy people. Make them, O Lord, such as thou wouldst have them to be, and such as thou wilt mercifully accept to thy favour here, and to thy kingdom hereafter. Look also upon our enemies; forgive them, and turn their hearts; and enable us to forgive them, as we hope for forgiveness at thy hands. Enable us to overcome their evil with good; and so to please thee in all our ways, that thou mayest make our enemies to be at peace with us.

Hear us, O God of the spirits of all flesh. Hear us both for ourselves and others; above all, O hear the Son of thy love, pleading for us at thy right hand; hear his all-prevailing intercessions for us, and for all the members of his mystical body. To him we commit our cause, and to thee through him; trusting in thy tender mercy, and ascribing to him, to thyself, and to thy blessed Spirit, all possible honour, might, majesty, and dominion, both now and ever. *Amen.*

A SECOND EVENING PRAYER FOR A FAMILY.

OUR ever blessed and most gracious God! thou art the Lord and Giver of our lives, and of all the blessings we enjoy. To thee we owe ourselves, and all that we are capable of rendering unto thee. For by thee, O Lord, we were created; and through thy good Providence it is, that we have been spared and provided for unto this present time. From thee, our God, comes all our help; and in thee is reposed all our hope. Thou art the bountiful giver of all the good that our souls desire, and the merciful withholder of all the evil that our sins deserve. We acknowledge thy great and daily goodness to us, and our own exceeding unworthiness of the least of all thy mercies. We take shame and confusion to ourselves, that we have so little improved, and so greatly abused, all thy patience with us, and all the various instances of thy bounty to us. We confess it to be a heinous aggravation of our offences, that we have done so much against thee, after all the great things thou hast done for us. But we desire, O Lord, to be humbled for our offences; and we entreat thy gracious favour, in Christ Jesus, for the pardon of them. Forgive us, we pray thee (for his sake), all the sins that ever we have committed against thee, and absolve us from all the evil whereof we now stand guilty before thee. And, being justified by faith, let us have peace with God, through our Lord Jesus Christ.

[And as we pray, that thou wilt be to us a Father of mercies, and a God of consolation; so we pray that thou wilt make us followers of God, as dear children; ever jealous over our hearts, and watchful over our ways; continually fearing to offend, and endeavouring to please thee; and enable us to keep our hearts with all diligence, that they may never be hardened through the deceitfulness of sin. Thou knowest, O Lord, our weakness, and our danger; thou knowest how unable we are of ourselves to resist the smallest temptation, while yet we are continually exposed to the assaults of our subtle enemy, to the allurements of an ensnaring world, and to the corruptions of our own treacherous heart. We pray, therefore, good Lord, that thou wilt arm us with the whole armour of God, and uphold us with thy free Spirit, and evermore watch over us for good. Especially in the times of our sorest trials, let us experience the strongest aids of thy heavenly grace, that we may never fall a prey to those deadly enemies that seek to devour us.

And teach us, O our God, to know the day of grace, and the time of our visitation, and to see the things of our peace, before they be hid from our eyes. And while we have time, O enable us to use and improve it to those great ends for which thou art pleased to continue it to us. Let us not neglect that precious talent, but employ it with all diligence and circumspection for the securing of our eternal welfare.]

And seeing thou art pleased yet to hold our souls in life, and to make us find and feel, by every day's experience, how abundantly gracious and merciful thou art, O give us hearts more sensible of thy love, more affected with thy mercy, and more thankful for those continued favours, which thou art pleased to multiply unto us. And help us to show forth thy praise, not only by speaking good of thy name, but by ordering our conversation aright, and by adorning the gospel of God our Saviour in all things.

And now, most merciful Father, we humbly recommend ourselves, and all that we have, to thy care and protection; beseeching thee, for thy dear Son's sake, to preserve and defend, to bless and keep us, both in soul and body. We know that by reason of our weakness and wickedness, we are exposed to many and great dangers; but we commit ourselves to thee, trusting that thou wilt sustain us. O be with us through the night season, and grant us comfortable repose; that our frail nature being refreshed, and our decayed strength renewed, we may rise again better fitted for the duties of the following day, if thou shalt be pleased to add another day to our lives. And as thou daily multipliest thy mercies to us, be pleased also to increase our repentance, and to renew us daily after thine image: that every day may not only bring us nearer to thy kingdom, but make us fitter for the enjoyment of that glory which thou hast prepared for them that love thee.

Accept these our prayers, most gracious and merciful Lord God: and, for all the good things we have received, or at present enjoy, or hope for in future from thy bountiful hands, enable us to render our grateful thanks: and let it be our employment now, as we hope it shall be hereafter, abundantly to utter the memory of thy great goodness, and to sing of thy praise without ceasing.—*Amen* and *Amen.*

A THIRD EVENING PRAYER.

O LORD, thou art our gracious God, our chief good, and our most merciful Father in Christ Jesus: in his great name, and through his prevailing mediation, we are encouraged still to present our persons and our prayers before thee. It is a privilege which we must acknowledge ourselves utterly unworthy to enjoy, that thou shouldst admit us into thy service, yea into fellowship with thy blessed self. We do not presume to appear in the presence of thy glorious Majesty, in our own name, or trusting in any righteousness of our own; being conscious of so much guilt, as might make us tremble for fear of thy judgments.

But we come in the name and mediation of thy dear Son, who has fully satisfied thy justice for our sins, and continually intercedes for us at thy right hand. Thou lovest him infinitely above all, and delightest to honour him in sparing and accepting the most unworthy sinners upon his account. O deliver us, most gracious Lord, for his sake, from all the transgressions, for which our hearts condemn us; and from all, of which thou, who art greater than our hearts, knowest us to be guilty. And seal to us a full pardon, in his most precious blood, which speaks better things on our behalf than we are able to speak for ourselves.

And may the time past of our lives suffice to have lived to ourselves, and to have served our own lusts and pleasures. O put an end to all our presumptuous and treacherous dealings; and grant us new and contrite hearts, that we may tremble at thy presence, and hate and abandon every evil way. Engage to thyself, O blessed Lord, the deepest thoughts of our minds, the choicest affections of our hearts, and the main tendency and activity of our souls. O let us delight in attendance upon thee, and in communion with thee; nor let the vanities of this world ever divert us from thy service, or interrupt our enjoyment of thee.

[Hear us, O Lord, for ourselves, and let our supplications also ascend before thee in the behalf of all men living. Send thy word, and the means of grace, to such as are yet destitute of them; and make them efficacious, and a savour of life, to those who now enjoy them. Convert the uncoverted, and perfect thy good work where thou hast begun it. Give a check to all profaneness and ungodliness, that presumptuous sinners may be ashamed, and that the wickedness of the wicked may come to an end. O make thy church to increase and flourish, and thy servants to prevail and rejoice. Be gracious and favourable to this our native land, to the head and governors of it, and to all the inferior and particular members. O do thou rule all our rulers, counsel all our counsellors, teach all our teachers, and order all the public affairs, to the glory of thy name, and to the welfare of our church and state. Avert from us, good Lord, the judgments which we feel or fear; and continue to us the many temporal and spiritual advantages which through thy favour we enjoy. And, notwithstanding all the devices of our enemies, and all the heinous provocations of our sins, O be thou still our reconciled God, and let us be thy happy, thy peculiar people.

Look down, O gracious Father, on all the sons and daughters of affliction: mercifully regard them under the pressure of their troubles, and think thoughts of pity and compassion towards them. O sanctify thy fatherly corrections to them, support them under their several burdens, and in thy good time deliver them from the furnace into which they are cast. Be gracious to all our friends and neighbours, reward our benefactors, and bless our relations with the choicest of thy blessings. Bless also our enemies, and reconcile them both to us and to thyself. Dwell in all the habitations which thou hast made houses of prayer, and with all the families who call upon thy name. Let thy heavenly blessings, and thy saving grace, descend and rest upon this family. O guide us, and keep us; make us wise and faithful in our duty, and prosperous in all our lawful undertakings. Bless all our present circumstances to us, and fit us for whatsoever changes we may be called to experience. O teach us how to want, and how to abound; and whether we be in a prosperous or suffering condition, secure our hearts to thyself, and make us upright before thee.]

And now, O Lord, be pleased to accept our evening sacrifice of praise and thanksgiving: we would glorify thee the Father of mercies, and the fountain of all goodness, for the mercies of the day past, and for the goodness that has followed us all the days of our life. Our lives have been filled with thy mercies, and thou hast abounded towards us in loving-kindness: infinite has been the variety of the sweet and comfortable blessings with which thou hast loaded us. Thou hast passed by our innumerable sins, as though thou hadst not seen them; and thou art still encompassing us with mercies on every side. Imprint, therefore, and preserve upon our hearts a lively and grateful sense of all thy kindness to us: let our souls bless thee; let all that is within us praise thy holy name; yea, let us give thee thanks from the ground of the heart, and praise our God, whilst we have our being. Thy patience with us, thy care over us, and thy continual mercy to us, demand our incessant praises: to thee, therefore, O our heavenly Father, let all thanks and praise, and love and obedience, and honour and glory, be rendered by us, and by all the Israel of God, henceforth and for evermore.— *Amen.*

A FOURTH EVENING PRAYER.

O LORD, the infinite, incomprehensible God, who wast before all, art above all, and wilt for ever be the same! Thou hast heaven for thy throne, and the earth for thy footstool. Thou art here and everywhere present; thou compassest our path, and our lying down, and art thoroughly acquainted with all our ways. Thou searchest our hearts, and triest our reins; thou knowest the dulness and hardness, the vanity and deceitfulness of our hearts; thou seest how difficult we find it to bring our souls into an holy frame, and to keep them in a state fit to attend upon thy heavenly Majesty. We were born in sin, and in sin have we lived: daily have we added sin to sin, and have made ourselves children of wrath still more by practice than we were by nature: every day of our lives have we transgressed thy laws, abused thy mercies, tempted thy patience, despised thy goodness, offended thee more, even for thy forbearance with us; and made the very abundance of thy grace an encouragement to continue in our sins. O Thou, whom we have so greatly provoked, what must we not expect if thou shouldst enter into judgment with us? How justly mightest thou withdraw thy tender mercies from us, and pour out upon us thy wrath and indignation to the uttermost! How justly mightest thou leave us to feel what an evil and bitter thing it is to trespass against thee; and make us to experience the same, in that place of torment, where is weeping and wailing and gnashing of teeth, and from whence there is no redemption!

But thou art a God of wonderful patience to bear with sinners; and a God of infinite goodness and mercy to forgive them, when they are truly penitent. Thou hast said, that if the wicked forsake his way, and the unrighteous man his thoughts, and return to the Lord, thou wilt have mercy upon him, and abundantly pardon. We humbly beg, therefore, that thou wilt be graciously pleased to stretch forth thy powerful hand, and to loose the chains of sin wherewith we are tied and bound. Let it be thy good pleasure to deliver us from every weight of sin, and from every yoke of bondage; that our souls may be fitted to serve thee with that sincerity and readiness and gladness, which thou requirest of thy people. O help us so to see and feel, so to hate and bewail, so to confess and forsake our sins, that we may have a well-grounded hope of thy forgiveness, and a comfortable persuasion that thou hast accepted us in the Son of thy love.

And for his sake, grant thou us, O Lord, an increase of thy grace, and such aids of thy Holy Spirit, as may enable us to mortify our sins, and fit us for all the duties of thy service. Make us, O our God, to serve thee sincerely, without hypocrisy; cheerfully, without dullness; universally, without partiality; and constantly, without falling away, or being weary of well doing. Thou art not weary in doing us good; O let us never be weary in doing thee service. But as thou hast pleasure in the prosperity of thy servants, so let us take pleasure in the service of our Lord, and abound in thy work and in thy love and praise evermore. O fill up all that is wanting, and reform whatever is amiss in us, and perfect that which concerns us; making us such in our hearts, and in our lives, that we may obtain peace in our souls, and be made partakers of thy heavenly glory. And be thou pleased to grant us now (out of the riches of thy grace) the comfortable sense of thy gracious acceptance of us, and of thy merciful intentions towards us. O speak peace to our consciences, and say to each of our souls, I am thy salvation; that so we may look upon thee as our reconciled God and Father in Christ Jesus.

[In his great name, and prevailing mediation, we enlarge our petitions, in behalf of the whole race of mankind. O that all the ends of the world may remember themselves, and turn unto the Lord, and see the salvation of our God! Do good, O God, in thy good pleasure, unto Zion, and build thou the walls of Jerusalem. Continue thy mercies to this guilty land, whereof we are sinful members. Teach us to know the meaning of thy dispensations towards us; and help us to improve by all thy dealings with us. O turn all our hearts to thee, as the heart of one man: and reform all our lives, according to the holy pattern and precepts of our Lord; that thou mayest cause thine anger towards us to cease; and mayest go on still to take the charge of us, and never leave nor forsake us.

Bless abundantly the queen's majesty, who now sways the sceptre of these realms. O Lord, preserve her life, prolong her days, and prosper her government. Give her the hearts of her subjects, and subdue her enemies before her. Make her the rejoicing of thy people, and a terror only to evil doers. O continue her long a zealous defender of the faith, a promoter of thy fear, and an assertor of our rights; that under her shadow we may be in peace and safety, enjoying the liberty of the gospel, and the free profession of thy holy religion. And grant unto all magis-

FOR A FAMILY. 43

trates and ministers continual supplies of thy Holy Spirit, for the conscientious and comfortable discharge of their several duties. O bring all our neighbours near to thyself; and be thou a friend to all our friends, a father to the fatherless, a husband to the widow, a refuge to the oppressed, a physician to the sick, a helper to the friendless, and a God of consolation to the distressed and sorrowful, whatever be their trouble and affliction. O bless to us, whatever thou art pleased to allot us, and everything that befalls us. Make all to work for our good; to build us up in thy grace, and to help us on to thy glory.]

And as thou hast been good and kind to us the day past, and throughout our whole lives, (for which we desire, O Lord, humbly and thankfully to adore thy name) so we beg, that we may experience the continuance of thy goodness to us, and of thy fatherly care over us, this present night. O preserve and defend, and bless and keep us, that no evil may befall us, nor any plague come nigh our dwelling. Give us sleep and rest, to refresh and strengthen us for thy service, and for the performance of all our duties; and prepare us, O Lord, for our last sleep in death, and for that great account that we must give at the judgment-seat of Christ. O instruct and assist us in that great work of preparation for our everlasting state; that we may (in this only time of preparation) finish the great work which thou hast given us to do, before the night of death overtake us, wherein we cannot work. that, whenever thou shalt be pleased to give us the summons of death, we may find nothing to do but to die, and cheerfully resign our spirits into thy gracious hands. Hear us, we intreat thee, through the riches of thy grace, and the worthiness of thy dear Son; in whose merits alone we trust; and to whom, together with thyself and the Holy Ghost, the one God of our salvation, be all praise, and honour, and glory, ascribed by us, and by all thy people, from this time forth for evermore.—*Amen.*

A FIFTH EVENING PRAYER.

O LORD, we desire to seek thy face, and to wait upon thee in the duties of thy worship; and we intreat thy gracious favour that we may be enabled to call upon thee with our whole hearts. To whom should we make our applications, but unto thee, the Father of mercies, and the Fountain of all goodness, who art able to do exceeding abundantly for us, even above all that we can ask or think; and who has declared thy willingness to be importuned by us, and thy readiness to hear and help us. O let our prayer be now set before thee as incense, and the lifting up of our hands be as the evening sacrifice, pleasing to thee our God, in the Son of thy love. It is in his blessed name alone that we have encouragement to approach thee, and boldness to ask of thee those things which thou knowest to be needful and expedient for us. There is in ourselves no good thing to recommend us to thy favour; but a proneness to everything which is displeasing to thy Majesty, and destructive to our souls. We are even by nature children of wrath, a seed of evil doers, the sinful offspring of rebellious parents: and ever since we began to act, we have been daily trespassing against thee, and adding to the heavy score of our offences. There is nothing in us, O Lord, but what may well provoke thee to reject us: but there is enough in thy beloved Son to procure for us the pardon of our sins, and peace with thee. Thou didst make him to be sin for us, that we might be made the righteousness of God in him; and that we might be saved by his merits, when we could not be saved by any desert of our own works. O see our sins punished in him, even in him who was wounded for our transgressions, and bruised for our iniquities: and, as the chastisement of our peace was upon him, so let the merit of his righteousness be on us; and by his stripes let our souls be healed.

Nor do we only beg for pardon of our sins, but also for power against them, and grace sufficient for us to break them off. We long to walk more acceptably before thee, in all the duties of righteousness and holiness, which thy word has prescribed to us. O never suffer us to be tempted above what we are able: but make our temptations less, or thy grace in us more sufficient to resist them; that no iniquities may prevail against us, nor any presumptuous sin have dominion over us. Make us more conformable to the pattern and the precepts of our blessed Saviour: transform us more into his holy image and likeness; that we may not dishonour his religion, nor cause the way of truth to be evil spoken of; but may make our light to shine before men, to the glory of thee our heavenly Father, and to the edification of those amongst whom we dwell.

And seeing the time of our abode in this transitory world is so very short and uncertain, and that after our departure hence we have an everlasting estate, where we must be happy or miserable for ever; O let us not set up our rest in this world, as if we were at home upon earth: neither suffer us to flatter ourselves with the hopes of a long enjoyment of these things which perish in in the using; but may we wait all the days of our appointed time, till our change comes; and not only live in expectation of it, but in the daily serious preparation for it: in the exercise of all those gracious and good works, that may make it unto us Christ to live and gain to die; that in life and death we may be always thine, safe in thy hands, and acceptable in thy sight.

And together with our own wants, we commend to thy mercy, O God, the necessities and distresses of all our brethren throughout the world. O enlighten the ignorant, quicken the careless, awaken the secure, convince the erroneous, reclaim the vicious, establish the wavering, and comfort the dejected. Bring all to the knowledge of thy truth, and to a cheerful obedience to thy holy will; that so they may attain to the blessed hope of thy glory, and the eternal salvation of their immortal souls. We pray (as more particularly bound) for the queen, for all our magistrates and ministers; for all our friends and relations; for all thy servants; and for all the afflicted throughout the world; and more especially for those for whose happiness and salvation thou knowest us to be chiefly concerned. O do thou for us, and for them, as thou knowest best, and most needful and expedient, for thine own mercy's sake in Christ Jesus.

[And as we pray to thee for what we want, so we desire to praise thee for all that we have received at thy hands. And blessed be thy name, O Lord, that we have anything (yea that we have so many things) to bless and praise thee for. O what shall we render to the Lord for all his benefits! Dear Lord! let not our hearts be shut and straitened towards thee, whose hand is every day so open unto us: but do thou possess and enlarge these hearts of ours with more love and greater thankfulness to thee, that we may both give thee thanks, and glorify thy name, for evermore.

And now that the night is upon us, and we are ready to betake ourselves to rest, we commit ourselves to thy gracious care and protection, well knowing that thou, who never sleepest nor slumberest, art the watchful guardian of thy favoured people. O watch over us, we pray thee, for good, that none of the evils, which our sins have merited, may befall us. Protect us both from the works, and from the powers, of darkness; and preserve us from all terrors and dangers through the night. Let all our sins, this day, or at any former time committed, be removed out of thy sight; and lift up upon us the light of thy countenance, that we may lie down with a sweet sense of thy favour, and a comfortable assurance that thou hast accepted us in the Son of thy love: for whom, and to whom, with thy eternal self, and Holy Spirit, be all thanks and praise, and honour and glory, ascribed by us and by all thy church, from this time forth for evermore.] *Amen.*

A SIXTH EVENING PRAYER.

O LORD, our God, most high and mighty, most wise and holy, most just and good! Thou art and ever wast, and ever shalt continue, unspeakably blessed and glorious, above all that we are able to express or to conceive. Thou dost not need the services of men or angels to make the least addition to thy glory or bliss. Men cannot be profitable unto God; nor can our goodness extend to the Lord. But, in kindness and love to our souls, thou hast been pleased to lay thy commands upon us, and to appoint that we should wait upon thee in the duties of thine immediate service; which is the blissful employment of all the hosts of heaven. Thou humblest thyself even when thou beholdest the things that are in heaven or regardest the worship of those blessed creatures above. O how wonderful is thy condescension, then, that thou shouldst look down upon us, poor sinful worms, who dwell in houses of clay, and whose foundation is in the dust! Lord, what is man that thou takest knowledge of him, and the son of man that thou makest account of him! Thou canst not at all need us, or anything of ours, O blessed God; but we all stand in continual need of thee, our only sovereign good; in need of thy mercy and forgiveness, thy grace and guidance, thy blessing and assistance; without which we can never hope to escape the misery, which is the wages due to our sins; nor ever to attain that glory, which is the free gift of God in Christ Jesus.

The desire of our souls, therefore, is to thy name, O Lord, and to the remembrance of thee. Our eyes are towards thee, and all our expectation is from thee; and still we wait, and call, and depend upon thee, till thou have mercy upon us, according to our several necessities, and according to the multitude of thy tender mercies. O remember not against us our former iniquities; enter not into judgment with us, according to our desert; but according to thy mercy remember thou us, for thy goodness' sake, O Lord. Blot out our transgressions as a cloud; and justify us freely by thy grace, through the redemption that is in Christ Jesus. And bless us, O God of our salvation, in turning us from all our iniquities, and in giving us grace, that we may repent and amend our lives according to thy holy word.

And to this end, be thou pleased to enlighten our dark minds with the beams of thy saving truth: O let us not be unwise, but understanding what the will of the Lord is. Reform our depraved wills, inclining them to a cheerful compliance with all the motions of thy good Spirit. Regulate our unruly passions; purify our corrupt affections; and convert all the faculties of our souls, that they may be instruments of thy glory, as they have been of thy dishonour; and make our bodies fit temples for thy Holy Spirit. Yea, sanctify us wholly, in body, soul, and spirit, that we may adorn thy gospel in all holy conversation and godliness.

And quicken us, O Lord, to hear thy voice, while it is called to-day; that we may make haste, and not delay, to keep thy commandments. O keep us frequently and affectionately mindful of the shortness of our time, the frailty of our lives, and the uncertainty of our continuance in this perishable world; where we have no continuing city, but are strangers and sojourners with thee, as all our fathers were. O let the remembrance of this have a prevailing influence upon us, to crucify the world to us, and us unto the world: let it make us more deeply concerned for our everlasting welfare, and more careful to improve every present good for our soul's eternal advantage. Let the work of thy grace be daily advancing in our hearts, that we may grow in grace as we grow in years, and be continually ripening for the full enjoyment of thy glory.

[The same things we beg also in behalf of all whom we ought to remember in our prayers. O forgive the sins, and relieve the miseries of thy sinful creatures throughout all the world. Enlarge* the borders of thy church, and add to it daily such as shall be saved. O that all who are called Christians may be Christians indeed, not only believing thy word, but walking as becometh the gospel of Christ. Let the *church*, which thou hast planted amongst us, be thy continual care: watch over it, O Lord, for good: preserve it night and day; let no weapon formed against it prosper. Give thy judgments also, O God, unto the *queen*, that she may judge thy people righteously and break in pieces their oppressors. Grant her still an interest in the hearts of her people, and thy protection from the hands of her enemies. May she so rule and reign for thee, that she may come to live and reign for ever with thee. Make all our *magistrates* to be men fearing God, and eschewing evil. And O that *all who are called to serve at thine altar,* may be in a more especial manner

SIXTH EVENING PRAYER

blessed with compassionate hearts, and exemplary lives. Make them wise to win souls; make them faithful, industrious, and successful in their sacred office, as workmen that need not be ashamed. Bless and prosper all the *seminaries* of sound learning and religious education. Bless *all orders and ranks* of people amongst us; let them all know thee from the least to the greatest; and so order their conversation aright, that they may see the salvation of God. Remember for good all *those who have been in any way instrumental to our good;* and let all *who have injured us,* receive forgiveness at thy hands. Look upon *all that mourn in Zion;* give unto them beauty for ashes, the oil of joy for mourning, and the garment of praise for the spirit of heaviness. Teach *those who are in health and prosperity* to remember and provide for the time of trouble, sickness, and death: and make *all of every condition* to be mindful of their duty; that thou mayest remember them in mercy, and be their God, and portion for ever.]

Our own unworthiness would make us despair of obtaining all these great and goods things which we beg at thy hands, O Lord; but the remembrance of thy tender mercy, and thy continual bounty, puts life into our hopes, and encouragement into our prayers, and leaves us no reason to doubt of finding mercy with thee. And blessed for ever be thy name, that we have so much to say of thy goodness by our own experience: that thou hast in so many things made us to differ from thousands of our fellow-creatures. O good Lord! continue thy gracious favour to us, and thy fatherly care over us, this night. As we go to rest after the labours of the day, so help us daily to do thy work, that we may enter into that rest which remains for thy people at the close of life. Renew to us day by day thy pardoning mercy, and supply us daily with thy grace; that we may finish our course with joy, and at the end of this life be received into thy glory. All of which we beg in the name and for the sake of our holy Redeemer: for whom we thank thee; and to whom, with thyself, O Father, and the Holy Ghost our comforter, in the unity of the ever blessed Trinity, be all praise, and honour, and glory ascribed by us, and by all the Israel of God, now and for evermore. *Amen.*

A SEVENTH EVENING PRAYER.

O LORD, thou great and glorious God, infinite in power, wisdom, and goodness! Thou hast created all things by thine almighty hand! thou sustainest and orderest all things by thy wise and righteous providence; and thy mercy is everlasting, and over all thy works. O who is able to express, who is able to conceive, the exceeding riches of thy grace and goodness! In what a plentiful measure have thy bounties been poured out upon us thy sinful creatures, who deserve nothing from thee, but to be forsaken and abhorred by thee! This day, and every day of our lives, O Lord, we have tasted largely of thy mercy, and been altogether preserved by thy fatherly care.

But, notwithstanding all thy patience and gracious dealings with us, and all the repeated pledges of thy favour towards us, O how ill have we requited thy love! And what unsuitable returns have we made for all thy great and continued goodness that we have experienced! Beside the guilt of our inbred corruption, which, as a sore burthen, hangs heavy upon us, we are amazed at the greatness and multitude of all our other sins that we have committed against thee; against the light and teachings of thy gospel; against the dictates and strivings of thy Spirit; against the love and sufferings of thy Son; against all the patience and forbearance which thou hast exercised towards us. O Lord, we have given thee so great provocation, that we have reason to fear lest thou shouldst forsake us utterly, and cause the day of thy patience to end. Well may we be afraid that thou wilt grant us no more of that grace which we have so greatly abused; nor any supplies of that Holy Spirit, whom we have so often resisted. And what have we now to expect from thee, O Lord! what but judgment, if it were not that thy mercy rejoices over judgment! Thy word assures us, that thou delightest not in the death of sinners, but rather that they should turn to thee and live: and therefore it is that thou still leavest us these opportunities to plead with thee for the life of our souls. But what have we to plead? Nothing, Lord, in ourselves: our hope is only in thee: we plead therefore thine own gracious nature, thy merciful inclinations, thine exceeding great and precious promises, which thou hast freely made to returning sinners. Thou hast sent thine only Son to be our almighty Saviour: and he that did no sin, was manifested to take away our sins. O then, for his sake, be pleased to pity us, to spare us, to forgive us. Turn away thy wrath from us; receive us to thy blessed favour; and comfort us with the sure persuasion, that our iniquities are forgiven.

And because such is the infirmity of our nature, that without thy grace we have not the least power to keep ourselves even from the greatest sins, O grant us the increase of thy grace, and the help of thy good Spirit; that we may be fortified against all temptation, and be made thy willing and faithful servants. And be pleased, O Lord, yet further to discover and manifest thyself to our souls, that we may know aright, thee, the only true God, and Jesus Christ whom thou hast sent. And give us power from on high that we may be able to live according to that light which thou art pleased to impart unto us; that we may not hold the truth in unrighteousness, but may walk in the light, as children of the light. O let us not only be almost, but altogether Christians: let us be true penitents, sincere converts, and sound believers. And O thou, that workest all in all, finish in us the work of thy grace, that we may have cause to give thee praise and glory to all eternity.

These things, Lord, we beg, not only for ourselves, but for all who partake of our nature, for all whom thou hast made capable of eternal happiness. More especially we pray for thy whole church, wheresoever or howsoever disposed of throughout all the earth: for the queen's majesty; and all our rulers and counsellors; for our ministers and teachers; for our relations and neighbours; our friends and benefactors; and for all thy afflicted, whatsoever be their trials and troubles. O supply all their wants, and fulfil all their desires, in such a manner as thy wisdom sees best, for thy own mercy's sake in Christ Jesus.

Thou, Lord, art the great preserver of men, who hast kept and blest us this day, and all our days. Praised be thy name for all thy goodness, which we have so long and largely experienced. O make us sensible of thy kindness, and thankful for it as we ought to be. Take care of us, O Lord, and be gracious to us this night. Give us not only bodily rest in our beds, but rest for our souls, in thy blessed self; and be thou our God and guide, our hope and help, our joy and comfort, our ALL IN ALL, this night, and for evermore. *Amen.*

FIRST MORNING PRAYER FOR THE LORD'S DAY.

O MOST blessed and gracious Lord God, whose almighty hand has brought us out of nothing, to enjoy the comforts of life; and whose free grace has called us out of a state worse than nothing to the hope of thy heavenly glory! We bless thy name, that thou hast conducted us safe, through all states and conditions of our lives, to see the comfortable light of this day; and we glorify thee that we have yet a day of grace wherein to seek the things belonging to our peace. We adore thee for having so far consulted the good of our souls as to set apart this day for holy uses, that we might engage in a solemn attendance upon thee in whose service consists all our honour and happiness. O how much higher might we have been in thy favour, how much nearer to thee our God, and fitter for thy heavenly kingdom, had we rightly used, and conscientiously improved, those means of grace, which thou hast been pleased to afford us!

But as we have been cruel to our own souls, as well as disobedient to thee, our Lord; many times losing the opportunities of appearing before thee; and shunning as a task what was our highest privilege: and even when we have set ourselves to seek thy face, it has been with such coldness and dulness, such wanderings and distractions, that thou mightest justly abhor our souls, and despise our services.

But be thou pleased to look upon us in the Son of thy love, who is the Lord our peace and our righteousness; and forgive us all that is past, wherein we have neglected thy work, or performed it amiss, or done what was inconsistent with it. Help us, O God of our salvation, and deliver us both from the bands and burden of our guilt; and purge away all our sins, for the glory of thy name: O let them not stand as a partition-wall, to hinder the ascent of our prayers to thee, or the descent of thy blessings upon us. But let thy peace and love shine into our souls; that we may see the felicity of thy chosen, and draw water with joy out of the wells of salvation.

O let us not rest in any forms of godliness, denying the power thereof; let us not take up with the name and profession of Christianity; but be swayed with its life and power. And let the gospel of our Lord, and the graces of thy good Spirit, shine forth in our lives, to the glory of thee our heavenly Father. O gracious God, be with us, and with all the ministers and stewards of thy mysteries, who are this day to speak in thy name: furnish them with abilities necessary for their great work; and enable them to suit themselves to the capacities and necessities of their several hearers. And grant, Lord, unto us, and unto all the hearers of thy holy word, humble and teachable spirits; that we may receive thy truth in the love of it, so as to profit and grow by it. O do thou remove all the hindrances of our spiritual improvement, that thy word may have free course, and be glorified amongst us. And let us this day go forth in the strength of the Lord God; and prosper and increase with the increase of God: let thy grace and blessing accompany all our endeavours; that having served thee imperfectly upon earth, we may attain to the full enjoyment of thee in heaven, and glorify thee in the perfection of holiness, for ever and ever.

And let thy grace and blessing, thy love and fellowship, thy direction and assistance, O heavenly Father, Son, and Holy Spirit, be with us and with all for whom we ought to pray, this day and for evermore. *Amen.*

A SECOND MORNING PRAYER FOR THE LORD'S DAY.

O LORD, the great almighty God; thou art the Giver of life and strength, and of all grace and goodness; without thee we can do nothing: but through thy gracious assistance we are enabled to do all things which thou requirest at our hands: we humbly pray thee to be graciously present with us, and powerfully assistant to us to every one his portion in due season. And let the word which they deliver be for the conviction and comfort of many souls. O thou that hast the key of David, that openest and no man shutteth, thou that speakest to the heart, and givest the increase, open our understandings to receive thy truth, both in the light and love of it: and set it home so powerfully upon our hearts, and root it so deeply in our souls, that the fruits of it may appear in our lives; and that we may not be forgetful hearers, but doers of thy word.

And grant, O gracious God, that our services this day may be such as may tend to our advantage, in the great day of thy appearing and glory: let us so hallow these sabbaths upon earth, that hereafter we may be admitted to the joyful celebration of the eternal sabbath in heaven; there, with all the church triumphant, to laud and magnify thy glorious name, and to enjoy thy love, and sing thy praise for ever. And now, Lord, for the addition of this sabbath we bless thee; for the benefit of thy word, and for the ordinances of thy worship, we glorify thy name: yea, for all the means of grace, and for the hopes of glory, to thee, the God of all grace, be praise and honour and glory rendered by us, and by all thy people, from this time forth, and for evermore. *Amen.*

A PRAYER FOR ANY INTERMEDIATE TIME OF THE LORD'S DAY.

O LORD the God of glory, who fillest heaven and earth with thy presence, fill my heart (I pray thee) with thy grace, and with a consciousness that thine eye is upon me: that I may demean myself as in thine immediate presence; and serve thee on earth as thou art served above, where thousand thousands minister unto thee, and ten thousand times ten thousand stand before thee. O happy are they who surround thy throne, and are ever occupied in the contemplation of thy Majesty, and the fruition of thy love: who have an everlasting period put to all their sins, and troubles, and temptations; and have their souls perfected in holiness, their hearts filled with joy, and their mouths opened to utter without ceasing the everlasting praises of their God. O Lord, look down from heaven, the habitation of thy holiness and thy glory, and behold with pity the poor remnant of thy heritage, who are yet upon their warfare and pilgrimage in this present evil world, beset with many and powerful enemies, and groaning for deliverance from the bondage of corruption, that they may be brought into the glorious liberty of the children of God.

O good Lord, pardon every one of us, who now prepare and set ourselves to seek thy face, and to meet and enjoy thee in the ordinances of thy worship. Though we be not cleansed according to the purification of the sanctuary, accept us in thy beloved Son, according to what we have; and fill us with thy good Spirit, to make us what we should be. O give unto me in particular, though the most unworthy of thy creatures, a devout and contrite heart; that I may not merely utter words of prayer, or rest in any forms of godliness, but may serve thee with my spirit, and lift up my heart to the Lord, and have (as much as possible) my conversation in heaven.

It is good for men to draw nigh to God: in whose service consists all our honour and bliss. O let my heart rejoice in seeking the Lord; and with great liveliness, and love, and cheerfulness let me frequent thy ways, and study thy word, and admire thy works and magnify thy name. I bless thee, my God, that thou hast given me an understanding to know thee, a heart to love thee, and a soul capable of waiting upon thee in the duties of thy holy service, and of enjoying thee in thy heavenly glory. I bless thee for all the opportunities and advantages which I have to serve thee, and to work out my salvation. I adore thee for the ministry of reconciliation committed to thy servants; for all their labours, and writings, and preachings: and for all other means of grace and assistances in this my warfare.

O give me such a love to thy word, that I may value it above all the wealth of the world, and relish it better than all the pleasures of the flesh;

and esteem it more than my necessary food. Enable me to receive it, not only in the light, but in the love thereof; that I may live and grow by it, and attain the salvation which it sets before me. And give me, Lord, a heart to fear thee, and to keep thy commandments always, that it may go well with me, both now and for ever. O let me so make thy word the rule of my life, that it may also be the ground of my hope: and while it is sounding in my ears, do thou apply it with an irresistible energy to my soul, that I may be made obedient to it in the day of thy power. And let there be such a transcript of the gospel in my life, that I may not only hear what it says, but be such as it describes. O gracious God! continue the light and joyful sound of thy gospel amongst us: and help us so rightly to use it, and to profit by it, that we may have reason to bless and praise thee for it to all eternity. O that every sabbath may add yet more and more to our stature in Christ Jesus; and that we may so sanctify thy sabbaths now, that in the end we may enjoy the sabbath of thine eternal rest; there to dwell in thy sight, and rejoice in thy love, and triumph in thy praise for evermore. *Amen.*

worship. Though we be not cleansed according to the purification of the sanctuary, accept us in thy beloved Son, according to what we have; and fill us with thy good Spirit, to make us what we should be. O give unto me in particular, though the most unworthy of thy creatures, a devout and contrite heart; that I may not merely utter words of prayer, or rest in any forms of godliness, but may serve thee with my spirit, and lift up my heart to the Lord, and have (as much as possible) my conversation in heaven.

It is good for men to draw nigh to God: in whose service consists all our honour and bliss. O let my heart rejoice in seeking the Lord; and with great liveliness, and love, and cheerfulness let me frequent thy ways, and study thy word, and admire thy works and magnify thy name. I bless thee, my God, that thou hast given me an understanding to know thee, a heart to love thee, and a soul capable of waiting upon thee in the duties of thy holy service, and of enjoying thee in thy heavenly glory. I bless thee for all the opportunities and advantages which I have to serve thee, and to work out my salvation. I adore thee for the ministry of reconciliation committed to thy servants; for all their labours, and writings, and preachings: and for all other means of grace and assistances in this my warfare.

O give me such a love to thy word, that I may value it above all the wealth of the world, and relish it better than all the pleasures of the flesh;

and esteem it more than my necessary food. Enable me to receive it, not only in the light, but in the love thereof; that I may live and grow by it, and attain the salvation which it sets before me. And give me, Lord, a heart to fear thee, and to keep thy commandments always, that it may go well with me, both now and for ever. O let me so make thy word the rule of my life, that it may also be the ground of my hope: and while it is sounding in my ears, do thou apply it with an irresistible energy to my soul, that I may be made obedient to it in the day of thy power. And let there be such a transcript of the gospel in my life, that I may not only hear what it says, but be such as it describes. O gracious God! continue the light and joyful sound of thy gospel amongst us: and help us so rightly to use it, and to profit by it, that we may have reason to bless and praise thee for it to all eternity. O that every sabbath may add yet more and more to our stature in Christ Jesus; and that we may so sanctify thy sabbaths now, that in the end we may enjoy the sabbath of thine eternal rest; there to dwell in thy sight, and rejoice in thy love, and triumph in thy praise for evermore. *Amen.*

FIRST EVENING PRAYER FOR THE LORD'S DAY.

O LORD, our God! thou art infinitely good, and thou hast showed us what is good, and what thou requirest of us, that it may go well with us, both now, and to all eternity. Thou sendest out thy light and thy truth amongst us; thou makest the way of life and salvation plain before us; and thou givest us many opportunities to further us in the knowledge of that way which leads to the kingdom of thy glory. We have line upon line, and precept upon precept; thou sendest thy messengers early and late, to open and apply thy word; to give us calls and warnings, directions and exhortations; and to promote by all possible means our edification here, and our salvation for ever. Thou hast not been wanting to us, O Lord; but we have been exceedingly wanting to ourselves: for, O! how have we loved darkness rather than light, and chosen to follow our own foolish and hurtful lusts, rather than to be guided by thy blessed word! So little have we improved the precious talents which thou hast put into our hands, that thou mayest justly take away the gospel of the kingdom from us, and give it to another people, who shall bring forth fruits more worthy of it. Because thou hast called, and we have refused; thou hast stretched forth thy hands, and we have not regarded; thou mayest leave us to our own perverseness and impenitence, to add sin unto sin, till our iniquities become our ruin.

But, O Lord God, merciful and gracious! we humbly beseech thee that thou wilt not so enter into judgment with thy servants; but in mercy pardon all our contempt of thy word, and our abuse of all the means of grace which thou hast afforded us. And help us, for the time to come, to use and improve such gracious opportunities to the glory of thy name, and the benefit of our own souls. As the rain descends from heaven and returns not thither, but waters the earth, and makes it fruitful, so let thy word not return unto thee void; but let it accomplish thy good pleasure, and prosper in that whereunto thou art pleased to send it. O make it instrumental and effectual to work thy grace, where it is not; and to establish and increase it, where it is; and let it build us all up in the fear and love of God, and in the knowledge and faith of our Lord Jesus Christ.

And though we cannot now find, upon the review of our services this day, that we have duly kept a day holy to the Lord; yet let it not be a lost day to us, nor thy word as water spilt upon the ground: but let thy good Spirit bring thy word to our remembrance, and cause it to be an engrafted word, able and effectual to save our souls. And as we have been taught how we ought to walk, and to please thee our God, so help us to walk more worthy of thee; and to be more ready to every good work, which may be pleasing in thy sight through Jesus Christ.

[At his hands, O merciful God, we beg thy gracious acceptance of our praise and thanksgiving, for all the blessings which thou hast so freely conferred upon us, and so long continued to us. Thou hast dealt graciously with us, O blessed Lord, and been exceedingly kind to us, not only beyond all that we have reason to expect, but above all that we are able to express. We bless thy name, O heavenly Father, that in so many respects thou hast made us to differ from multitudes in the world, who are destitute of the comforts of this life, and the hopes of a better; which through thy special favour we enjoy. We acknowledge thee in all: and we desire to ascribe unto thee all the praise and glory. Particularly would our souls now bless thee for the mercies which we have experienced this day; for thy house open to us; for the word of salvation sounding in our ears; and for thy blessed Spirit striving with our hearts. O that we may not receive the grace of God in vain; and that thy mercies may not be lost upon us! But let us act worthy of that care and kindness, which we have so long and largely experienced; let us thankfully receive and carefully improve thy distinguishing favours; let us not provoke thee to withdraw thy tender mercies from us: but do thou still continue thine accustomed goodness to us; increase and multiply thy blessings upon us; and rejoice over us to do us good.]

In mercy pardon all which thy pure and holy eyes have seen amiss this day, in any of our thoughts or desires, our words or actions. O pardon our neglect of what we should have done, and the guilt which we have contracted in all that we have attempted to do: forgive the iniquities of our holy things: and enter not into judgment with us, even according to the best of our works and services: but overlook all our sins, and failings, and imperfections, for the sake of our great Mediator and Redeemer; who appears in thy presence, and ever lives at thy right hand, to make intercession for us. To Him, as the blessed author of our hopes and happiness; and to Thee, who didst vouchsafe to deliver him up for us; and to that blessed Spirit who has revealed him to us, be all praise, and honour, and glory, humbly and heartily ascribed by us, and by all thy church, now and for evermore. *Amen.*

A SECOND EVENING PRAYER FOR THE LORD'S DAY.

O LORD, thou art good to the soul that seeks thee. By numberless invitations, and by all the endearments of thy love, thou encouragest poor sinners to come unto thee. Thou dost not bid us seek thy face in vain, or serve thee for nought: thou hast pleasure in the prosperity of thy servants, and givest not according to our poor imperfect services, but according to thine infinitely rich and tender mercies: thou givest us eternal life through Jesus Christ our Lord. It is not any thing in thy laws, O gracious Lord, but the sinfulness of our depraved nature, that makes any of them seem grievous to us: they are all holy, and just, and good, tending only to promote our present and eternal happiness. Nor is it anything in thy blessed service, but the indisposedness of our own vile hearts, that makes any part of that employment tedious to us, which is the work and joy of angels; and which it is our wisdom, our honour, our interest, and our happiness to perform. Holy God, we are all as an unclean thing, and all our righteousness are as filthy rags; nor can we ever hope to be justified in thy sight upon the account of any works or worth of our own; for by our own hearts and deeds we are reproved and condemned; and should be left speechless in the judgment, if thou, O Lord, shouldst call us to account, according to the merits even of our best services. But we desire to take refuge under the shadow of our crucified Saviour; and to be found in him, not having our own righteousness, but that which is by the faith of Jesus Christ; that the shame of our nakedness may be covered, and all our sinful deformities be hid from thine eyes. And we intreat thee to forgive us mercifully, and receive us graciously, and love us freely, in the Son of thy love, in whom thou art well pleased.

Command a blessing, we pray thee, O Lord, upon the word which this day we have heard, and upon all the means of grace that have been used for the good of our souls. It is not of him that planteth, nor of him that watereth, but of thee our God, who givest the increase. O be thou pleased to second the preaching of thy word with the powerful influences of thy grace and Holy Spirit; that it may be the savour of life to our souls, and the power of God to our salvation. O let us so hide thy word in our hearts, that we may not (as we have done) sin against thee, but may have it as a treasure within us, to aid us in every hour of temptation, and in every time of need. Apply it to our hearts, that we may walk more humbly and closely with our God, and more conscientiously and circumspectly before thee; and be so obedient to the holy precepts of thy word, that finally we may enjoy the great and precious promises contained in it.

Supply, O Lord, by the immediate teachings of thy Spirit, the want of thy public ordinances to all such as through any unavoidable impediments are kept from them. And continue to us, O gracious Lord, the light of thy gospel and all the happy opportunities which we enjoy for our soul's advantage. Preserve us also by thy grace, from the curse of barrenness; and that thine ordinances may not rise up in judgment against us,

O make them now effectual for our good : cause them to accomplish in us all the purposes of thy grace ; and let their sanctifying efficacy shine forth with a convincing splendour in our lives.

[And now we give thanks (as we are infinitely bound) to thee, O Lord God, our heavenly Father, for the mercies of this day : and for thy great mercy and goodness that has followed us all the days of our lives. O how wonderful is thy patience and long-suffering, that thou shouldst all day long stretch forth thy hands to a rebellious and gainsaying people ! And how unwearied thy kindness and love, that thou still loadest us with benefits, notwithstanding our past abuse of them, and impartest even the greatest mercies to us, who have deserved nothing but judgments at thy hands ! Blessed be thy name, O most merciful Father, that thou hast defended us from so many dangers in our lives, which threatened to destroy us; and delivered us out of so many troubles, under which we should have sunk and perished, if thou hadst not been nigh to us, and done great things for us. We bless thee for our health and plenty, peace and liberty ; for the use of our reason, limbs, and senses ; and for the comforts of all thy good creatures ; for the kindness of friends, and safety from our enemies ; for the benefits and refreshments of society, and the success and prosperity of our affairs in the world. But, above all, we bless thee for the mercies and blessings relating to the world to come ; for Jesus Christ, and all spiritual blessings in heavenly things in him; for remembering us in our low estate, and sending eternal redemption to us by the hands of thy dear Son; for the light and direction of thy word; for the teachings and strivings, the aids and consolations of thy Spirit; for all the means and helps which we have to do us good; for all thy grace wrought in us, and bestowed upon us; and for all the discoveries and hopes of eternal glory, which thou hast given to us. O how infinitely indebted are we to the kindness and love of God our Saviour! O that we may ever be sensible and thankful as we ought! And with all that thou hast given us, blessed Lord, give us hearts filled with thy love, and lifted up in thy praise, and devoted to thy service.

We can only acknowledge the debt, which we can never pay. We cannot praise thee according to the riches of thy grace, and the multitude of thy mercies: but we desire to bless and praise, with all the capacities and abilities wherewith thou hast blessed us. And help us, O Lord our God, to glorify thy name, not only in speaking to thy praise, but in so entirely devoting ourselves to thy service, that we may be thine in faithfulness, and in the sincerity of our hearts, even all the days of our lives.]

O make us truly penitent and humbled for all which this day we have done amiss; and make us unfeignedly thankful for all the good that we have received; and for all which thou hast, in any manner or measure, enabled us to do aright. The evil is from ourselves alone, and to us belongs shame and confusion of face for it; but all the good is of thy free grace, and thy mere mercy; and to thy blessed name, O Lord, our God, be all the praise and glory rendered, with the most sensible and grateful hearts, now and for evermore. *Amen.*

A CONFESSION OF THE SINS FORBIDDEN,
WITH PRAYER FOR GRACE TO PERFORM THE DUTIES ENJOINED IN THE COMMANDMENTS:
[Preparatory to the Sacrament, or at any time of humiliation.]

O LORD, the great and glorious God! against whom I have grievously offended; and who for my sins art justly displeased: I know not where to begin or end the rehearsal of all my transgressions; which are more than I can remember, and greater than I can express.

Thou art God alone, and there is none beside thee. Thou hast an absolute right over me; and thou alone art worthy to be worshipped and served by me. But, O Lord, my God, other lords beside thee have had dominion over me. I have idolized things in myself, and in this present world; and have set them in the stead of God; either disbelieving thy being, or forgetting thy presence, or disliking to retain thee in my thoughts, or living without thee in the world. I

A PRAYER UPON THE COMMANDS. 75

have not improved in thy knowledge, answerably to the means of instruction wherewith thou hast blessed me. And that I have no better knowledge of God, it is my shame; it is altogether owing to my sinful dulness and negligence in that which most of all concerns me. I have not had all my expectation from thee, nor my whole dependence upon thee, nor my chief hope and delight in thee; but have sought my happiness in creature comforts and worldly enjoyments. O how have I hardened my heart against the fear of thee, who couldst in one moment destroy me, both body and soul, in hell! How have I sinned against the clear light which thou hast caused to shine upon me! And how have I shut my heart against the love of thee, my chief good; notwithstanding thou hast been doing me good, and laying fresh obligations upon me, with thy renewed favour, every day.

I have conceived injurious, unbecoming thoughts of thine infinite greatness and goodness, till I have become vain and wicked in my imaginations; thinking the most high and glorious God to be even such a one as myself. And instead of worshipping thee in spirit and in truth, it has been after my own fancy and humour; in a formal and customary manner.

O what light account have I made of thy great name! And what little zeal have I showed for thine honour and glory! How have I disregarded thy word and works, thy mercies and judgments, thy calls and warnings, and all thine offers and invitations; and either neglected the offices of thy worship, or profaned thy holy things, and abused religious duties, to cover my own offences: drawing nigh to thee with my mouth, when my heart has been far from thee!

Thy day I have not remembered as I ought, to keep it holy: but have used as common, what thou hast set apart for sacred; and borne the holy season as a burden, and made bold with thy hallowed time, to spend it upon my sloth, and lusts, and worldly trifles, and carnal indulgences.

O how have I failed and sinned in all my relations. As a superior, in pride and vanity; as an inferior, in stubbornness and envy; as a parent and child, master and servant, friend and neighbour: not discharging my duty in any capacity as I ought!

How careless have I been of my own and others' souls! How passionate and unmerciful, contentious and revengeful! Bitter in my words; malicious in my heart; tempting some to commit sin; neglecting to keep others from the commission of it: and not exerting my utmost endeavours to do good unto all!

O Lord! I am unclean, unclean! defiled with filthy imaginations in my head, and lustful desires in my heart, which have often broke out into corrupt communication, and indecent levity and intemperate living after the flesh. Yea, I have been guilty of the spiritual whoredom, in forsaking the blessed bridegroom of my soul to cleave to lying vanities; and to keep up that friendship with the world, which is enmity with God.

I have been unfaithful in the unrighteous mammon, and not honoured thee with my sustance; nor done the good which thou hast made me capable of doing; but by idleness and injurious entrenching on the rights of others, or by profuse consuming my portion on my own lusts, I have been a sacrilegious usurper of thy good creatures.

O! what sinful liberties have I taken, in speaking evil of my neighbours! Using them in my words, as I would ill resent to be used; slandering and reviling, dissembling or rash judging; and often wronging the truth, to avenge, to excuse, or exalt myself.

O what a nursery of covetous and carnal desires has been this corrupt and wicked heart of mine! cherishing and delighting in evil motions; repining at others' welfare: coveting all to myself, and making provision for the flesh, to fulfil its lusts.

Such sins I have committed against thy holy laws; and I have also sinned against thy gracious gospel, O Lord; not acquainting myself with the way of salvation by Jesus Christ; but neglecting his great salvation; and disregarding the only Saviour, whom to know and win should have been all my desire; and in comparison of whom I should have accounted all things else but loss and dung. I have not been awed by thy threatenings, nor allured by thy promises. I have not listened to the calls of thy word, nor yielded to the motions of thy Spirit; nor believed thy truths; nor loved thy days; nor improved the opportunities which thou hast graciously set before me. I have even shut my eyes against the things of my peace; and made light of all my Saviour's invitations, and of all the wonderful things which he has done and suffered for the salvation of my soul; taking pleasure in the enemies of his cross; little concerned for the success of his gospel; nor laying to heart my own, or others' sins; nor seriously repenting, nor fervently praying; but doing all these things as if I did them not.

Such is my heavy charge; this is my heinous guilt: O that I may not only confess it, but be duly humbled for it, and lay my mouth in the dust, if so be there may be hope! And is there hope for such a great and provoking sinner? Lord of love, thou hast helped many poor miserable souls in a low and desperate condition: and many (I believe) are now triumphing and praising thee in glory, who long and grievously rebelled against thee here below. Such are the wonders of thy grace; and thus hast thou glorified thyself in seeking and saving that which was lost. And is thy hand shortened, that thou canst not save, or thy mercy exhausted, that thou wilt not hear? O be merciful unto me also, even unto me, the

A PRAYER UPON THE COMMANDS.

chief of sinners. Put me in the way where all thy goodness may pass before me: and help me to exercise such humiliation and repentance in thy sight, that thou mayest exercise thy pardoning and saving mercy towards my soul: and never lay my sins to my charge; but accept me for HIS sake, who, though he knew no sin, was made sin for us, that we might be made the righteousness of God in him.

Nor do I beg only for the pardon of my sins, but also for power to subdue them. For thy truth and mercy's sake, let thy *preventing* grace guard me from temptations in their first approach; and thy *assisting* grace enable me to withstand them, whenever I am called to the conflict: that so, through thine effectual help, I may overcome that cruel adversary, who walks about as a roaring lion, seeking whom he may devour. Turn my feet, O blessed Lord, to thy testimonies; and help me, with an enlarged heart, to run the way of thy commandments. O give me grace to take and choose thee for my God: and to know and trust, and fear and love, and serve and worship thee as it becomes me. Give me a deep reverence for thy name; an ardent zeal for thy glory; a devotion and constancy in all the duties of thy holy religion; a conscientious care to sanctify thy sabbaths; and a due veneration and affection for all thy holy things.

Help me also, O my God, rightly to discharge all relative duties towards my superiors, equals, and inferiors, even towards all with whom I have my conversation in the world: that I may give no just offence to any, but may rather win others by the amiableness and excellence of my deportment. O make me careful of my own, and of others' souls; make me peaceable and patient, merciful and kind, and studious (as far as in me lies) to promote the good of all: make me in all things to love my neighbour as myself. Enable me to be chaste and continent; pure in heart; sober and modest in speech and carriage; temperate in the use of thy good creatures; given to prayer, and to all the exercises of godliness, that tend to mortify the lusts of the flesh. Make me also faithful in the unrighteous mammon; contented with my portion; industrious in my calling; upright in my dealing; honouring thee with my substance; and doing good, and not hurt, with that portion which thou hast been pleased to bestow upon me. Help me, O righteous God, ever to love and own, to confess and maintain the truth: candidly to interpret the words and actions of others; not delighting in their shame, but being as tender of their reputation as I would desire they should be of mine. And help me, O my Lord, to resist the beginnings and first risings of evil motions in my mind; and to keep my heart with all diligence, so that it may never harbour or indulge any covetous or unclean desires. O let me not give my mind to earthly things; nor be carnally minded, which is death; but spiritually minded, which is life and peace. And incline me, O good God, to meditate on thy holy laws, yea to love and keep them with my whole heart.

O make me resolved to live a life of holiness, according to thy blessed will and word. And let me not only think and purpose to live godly in Christ Jesus, but bring my purposes into actions, my actions into habits, and my habits into an uniform perseverance; so enduring to the end, that I may be saved. And through the ways of thy holy commands, O Lord, lead me to the joys of thy heavenly kingdom; that, having my fruit unto holiness, I may, in the end, attain everlasting life, through Jesus Christ our Lord. *Amen.*

A PRAYER BEFORE THE SACRAMENT OF THE LORD'S SUPPER.

O WHAT am I, poor unworthy sinful wretch, that I should go to the table of the Lord, and take to myself the portion of his saints! Great God! my guilt, and shame, and fear do pull me back, and make me ready to conclude that it would be presumptuous and vain for me ever to expect such high honour and favour from thy hands. I could not presume to make such near approaches to thy divine Majesty, but that thou art pleased to invite and command us to come unto thee. Nor could I ever hope for such heavenly blessings at thy hands, O Lord, were it not that thou art infinitely good and kind, even to such as deserve nothing but to be forsaken and abhorred of thee. Instead of stretching forth a sceptre of mercy to invite me to thy table, thou mightest with the rod of thy wrath dash me in pieces as a potter's vessel: and, instead of entertaining me with the bread of life and the cup of blessing, thou mightest give me the bread and water of affliction; and cast me into the lowest pit, where I should in vain cry for one drop of water to cool my tongue.

But seeing thou art pleased to command, that they who have undone themselves should come unto thee for help; and hast appointed this sacrament as a means of conveying to them pardon and grace: and since I so extremely need thy pardoning mercy, and thy sanctifying grace, I come (Lord) though polluted and unfit to appear before thee; and I dare not but come, knowing that I shall be undone, if I keep away from thee. I come not, Lord, because I am worthy; but because thou art rich in mercy. I come as the hungry to be fed; and as the sick and maimed, to be recovered and healed. I come that I may wash in the blood of thy dear Son, and be cleansed; that I may receive out of his infinite fulness, all that is wanting in my wretched self; and that I may so touch my Saviour, as to derive virtue from him, to heal my infirmities, and to fit me for thy service.

O that I may come in the humblest manner, with all reverence and godly fear; and with the most earnest longings after Christ Jesus; and the heartiest resolutions to live unto him, who, of his infinite mercy, was pleased to die for me! And do thou instruct me, O Lord, and assist me in the examination and preparation of myself; in order that I may safely and comfortably partake of this holy ordinance. Before I compass thine altar, do thou purify my heart by repentance, and by faith in the blood of our adorable Redeemer. O let me receive a crucified Saviour into a broken and contrite heart. And make me so willing and obedient, that I may derive good from the ordinance, and enjoy in it, not only a representation, but a rich participation also, of his dying love. O turn in, my Lord, and be not as a stranger to the soul that has been purchased by thy blood. Enrich thine ordinance with thy presence; that I may find him whom my soul desires to love, and whose love is better than wine. Blessed Jesus, make thyself known to my soul in this breaking of bread: and let me receive such life from thee, as may enable me to live unto thee: and make me know, that thou abidest in me, by the Spirit which thou hast given me.

Blessed Saviour! weigh not my merits, but thine own; for I have deserved nothing at thy hands but wrath: nor could I presume to ask anything of thee, if thou hadst not redeemed me with thy precious blood. I can never be worthy of thee; but thou canst give me such views, dispositions, and affections, that I may eat and drink worthily of the feast to which I am invited. Come to my help, O thou blessed Emmanuel, that I may participate of thy sacred body crucified, and thy precious blood shed for us, with such discernment, and reverence, and penitence, and faith, and love, and thankfulness, as I ought to do; and may receive these symbols of thy love to my present consolation and my everlasting salvation.

O thou that hast prepared a table in this wilderness, with heavenly provisions for our souls, prepare my soul, dear Lord, for these provisions; and give me spiritual appetite, as well as spiritual sustenance: that as the hart panteth after the water-brooks, my soul may pant after thee, O God. Let me feel a vehement desire to eat this passover. Make me so to open my mouth, that thou mayest fill my hungry soul with thy good things; and so to lift up the everlasting doors of my heart, that the King of Glory may come in. Come thou, and dwell in my heart by faith; and abide with my spirit to the latest hour of my life.

O make thine ordinance healing, and a savour of life to my soul. And make it also a sealing ordinance, to clear up to me the pardon of my sins, and the assurance of thy love. And as thou sealest the covenant of grace, O let me seal the covenant of obedience: and in such a devout and acceptable manner come unto thy table, that I may return from it with my conscience quieted my corruptions subdued, my graces increased, and my soul encouraged, with an enlarged heart, to run the way of thy commands.

Ah Lord! to whom should I repair but unto thee, my life, my strength, and my Redeemer! O thou that callest unto thee the labouring and heavy-laden sinners, help me so to come to thee, that in thee I may find rest for my soul. Thou that hast commanded us to break our bread to the hungry, O break the bread of life to all of us that hunger and thirst after righteousness: and give us, O Lord God our heavenly Father, evermore give us this bread. And since thou art pleased still to continue to us the liberty and advantage of this ordinance to nourish and revive our souls, O work in our hearts a higher esteem for it, and a greater love to it. And in our preparations before we eat and drink at thy table, in our communicating there, and our conversation after, O teach and help us to act as becomes the redeemed of the Lord, and the living members of Jesus Christ.

Hear me, O Lord my God, and forgive me; bless and direct me, quicken and assist me, in the work now lying before me: and deal graciously with me, that I may discharge all my offices heartily as to the Lord, and with good acceptance in thy sight, through Jesus Christ, thy beloved Son, my only mediator and advocate. *Amen* and *Amen.*

SOME DEVOUT EJACULATIONS AND ELEVATIONS OF THE SOUL,

BEFORE RECEIVING AT THE LORD'S TABLE.

I. Blessed be my God, that again is pleased to call me to the reconciliation feast; and after all my breaches with him, and all my offences against him, yet to grant me a new indulgence; and to seal my pardon afresh in the precious blood of his dear Son, that was shed to take away the sins of the world.

II. At thy gracious invitation, Lord, I am bold to come, looking for that blessed benefit, which I know myself so unworthy to receive, that thou mightest justly bar up the doors of mercy against me, and withhold thy saving good from me. But thy mercies, blessed God, are not to the deserving and worthy, but to the miserable and needy. O let me find them, (needy and miserable as I am) according to the riches of thy bounty, and according to the greatness of my necessity.

III. I have no might for this great work: but I will go in thy strength, O Lord my God. Give me, I beseech thee, the dispositions which thou approvest; and work in me what thou requirest from me. O let me find thy hand upon me, thy help with me, and thy grace sufficient for me.

IV. O that I may see thy power and thy glory, so as I have seen thee in the sanctuary! That I may share in the heavenly entertainment of thy children, and eat and drink in thy presence that bread of life and that cup of blessing, which may be the life of my soul, and make my heart glad with the joy of thy salvation.

V. O what shall I do at thy house, and thy table, Lord, if thou dost not appear, to receive and entertain me? O that thou wouldst, in wonderful condescension, bow the heavens and come down; and make me experience thy presence with me, and the power of thy Spirit upon me, and that loving kindness of thine, which is better than life.

VI. O let not the great Lord and lover of souls keep off as a stranger to my soul; but look forth at the windows, and show himself through the lattice, and remember me in saving mercy, where he feeds, and where he makes his flock to rest: and let me now taste, and see (to the satisfaction of my soul) how good the Lord is.

VII. I desire to take shelter under the shadow of my Redeemer's wings; and to be found in Christ Jesus, clothed with that righteousness of his, which is sufficient both to atone for all my guilt, and also to fill up all my wants; yea, to make me complete in the sight of God, and meet for the felicity of his chosen. O God of all grace! give me, I beseech thee, a saving interest in that great redemption which thy beloved Son has purchased for a ruined world: that my soul may magnify the Lord, and my spirit may rejoice in God my Saviour.

VIII. O thou that art able to do it, bring me into the bonds of the covenant: and let me voluntarily and cheerfully enter into it; not as one who is averse to the terms that it proposes, but as one who longs to enjoy the blessings which it offers.

IX. O make me willing in the day of thy power; and may I this day experience, Lord, the powerful workings of thy blessed Spirit, to open and enlarge my heart, and to make me ready and fit to receive him who stands at the door and knocks, even to receive into my soul Christ Jesus the Lord.

X. O how unworthy am I, Lord, that thou shouldst come under my roof; unworthy to eat the crumbs that fall from thy table! But thine infinite merits can cover all my sins and unworthiness; and recommend me to the just and holy Majesty of heaven, even as if I had not sinned. O deal graciously with me, my Lord and my God. I beseech thee; and forgive, and heal, and help me; and exercise thy power and pity towards me; and come into my soul, with all the blessings and consolations which thou hast taught us to expect at thy hands.

XI. O Lord! my soul is polluted and unclean; but thy precious blood can cleanse me from all my sins and defilements, and make me a fit habitation for thy Holy Spirit. O speak thou the word, and I shall be clean and whole: and my soul shall live, and for ever bless thy name

XII. Assist me mercifully, O Lord, in my designs and endeavours to obtain the blessed fruitions, whereof thou hast made me capable. O forgive my unworthiness; cover my sins; help my infirmities; quicken my dulness; prepare me for thee; draw me unto thee; bring me into the enjoyment of thee; let me possess thee *now*, as far as my poor capacity will admit of, and *hereafter*, in all thy fulness, for ever and ever.

XIII. O that thine ordinance now may be the means of my establishment! Let it impart unto my soul, out of the fulness of Christ Jesus, grace sufficient for me. Let it be the means of rendering me lively and constant in the discharge of every duty. And what I *have* not in myself, Lord, do thou give me: and what I *am* not of myself, O do thou make me, for thy own mercy's sake. *Amen, Amen*

SOME DEVOUT EJACULATIONS AND ELEVATIONS OF THE SOUL,

AFTER RECEIVING AT THE LORD'S TABLE.

I. GLORY be to thee, O Lord our God, that in our extreme need of a Redeemer thou hast made such gracious provision for our souls; that thou hast sent thy Son to die for our sins, and to save us, after we had destroyed ourselves. Blessed be thy name, that he who offered himself upon the cross for us, is pleased to offer himself at his table to us: there have I been tasting the fruits of his love, and receiving my share among the redeemed of the Lord. O blessed be God for so great a mercy!

II. I bless thee, my God, for the mercies of a Saviour; without which all other mercies would be of no avail, would do me no good. I bless thee, that thou hast not withheld thy Son, thine only Son from us; but hast given him to be the propitiation for our sins, and the life and food of our souls.

III. I sat down under his shadow, and his fruit was sweet to my taste. I have been entertained at the table of the Lord: and there his banner over me was love. It was love that gave me the Saviour whom I have been receiving, and the opportunity to rest and feast my soul upon him.

IV. Return to thy rest, O my soul, for the Lord has dealt bountifully with thee. Thy life is given thee at his hands, who forgiveth all thy sins, and healeth all thy diseases: and not only redeems thee from destruction, but crowns thee with loving-kindness and tender mercies; and satisfies thy mouth with good things, even with pardon and peace, yea, with the riches of his grace, and the pledges of his glory.

V. Blessed be my God, for that bread which came down from heaven, to give life unto the world. And blessed be thy name, O gracious

Lord, for my share in this highest expression of thy wonderful love and bounty.

VI. Eternal thanks and praise be unto thee, O blessed God my Saviour, for all thy glorious achievements, in laying the sure foundation for our hope and everlasting consolation.

VII. Thou hast loved us, and redeemed us, and washed us from our sins in thine own blood. And O how infinitely indebted am I to thy mercy, that thou callest me to this sweet heavenly entertainment; which thou hast purchased and provided for us at so great a price!

VIII. O make me more sensible of thy love, and more thankful for all its blessed effects. And let me now find the happy fruits of strength and refreshment to my soul: even strength against all the temptations that would pluck me from thee; and refreshment, that may render all the pleasures of sin distasteful to me, and make it my meat and drink to do the will of my heavenly Father.

IX. After I have tasted the pleasures of my Father's house, O let me not go to feed upon husks. Let nothing take away from me the savour that I have had of heavenly things nor let a world separate between me and the blessed Saviour of the world.

X. Let me not turn my back upon the Lord of love, that has been so good and kind to my soul. O let me never more take up arms against my heavenly Sovereign, to whom now again I have vowed allegiance.

XI. Whither shall I go from thee, O blessed Jesus, who hast the words and the gift of eternal life? All is in thy hands: and thou art the best of all lords, who rulest us only that thou mayest bless us; and layest thy commands upon us only that thou mayest keep us from ruining ourselves, and secure to us the highest happiness.

XII. I will admire, and love, and praise my Lord: I will believe and trust in his tried mercy: I will rejoice and glory in his great salvation. And who shall pluck me out of his hands? What shall separate me from his love? My beloved is mine, and I am his. Thine I am, O Lord, and thine I will be, while I have my being.

XIII. Yet, Lord of all power and love! I beseech thee keep thy servant from falling; and preserve me in every time of danger. O do not suffer me to destroy myself; but pity my frailty, and relieve my infirmity: and in thy hands let me be safe, and never perish, but attain everlasting life; through Jesus Christ, my great Redeemer and only Saviour. *Amen, Amen.*

THANKSGIVING AND PRAYER AFTER THE SACRAMENT OF THE LORD'S SUPPER.

I DESIRE with all my soul to adore and magnify thy blessed name, O Lord God, my heavenly Father, for all the expressions of thy love and bounty to me, a poor unworthy sinner.

Particularly for thy precious favours, and the renewed pledges of thy love in Christ Jesus, which I have received from thee this day: that thou hast admitted me, not only into thy house, but to thy table; and used me as thy friend, and the child of thy family; even me, who deserve to be cast out as an enemy, and to be abhorred by thee as the off-scouring of all things. O what manner of love is this, that I should fare so well, who deserve so ill at thy hands! O that it should be done to wretched sinful men! That the God so greatly offended by us, should not only forgive us, but entertain and feast us with all the good things, which our blessed Saviour has merited and prepared for us! Lord, what is man, that thou art so mindful of him, and the son of man that thou so visitest him! And what am I, one of the vilest and most sinful of men, that the great Lord, so often dishonoured by me, should deal so exceeding graciously with me! O make me to know the things that are freely given me of God, and to see how much I owe unto the Lord for all thy kindness to my soul. O give me a heart deeply sensible of thy mercy, and steadfastly purposing to live to thy glory; that I may show my thankfulness for thy benefits by my obedience to thy precepts. O keep me mindful of the vows which are upon me: and help me to live, as having my holy Redeemer now dwelling in me.

And as I have received Christ Jesus the Lord,

so enable me to walk in him; to walk more worthy of the Lord unto all well-pleasing; to walk in love, as Christ hath loved us; and to go on in the strength of what I have received from thee, following after holiness, and perfecting it in thy fear.

As I have eat and drank the sacramental bread and wine, to the nourishment and refreshment o. my frail body; so let the body and blood of God my Saviour nourish and sustain my immortal soul unto life eternal.

And O that the sacrifice of Christ Jesus (that sacrifice of himself which he offered upon the cross, and which I have this day been commemorating at thy table,) may atone for all the failings and defects of my preparations and performances! and that, upon the account of that grand propitiation for the sins of the whole world, I may be spared and accepted with thee my God! O grant it, I beseech thee, through him that loved us, and gave himself for us, even the Son of thy love, the great lover of our souls: for whom, and to whom, with thy eternal self and Holy Spirit, be all thanks and praise, and honour, and glory, ascribed of me, and of all thy church, now and for evermore. *Amen.*

A PRAYER FOR GRACE TO RESIGN, AND GIVE UP OURSELVES TO GOD.

O MY great and glorious Maker and Redeemer, my continual Preserver, my only Lord and Owner! Thine I am every way, by all the ties of duty and love. I am not at my own disposal; for thou hast formed me for thyself; and dearly ransomed me, after I had destroyed and sold myself. I have been solemnly devoted to thee, and have vowed to renounce all tempters that would rival my blessed Lord : and obediently to serve thee, my God, and to walk in thy holy ways all the days of my life. Nor is this a matter of duty only and obligation, but it is my honour and interest, my highest perfection, and my greatest bliss.

But with confusion and remorse I must acknowledge, O Lord, that I have sacrilegiously alienated myself from thee, and most foolishly and wickedly forsaken thee, to serve other lords; yea, to be under the power and servitude of my own vain humours and sinful passions ; not concerned so much to honour thee, as to please myself: as if I were altogether my own, and had no Lord over me. O my God! forgive, and mortify in me, this wicked and pernicious selfishness: and let me no longer unjustly withhold myself from thee ; nor madly expose myself to ruin, by living in the world without thee; nor vainly hope to unite the inconsistent services of God and mammon: but make me so mindful both of my duty and happiness, as willingly and cheerfully to devote myself to the blessed Author of my being: that so I may both answer the end for which I was made, and also attain the happiness whereof I am capable. Seeing that all who are far from thee shall perish, as branches cut from the living root that feeds them; and that I have no sufficiency in myself, but derive all my good from union with my God; I am convinced, O Lord, that I ought to yield up myself to thee, by my own free choice and voluntary act. O bring me to this surrender of myself to thee; and make me faithful and hearty in it.

My Lord! break all the ties that detain me from thee: and take me for thine own: yea, keep and continue me in thy fear and love, to my life's end. And upon my mind and memory, upon my will and affections, upon my heart and conscience, write Holiness to the Lord; and every way make me willing to be wholly thine. Let thy will ever be a law to me in all things: and melt down this stubborn will into a ready compliance with thy holy pleasure. O let me love what thou lovest, and hate what thou hatest. Let my soul and body, and all the faculties and powers of both, be under thy control, and be employed to thy glory. Let all that I am, and all that I have, be thine; not in pretence only, but in deed and in truth. And never let me think it hard to renounce all for thee, who art infinitely better to me than ten thousand worlds.

O help me so sincerely to deny myself; that I may own no guide and ruler, but my great Lord and Proprietor: that my eyes may be ever towards thee, and my whole dependence upon thee; and that in all things thou mayest ever be regarded and preferred and glorified by me, through Jesus Christ. *Amen.*

PRAYER AND HUMILIATION FOR A PUBLIC FAST-DAY.

[SEE ALSO PAGE 74.]

O LORD God, glorious in holiness, and of purer eyes than to behold iniquity without abhorrence of it, and indignation against it! how shall man, sinful man, that drinks iniquity like water, appear before thee! And how shall we, vile and frail, polluted and depraved as we are, show ourselves in the presence of such a just and holy God as thou art! When we look upon thy perfect law, and see what we should be, what manner of persons in all holy conversation and godliness; and when we reflect on our own hearts and lives, and find what we are, how wanting in our duty, and how contrary to what thou requirest of us; we cannot come into thy presence, O Lord, without confusion of face, and anguish of soul, and remorse of conscience, to think how foolishly and wickedly we have acted; and how abject and wretched we have made ourselves.

Besides that we brought with us a corrupt nature into the world, full of strangeness to thee our God, and full of enmity against thy holy, good, and righteous laws; we have mis-spent the most of our time here in a neglect of thy work, and in disobedience to thy word: daily multiplying our offences against thee, as thou hast multiplied thy blessings unto us. O the precious time that we have lost, the means that we have neglected, the mercies that we have abused, the calls and warnings, the offers and invitations, that we have disregarded! What little regard have we had of thee! what little fear of offending thee! Alas! O Lord, we have grievously insulted thy glorious Majesty, and daringly trampled upon thy holy laws.

O the crying sins and abominations that prevail in every place! [The swearing and drunkenness, the pride and uncleanness, the cruel enmity and injustice, the corrupt communication and ungodly conversation whereby God is so greatly dishonoured and provoked every day.] And O how large a share have we had in adding to the public guilt; sinning, as we have done, in all estates and affairs, in all relations and circumstances of our lives! And not only through weakness and surprise, and the violence of temptations; but many times knowingly, wilfully, and presumptuously; with a high hand, and stiff neck, against thee, our Maker and our Judge! And O how great a weight have we added to all our other sins, by the hardness of our hearts, and our impenitent continuance in our sins! committing great sins with little remorse, little penitent concernment for all the evils whereof we have been guilty! Yea, Lord, how unsuitable still are our hearts and lives to those holy rules, which thy word gives us in charge to follow! So much is there still amiss with us, and wanting in us, that it is of thy great mercy we are not consumed: it is because thy compassions fail not, that we have still these opportunities to humble ourselves before thee and to cry for mercy.

We have not glorified thee, O Lord, in bearing fruits of holiness answerable to thy revealed will; but we desire to give glory to God, in confessing our sins, and humbling our souls, and acknowledging our desert; and more especially would we admire and magnify the riches of thy grace, which has spared us so long a time, and showed us such marvellous kindness still, notwithstanding all the high provocations of our sins. Lord, we have heard (and, blessed be thy name, we have found) that the King of heaven is a merciful king; that with thee, our God, there is mercy; that our sins, though great and manifold, may be pardoned; and that our souls may yet be recovered, and healed, and saved. O help us so to judge and condemn ourselves, that we may not be judged of the Lord, and condemned with the world. Lay not our sins to our charge; but put them to the account of thy Son, our Saviour, whom thou hast given to be the propitiation for our sins, and in whom thou art reconciled to a guilty world. For his sake, O good Lord, give us repentance and pardon for all the sins whereby we have offended thee: whether they be our sins of omission, or commission; our sins of weakness or wilfulness; our failings or presumptions; our sins of ignorance, or such as we have committed against light and knowledge: O gracious Lord, humble us duly under the sense of them, and absolve us thoroughly from the guilt of them. O set our sins in order before us, and make us to know our transgressions; make every one of us to search and try our ways, that we may turn to the Lord, and bring forth fruits meet for repentance. May we not only loathe ourselves in our own sight for all the evils whereof we have been guilty, but also loathe, as much as ever we have loved, the things which have displeased thee. O that we may forsake our sins, not only in the outward commission, but in the inward affection; not reserving to ourselves any sin or lust to be spared, but keeping at a distance from every evil and accursed thing: cleansing ourselves from all filthiness of flesh and spirit, and endeavouring to perfect holiness in the fear of God!

We have been accessary to the accumulated heinous guilt that endangers us all, and calls for judgment on the land. O that we may now contribute our help, by the humiliation of our souls and the reformation of our lives, to save our nation, and to turn away the anger which is gone out against us, that we perish not! Save us, O Lord, from our sins, which are the enemies of our own house; more mischievous to us than any other evils or enemies abroad. O pour out a spirit of serious repentance and reformation upon the whole nation; to heal the distempers of our souls, to curb the disorders of our lives, and to recover the decayed power of godliness in the land: yea, Lord, prepare and dispose us, not only for thy temporal mercies, but for the mercy of our Lord Jesus Christ to eternal life. Help us so to turn from the evil of our ways, that thou mayst turn from the fierceness of thy wrath, and cause thine anger towards us to cease. O that we may fear the rod, and him who has appointed it! and so prepare to meet thee, in the way of thy judgments, that thou mayst have thoughts of peace towards us, and not of evil; to give us an expected end, and the desired issue out of all our troubles.

Thou canst show us great and mighty things, which we know not, and canst exceed all our expectations, as well as our deservings, by thy bountiful favours: and though thou mightst make us know the worth of slighted mercies, by the want of them, and deprive us of all the good, which we have so greatly abused, yet, O how do the promises of thy word, and the frequent experience which we have had of thy mercy, encourage us still with hope to look unto our God, and to wait for the salvation of our Lord! O how long (in all provocations) hast thou spared us! And how often (in our distresses) sent a wonderful redemption to us! To thee, who hast helped and delivered, we still look for help and deliverance. O our God! arise and help us, and deliver us, for thy mercy's sake; for the sake of that mercy which first made us thy people, and still has owned us for thy peculiar care. O do not abhor us, nor forsake us, for thy name's sake; but be jealous for thy land, and pity thy people. Turn us again, O Lord God of hosts; and cause thy face to shine, and we shall be saved.

But, O our God, if thou dost not see fit to turn away the evils from us, prepare us for them, and support us under them, and bring us out of them purified as gold. Let us not sink and perish in our calamities, but receive spiritual good from temporal evils; and find the light momentary afflictions to work for us a far more exceeding and eternal weight of glory. And though thou shouldst feed us with bread of adversity and water of affliction, yet let not our teachers be removed into corners: bring us not under a famine of the word; nor give us over to the formality o a lifeless profession: but whilst thou continuest to us the means of grace, O continue thy blessing upon them, and send not leanness withal into our souls. Though thou permit the floods and storms to arise, yet fortify us so by thy grace, that we may not be moved by any of the afflictions; nor turn the advantage of suffering for thee, into an occasion of falling from thee.

Seeing the truth itself will not make us free if we are not true to it; nor the purest religion be our defence if we continue to walk unworthy of our profession; O help us, Lord, to rid our hands and our hearts of all the accursed things that provoke thy wrath and indignation against us. Let us wisely consider of thy doings, and know the time of our visitation: give us grace that we may hearken to thy calls, and take thy warnings, and improve thy mercies, while we have them: let us now follow the conduct of thy good providence, and comply with all the gracious methods which thou art using to reclaim us, that we may be delivered from the evil to come, and be for ever happy in thy presence. Hear, Lord, and answer us for the sake of Jesus Christ our blessed Lord and Saviour. *Amen.*

CONFESSION AND PRAYER FOR THE EVENING OF A PUBLIC FAST-DAY.

O LORD most high and holy, the God of all power and glory, against whom we have greatly sinned, and who by our sins hast been highly provoked, we are under a necessity still to come and appear before thee; nor dare we keep away from thee. But O! with what confidence can we look up to the Majesty of heaven, whom we have so much offended!

Well may we be abashed and struck down, to bethink ourselves of all the evil that we have done, and all the sins of heart and life which we still commit: when we remember, O Lord, and consider thy perfect understanding of every particular, thy holiness to hate, thy justice to requite, and thy power to punish every wicked thing, we are even confounded before thee.

We fall down, and humble ourselves at thy footstool, O blessed and glorious God, confessing the grievous guilt of all our sins, and our just desert of thy heavy judgments. For we cannot but own ourselves to be some of those degenerate children whom thou hast nourished and brought up, and that have rebelled against thee. Yea, the very forbearance which thou hast exercised, has emboldened us to sin the more against thee.

Holy Father! we are filled with confusion, to think how inconsistent we have been with ourselves: we call ourselves children of God, members of Christ, and heirs of glory; we profess to take the gospel as our rule, and to believe all the great eternal things contained in it; and yet we walk as if we did not know the privileges that we enjoy, or regard the relations in which we stand; alas! how unsuitable is this conduct to our profession.

Surely this may not only fill our faces with

shame, but our hearts with dread; lest our very profession of thy holy religion should rise up in judgment against us, to aggravate our condemnation.

We have been vain and carnal, proud and unthankful in our health and prosperity; and sullen and froward, murmuring and desponding in seasons of adversity. The kindness that should have allured us unto thee, and encouraged us the more faithfully and cheerfully to serve thee, has caused us rather to be forgetful of thee, and to wax wanton against thee. And the correction that should have driven us out of our sins, and hastened us to flee for the life of our souls, has but put us out of patience, and filled us with prejudice against thy righteous hand, and with hard and unworthy thoughts of our God. In this manner we have held fast our sins, notwithstanding all thy various methods to alienate us from them.

Yea, to thee, O Lord, who searchest the heart, and triest the reins, we must acknowledge and bewail the sins of our hearts and minds; our vain thoughts and proud imaginations, our impure and covetous desires, our envious and malicious projects. These have corrupted the fountain, and defiled the habitation of thy blessed Spirit. These are the seeds and roots of all the other evils in our lives; and render us even as criminal in thy sight, as if we had outwardly acted, what we have thus inwardly devised. These vile inclinations, this proneness to evil, (this approving of it, consenting to it, and delighting in it) carries so much guilt and malignity along with it, that even for this, thou mightst justly abhor us, and condemn us in that day when thou shalt judge the secrets of men by Jesus Christ.

Thus we must criminate and arraign ourselves before thee; confessing that iniquities prevail against us, and that our sins still retain in great measure the ascendant over us! Still we are offending our holy Lord; and still we carry in us the corrupt nature, the carnal mind, which are enmity against God, and which justly expose us to thy heaviest displeasure.

We read of such as cannot cease from sin: and such, O Lord, thou knowest us in a great measure to be; that have brought ourselves under the sad necessity of sinning against thee; and so entangled our guilty souls in the tempter's snare, as to be taken captive by him, even at his will.

We call to mind with shame and remorse, how we have provoked thee to jealousy, and affronted thy glorious Majesty by the frequency of our sins and the heinousness of our offences.

But though we are constrained to acknowledge what great and provoking sinners we have been, yet O how superficial and hypocritical has been our repentance! Even when we talk of humiliation, and pretend to it, and argue for it, O Lord, thou knowest how seldom we have engaged in it, and how slightly we have performed it, even on the days that were more especially set apart for it. How hard and unrelenting have been our hearts! and how loth and backward have we been to this most needful work!

O merciful God! humble us, for that we have been no more humbled; and lay not to our charge the sins of those services which we have so ill performed. And seeing that unrepented sins are the cause of thy dreadful judgments, O that the fear of thy judgments may drive us out of all such sins! And when the wrath of God is revealed from heaven against them, O let us not dare to continue in them. When the axe is laid to the root of the tree, and thy hand is lifted up, as ready to execute vengeance upon us, O that we may be so warned as to be reclaimed; and bring forth such fruits meet for repentance, that we may not be hewn down and cast into the fire, nor die and perish in our sins; but may find a way of escape, and mercy from the Lord, and grace to help in every time of need.

And the Lord in mercy pity our frailties and infirmities, and forgive us all our sinful neglects and iniquities. And for what is still wanting in us, O be thou graciously pleased to accept the full and perfect merits and righteousness of thy dear Son, our most holy Saviour: and let his precious blood be heard speaking for us, where we have nothing to say for ourselves: and where we are so unworthy to be heard on our own account.

Be merciful, O God, to this sinful nation, that has so long enjoyed and so much abused thy rich blessings, and still goes on to provoke thee daily.

O forgive the many crying sins, for which thou mightst justly abhor us, and reject us, and lay us desolate, and so forsake us utterly, as to be favourable to us no more. Yet grant us thy grace, we beseech thee, so to repent and amend, that we may be spared, and saved from all the judgments which we have so richly deserved.

O that all thy warnings and threatenings and chastenings, may not leave us still an unrelenting, incorrigible people, nor pass over us, without working an humble submission and unfeigned repentance in us! O that we may find reconciliation with our God, in humbling ourselves before thee, returning unto thee, and bringing forth such fruits of new and better obedience, as (through the Lord our righteousness) shall be favourably accepted by thee. Let us not sink under our fears, nor be ruined by our sins; but let us be plucked as brands out of the fire; to survive our dread and danger, and to see the good of thy chosen, and rejoice in the gladness of thy nation, and to glory with thine inheritance.

And for all the mercy which thou hast still remembered toward us; and for all thy wonderful patience with us; and for that continued matter and occasion of thankfulness which we have yet daily before us; not unto us, O Lord, not unto us, but to thy name be all praise and glory rendered, with humble and grateful hearts, by us, and by all thy people, now and for evermore. *Amen.*

PRAYER AND PRAISE

UPON THE OCCASION OF OUR BLESSED SAVIOUR'S
COMING INTO THE WORLD.

BLESSING, and honour, and glory, and power be to him that sitteth upon the throne, and to the Lamb, for ever and ever! O Lord God of our salvation! thou hast remembered us in our low estate: thou hast raised up a great salvation and a mighty deliverance for us; thou hast sent thine only-begotten Son to heal the sinful, to help the miserable, and to save the lost. None but thy blessed self, O Lord, knoweth the greatness of that gift, which thou hast conferred upon us; (the greatest that thou couldst give, or man receive;) none can duly estimate thy mercy in giving thine only Son, to be our almighty Saviour, to deliver us from the miseries of hell, and to exalt us to thrones of glory. O how wonderful have been the designs of thy love, and the counsels of thy wisdom! that thou shouldst recover our lost souls, and work for them a salvation so worthy of thyself! That he, who is thy fellow, should be manifested in the flesh, to destroy the works of the devil! and that the eternally beloved of thy soul should be made the Son of man in order that we might be made the children of God! O what manner of love has the Father bestowed upon us! how infinitely does it exceed all that we can ever say of it! O that all might praise thee, O Lord, for thy goodness, and for thy wonderful works unto the children of men! O that we in particular might receive this great mystery of godliness with the deepest reverence and most lively gratitude! Let our souls magnify the Lord, and our spirits rejoice in God our Saviour! Yea, for ever blessed be the Lord God of Israel, that has so visited and redeemed his people.

And now that thou hast laid help upon one that is mighty, and found a ransom for us, O help us, blessed God, to entertain and welcome the joyful news, that Jesus Christ is come into the world to save sinners. Father of mercies! prepare our hearts to embrace that thine inestimable gift. Let him who came into the world in the fulness of time, now come into our souls in the fulness of his grace. Let him who was miraculously formed in the virgin's womb, be spiritually formed in our hearts. O thou great Lord and lover of souls; remember us with the favour which thou bearest to thy people, and visit us with the joy of thy salvation. O make the way of salvation plain before us, that we may know where our help lies, and what we must do to be saved. And incline and quicken us, O Lord, to comply with the gracious designs of thy mercy, and to receive with all thankfulness that grace of thine which bringeth salvation. O blessed Saviour, be thou an effectual Saviour unto us: save us from our sins, that thou mayest also save us from the wrath to come. Redeem us from all iniquity, that thou mayest also redeem us from everlasting misery. Thou camest down to earth, to raise us up to heaven: thou tookest our nature, that we might partake of thine: O let us then experience the mighty power of thy grace; let it heal our depraved natures, let it sanctify our sinful souls, let it make us lovers and followers of thy holy ways; and let those good things, which accompany salvation, be multiplied unto us exceedingly, through the knowledge of our incarnate Lord. Let the great and wonderful things which thou hast done for us, in revealing thy salvation, and in opening a door of hope to us, dwell richly in our minds; and let a sense of thine infinite loving-kindness ever constrain us to love and serve thee with all our heart, and mind, and soul, and strength: even so, O God and Father, for thy dear Son's sake; to whom, together with thyself and the Holy Ghost, Three Persons in one glorious Godhead, be equal and everlasting glory. *Amen.*

A PRAYER ON THE OCCASION OF OUR BLESSED SAVIOUR'S DEATH.

O GOD, the Father of mercies, and of our Lord Jesus Christ, through whom every mercy is vouchsafed and derived unto us; thou didst create us after thine own blessed image, in a holy and happy state: but we have defaced the work of thy hands, and have brought ourselves into a state of alienation from thee, and of enmity against thee. Yet thou hast not dealt with us as enemies, or left us in the sad ruins of our fall; but hast pitied us when lying in our blood, and hast bid us live. Thou hast even given thine only-begotten Son to die for us, to save us from that everlasting death, which is the due wages of our sins. Him, O most holy Lord God, thou sparedst not, that thou mightst spare us, and make us eternal monuments of thy saving mercy. O what amazing unspeakable love is this, that, even when enemies, we should be reconciled to God by the death of his Son! But O the cursed nature of sin, that needed such an atonement; and the inexorable justice of my God, that required it; and the incomprehensible love of my Saviour, who offered it upon the cross! O that we could bear these things always in remembrance! that we could hate sin with a perfect hatred! that we could stand in awe of our God, and fear to offend him! and that we could love that adorable Saviour, who bought us at the inestimable price of his own blood! Most blessed God, we desire to bless and magnify thy name for revealing to us this stupendous mystery. By it we abide; and upon it we depend for the pardon of our sins, and for our whole acceptance with thee, both here and for ever. We believe, O God, that thy dear Son has fully discharged our debt; and that nothing at all remains to be paid by them, for whom thou art pleased to accept his infinite satisfaction. And seeing that there is balm in Gilead, and a physician that is able to heal us, O let not our souls be unhealed; let not the great things which our Lord Redeemer hath done and endured for perishing sinners, be lost unto us: but let the same be mercifully accepted upon our account, as the payment of our debt. O let not the blood of Jesus Christ (as to us) be shed in vain; but let it purge and purify us from all our sins, and make our peace with thee, against whom we have so greatly transgressed: let us be healed by his stripes, and find his death unto us a savour of life.

Though we are sinful and unclean, yet what pollution and defilement cannot this fountain, opened for sin and uncleanness, wash and cleanse us from! Having therefore such an all-sufficient Saviour to repair to, let us not be faithless, but believing that Christ is our Lord and our God, who loved and redeemed us, and washed us from our sins in his own blood. O that we may know him, and the fellowship of his sufferings, and be rendered conformable to his death! Let the cross of Christ be the means of crucifying the world unto us, and us unto the world. Pardon, O good Lord, all our forgetfulness of thee: and make us to know more of the love wherewith thou hast loved us; and touch our hearts with such a powerful sense of thy love, that we may make better returns of love to thee, who hast done such great things for our souls. Let us never forget or slight such unparalleled kindness, but be constrained by it to live unto him who died for us, and rose again. O that the life which we now live, may be by the faith of the Son of God, who loved us, and gave himself for us! Let us more and more abound in thy love. Blessed Lord! let the serving and enjoying of thee be ever preferred above our chief joy. And let nothing in the world ever be so dear to us as the name of our adorable Emmanuel, who has given the highest demonstration of love that ever could be given to our perishing souls. And for what thou hast done for us, be all possible glory and honour and praise ascribed unto thee. O most blessed Saviour and Redeemer, by all the Israel of God, both now and evermore. *Amen.*

PRAYER AND PRAISE ON THE OCCASION OF OUR BLESSED SAVIOUR'S RESURRECTION.

BLESSED be the God and Father of our Lord Jesus Christ, who, according to his abundant mercy, has begotten us again to a lively hope, by the resurrection of Jesus Christ from the dead. Blessed be he, who liveth and was dead; and behold, he is alive for evermore; *Amen:* and has the keys of death and hell. The Lord liveth, and blessed be our rock, and let the God of our salvation be exalted. He hath borne our griefs and carried our sorrows, and has wrought eternal redemption for us; with his own right hand and holy arm hath he gotten himself the victory: having loosed the pains of death; because it was impossible he should be holden of it. Adored be that glorious Sun of Righteousness who is risen with healing in his wings; and hath showed that he is able to save himself; and to save to the uttermost all that come unto God through him. Our eyes are unto thee, O Lord, our life, our strength, and our Redeemer, who hast all power in heaven and in earth; to whom nothing is impossible or difficult: who quickenest the dead, even souls dead in sin, as well as bodies dead in the grave; and hast life in thyself, to give it to whomsoever thou wilt. O that we may know thee, and the power of thy resurrection! Let us find it effectual to raise us out of the grave of our corruptions, to newness and holiness of life; that, having part in the first resurrection, we may never be subjected to the second death. Speak death to our sins, O Lord, that our souls may live, and for ever bless thy name. Thou, O Christ, art our life; and in thee is all fulness of whatever we want: O give us the life, which thou camest to impart: and let us have it more abundantly. Let us have such life from thee, as may enable us to live unto thee, and *that* entirely and cheerfully; even as long as we have any life and being. *Amen*

PRAYER AND PRAISE ON THE OCCASION OF OUR BLESSED SAVIOUR'S ASCENSION.

THOU art the King of Glory, O Christ: thou hast ascended on high, and led captivity itself captive; dragging after thy triumphant chariot thy vanquished enemies. Thou art exalted far beyond all principalities and powers, and enthroned in the highest glory in thy kingdom, where saints and angels, even all the host of heaven, admire and adore thee. Be thou exalted, Lord, and reign in the greatness of thy power and majesty, until thou hast brought all enemies into subjection under thy feet. But, Lord, remember us, now thou art in thy kingdom. O regard the supplications, and relieve the necessities, of thy poor servants here below. Save, Lord, and let the King of heaven hear us when we call. And O that we may feel the powerful attraction of thy grace, to draw up our minds and desires from the perishable enjoyments of this world, to those unspeakable and everlasting glories above, where thou sittest at the right hand of God. O let us lay up our treasure, and have our conversation, with thee in heaven; and so love thine appearing, as to be ever looking for and hasting to the coming of that blessed day, when we shall be dissolved and be with Christ; that when Christ, who is our life, shall appear, we also may appear with him in glory. Enable us now to ascend and dwell with thee in the constant exercise of faith and love; that, in the last day, we may personally ascend in soul and body, to be for ever with the Lord; there, together with thy whole triumphant church, to see and admire, to love and bless, to praise and glorify thee, O blessed God our Saviour, world without end. *Amen.*

A PRAYER ON THE OCCASION OF THE COMING OF THE HOLY GHOST.

O THOU infinite, eternal Spirit, the Lord and giver of life, who workest all in all; and especially workest and abidest in the souls of men! pardon (we beseech thee) all the guilt we have contracted in resisting thy motions, and quenching the flames which thou hast at any time enkindled in our breasts. And be pleased so to enlighten our minds, and pur fy our hearts, that we may be fit to receive and entertain thee, as the guide and comforter of our souls. O thou Spirit of truth, lead us into all truth; and bring all needful things out of the word to our remembrance; and set them home powerfully upon our hearts, to influence our lives, and to do us good in every time of our need. Whatsoever grace is lacking in us, O form it in our hearts by thy Holy Spirit: and establish and increase what thou hast already wrought in us. Excite and stir us up to all good; and enable us for the performance of it, and engage us to continue and persist in it.

O come down, Lord, as fire, upon us, to consume our dross, and to make clean our hearts, and inflame them with heavenly love; that we may devoutly relish thy holy things, and be lively in following thy holy ways. O be thou a powerful principle of life, and light, and love, and of all grace and holiness in our souls; to illuminate our minds; to spiritualize our affections; to pacify our consciences; and to bring our souls out of every dangerous, self-destroying course, into the paths of righteousness, even to that way of life, which is above to the wise, to depart from hell beneath. O blessed Lord, restrain us from grieving thy Holy Spirit, whereby we are sealed to the day of redemption. And cast us not away from thy presence. Take not thy Holy Spirit from us. O make us so tractable under his holy motions, that we may experience his heavenly consolations. And let the joy in the Holy Ghost be more to us than all the pleasures of the world. O blessed Spirit! be thou ever with our spirits; to heal our distempers, and help our infirmities, and work mightily upon our hearts by thy grace; until our souls are fitted for that glory, which is unspeakable and everlasting. *Amen.*

A PRAYER ON THE COMMEMORATION OF ANY SAINT.

O GOD of all grace, who art pleased to call out of this present world a peculiar people to thyself, and to pour out thy Spirit upon them, and to make them shine as lights in the midst of a crooked and perverse generation, and to set them forth as examples to the rest of mankind; we bless thy holy name, that thou hast not left us destitute of such helps and patterns, as might serve to show us how practicable is our duty, and what encouragement we have to set ourselves to the performance of it. Stir us up, we pray thee, to take that more excellent way, wherein they (with such happy success) have gone before us; and constrain us to become followers of them, as they were of Christ. And seeing that we are encompassed with so great a cloud of witnesses, O that we may lay aside every weight, and the sin that does so easily beset us; and run with patience the race that is set before us! Teach and enable us, O King of Saints, to make a right improvement of those gifts and graces, whereby thy servants of old adorned their holy profession; and so to imitate their virtues, as to convince the world, that the righteous is indeed more excellent than his neighbour.

O that we may never persecute thy saints, nor madly despise those who are as the apple of thine eye; whose great care is to approve themselves faithful in thy covenant, and zealous for thy glory. May we ever hold such in the highest reputation whilst living, as well as count their memories precious when they are dead. O heavenly Father, let them be dearest to us that are dearest to thyself. And let all our delight be in the saints that are in the earth; of whom the world is not worthy; notwithstanding that they are so abused by the world, as if unworthy to live in it. O let us not be conformed to this world; nor follow the multitude, to do evil; but be followers of those who (through faith and patience) do already inherit thy glorious promises: and may we so live the life of the righteous. that we may also die their death. Help us, O Lord our God, so to imitate thy saints here in their holy living, that hereafter we may be numbered with them in glory everlasting. As we desire and hope for their blessed end, O let us love and follow their godly way; and make the communion of saints an object of our pursuit, as well as an article of our faith. Let us be lovers of all good men, honouring them that fear the Lord, and esteeming them very highly in love for their work's sake. And, O Lord, increase the number of thy faithful people in all places, and add daily to the church those who shall be followers of God, as dear children. Let thy kingdom come; and thy will be done on earth as it is in heaven; that thy church may grow and flourish; until we, with all thy servants departed in the Lord, meet together in the kingdom of our Father, to live in thy presence, and to enjoy thy love, and to glorify thy name, world without end. *Amen.*

A PRAYER UNDER ABUSES AND PROVOCATIONS.

O MOST high and wise, holy and righteous Judge of all the earth, the great author and lover of peace and truth: thou knowest my foolishness; and my sins are not hid from thee. How far I have been accessary to bring down these troubles upon my own head, and how much worse than these I deserve at thy hands, is all naked and open before thee. I submit, Lord, to thy correction, whomsoever thou shalt use as the instrument of thy displeasure. And O that the ill-will of men may quicken me the more to examine myself for that which is offensive in thy sight; and make me more careful to have my heart right with God, and to be approved in thy sight.

But seeing my heart condemns me not in the present case, for being the cause of all this wrath and clamour, and malice and vengeance; and that I apprehend myself now to suffer wrongfully; being slanderously reported, falsely accused, shamefully and despitefully used, and hated without a cause; I come with boldness to pour out my complaint before thee, O God, and to shelter myself under the shadow of thy wings. Plead my cause, O Lord, with them that strive with me; and save me from those that rise up against me. Though, for my love, they are my adversaries, let me give myself unto prayer; and not avenge myself, but rather give place unto wrath, and commit my cause to thee, who judgest righteously. O convince my adversaries of the error of their judgment, and the evil of their way. And the remainder of their wrath, O do thou restrain; and make a way for me to escape from the stormy wind and tempest.

I confess, O Lord, thou mightst justly use them that provoke me, as thy scourge to chastise me for provoking thee: and I know not, but such now may be thy pleasure. O help me then patiently to bear the indignation of the Lord; because I have so greatly sinned against thee. And however I am pursued and injured, O let me not render evil for evil, or railing for railing, but contrary-wise blessing: and make me duly to consider him, who endured so great contradiction of sinners against himself; that I may be not wearied or faint in my mind. If the man after thine own heart had so many implacable enemies, that not only traduced his name, but sought his life; if thy holy apostle was called a babbler and troubler of the world, and a pestilent fellow, not fit to live; yea, if the Son of thine eternal love had the character of a wine-bibber, a friend of publicans and sinners, a deceiver of the people, and a dealer with the devil: if he that deserved so well of men, fared so ill at their hands; if he that did no sin was persecuted, as if he had been the chief of sinners; if he suffered so much evil, who never deserved any; O why should such an unworthy sinful wretch as I, to whom belongs shame and confusion of face, so heinously resent it, when called to endure what is only the correction of my own wickedness! Though I deserve it not from them, yet, O how much worse do I deserve from thy heavenly Majesty, whom I have offended by my sins, and who mayst justly punish me by their hands. Whatever then men may say or do against me, let me be as a deaf man that heareth not; and as a dumb man that openeth not his mouth; little regarding the anger of man, if I can but be happy in the favour of my God. O Lord, keep back thy servant from giving any just provocation : and let me not suffer as an evil doer; nor let any offence come by me, that shall bring down thy displeasure upon me. Then, when persecuted for righteousness' sake, I shall rejoice and bless thy name, and give thee thanks and praise, for all thy grace and goodness to me in Jesus Christ. *Amen.*

A PRAYER UNDER INFAMY AND DISGRACE.

O LORD! righteousness belongs to thee; but to me confusion of face, as it is this day. Shame is the portion of my sins; and I deserve no better than to be slighted and despised myself, for having slighted thy laws, and despised the glorious Majesty of heaven. If I had been innocent, I might have been confident, to lift up my face without spot: but woe is me, that I have sinned: I have made myself vile, and fit only to be trampled on. As far as I am guilty, I take shame to myself, as the reward of my folly and wickedness. And O that I may so feel it here, that I may not hereafter awake to shame and everlasting contempt! And let not any that wait on thee, O Lord God of hosts, be ashamed for my sake: yea, where I suffer wrongfully, yet, Lord, help me to take it patiently. Though I am reproached for the name of Christ, and persecuted for righteousness' sake, I shall not droop under the censures and scorns of men, if I can but find acceptance and favour in thy sight. It is not men's applause or reproach that can make us happy or miserable: though we have their good opinion and commendation, what are we the better, if we have made thee our enemy? And though we are detested by them, what are we the worse, if only we have approved ourselves to thee our God? Thy word, O Lord, teaches us that if we suffer as Christians, we should not be ashamed, but glorify thee on this behalf. And thine apostles, who were made as the filth of the world and the offscouring of all things, rejoiced that they were counted worthy to suffer shame for the name of Jesus. Though therefore I pass through evil report, as well as good, let me account it but a small thing to be judged of man's judgment. And if thou, my God, wilt have me to be low in the world, yea, even a hissing and proverb of reproach, let me not be so much concerned to avoid the disgrace as to cut off all just occasion for it; and to be more careful and diligent in seeking the honour that cometh of God.

If men speak evil of what they understand not, if perverse scoffers, walking after their own lusts, oppose and deride me, O let not thy holy religion ever sink in my estimation on account of their hard speeches, or cruel usage, but enable me to look unto Jesus the Lord of glory, who was despised and rejected by those whom he came to save: and let me little regard what indignities they cast on me, if only I may be thereby rendered more conformable to his blessed image. Enable me to follow him in meekness and patience: and let my eyes be ever towards him as the author and the finisher of my faith: who having himself despised and surmounted the shame, now sitteth on the right hand of the Majesty on high; from whence he shall quickly come, in all the glory of his Father, to judge the world: to whose name be all blessing and praise, world without end. *Amen.*

A PRAYER UNDER CROSSES AND DISAPPOINTMENTS IN OUR AFFAIRS.

O MY Lord! I live by thee; and on thee I continually depend for life, and breath, and all things. Thy providence has appointed my station, and ordered whatever concerns me in the world. If not so much as a sparrow falls to the ground without thee, and the very hairs of our head are all numbered, thou canst not be unconcerned in the changes and accidents that befall thy servants: and the things that appear casual to us are the appointments of thy good pleasure. Restrain me, therefore, O Lord, from fretting myself in any wise to do evil. And help me to take up my cross, and follow my meek and lowly Saviour, in self-denial, and in quiet submission to the will of my heavenly Father.

O who am I, sinful wretch, that I should never be crossed, nor have anything to trouble me? Thy will be done, O Lord, how much soever my own corrupt will may be opposed and mortified. Let me desire nothing but the glory of thy name: and, if thou seest it needful to try me in the furnace of affliction, enable me to kiss thy rod, and to learn obedience by the things which I suffer. And O grant, that the things which disappoint

my carnal wishes, may indeed be over-ruled for
the glory of thy name, and for the furtherance of
my own welfare in the great day of our Lord
Jesus Christ. *Amen.*

UNDER ANY GREAT DIFFICULTIES AND ARDUOUS AFFAIRS.

O LORD, thou art a God of knowledge; thine understanding is infinite; nor art thou ever at a loss to effect what is best for us. But thou knowest our thoughts, O Lord, that they are vain. Our wisdom is often at a stand, so that we know not what to do for ourselves. At this time especially our affairs are entangled; we are perplexed in our counsels; nor can we find how to extricate ourselves from the difficulties in which we are involved. But a man's goings are of the Lord; how then can man understand his own way? his heart may advise his way, but the Lord directs his steps: there may be many devices in his heart, but the counsel of the Lord, that shall stand. If we lean not to our own understanding, but in all our ways acknowledge thee, thou hast promised, O Lord, to direct our paths: and when we commit our way to thee, and trust in thee, we have thy word, that thou wilt bring it to pass. But thou hast pronounced woe to them that take counsel, but not of thee; that cover with a covering, but not of thy Spirit, and that have not asked at thy mouth.

Our eyes therefore are unto thee, O God; and to thee we seek now for wisdom, that we may be able to discern the path of duty. Without thee, O Lord, our wisdom is folly: be thou therefore graciously present in our counsels: and let us now be taught of God, which way to take, and how to act most agreeably to thy blessed will, and most for our present and eternal welfare: we ask it for Jesus Christ's sake. *Amen.*

A PRAYER UNDER LOSSES AND DAMAGE IN OUR GOODS AND ESTATE.

BLESSED Lord! thou art the great Proprietor and Owner of all that we possess: the world is thine, and the fulness thereof. And whether thou givest, or takest away, it becomes us to bless thy name in all. Thou hast made me to abound with many things, of which others are destitute: and if thou also makest me to want what others abound with, yet teach me, O my God, how to suffer need, as well as to abound; and in whatsoever state I am, therewith to be content. And seeing that all things come alike to all, and that no one knows love or hatred by all that is before him, let me not hastily conclude that thou art my enemy; but rather hope that thy chastisements are tokens and expressions of thy love. Whatever I may lose, let me never grieve, as one that has no hope of better things; but cheerfully commit myself to thee, to choose my inheritance for me: and not to be anxious about my worldly portion, so that I may but see the joy of thy salvation. And, Lord, repair to me these losses, in an infinitely better way, out of thine own fulness, with the more precious things that accompany salvation. Let me imitate thy servants of old, who took joyfully the spoiling of their goods, knowing that they had in heaven a better and an enduring substance. O make me now the more solicitous and industrious to lay up treasure in heaven. And since I see how little any thing is to be confided in here on earth, O let me look less upon these temporal things that are seen; and be most of all concerned about the things that are unseen and eternal. Let it be henceforth my continual labour to provide well for my soul, and to be rich towards God; that when all things here shall fail me thou mayst never fail me; but be the strength of my heart, and my portion for ever. *Amen.*

A PRAYER IN TIME OF THREATENING DANGERS.

GREAT God, holy and just! I am amazed to think of the dreadful wages which my sins have merited. Fearfulness and trembling are come upon me, and my spirit is overwhelmed, and my heart fails me for fear: so that I know not what to do. But mine eyes are upon thee, my great Saviour and mighty Deliverer, to give me that help, which it is in vain to expect from man. Now that I am afraid, I will trust in thee; and under the shadow of thy wings will I make my refuge, until these calamities be overpast. O my Lord, take me under thy fatherly care and almighty protection: and save me from the hands of my enemies, and from the evils which I dread. O dispel the clouds; and turn away the storms; and clear up the face of heaven, which is now so blackened over my head. Thou, Lord, who knowest how to deliver, and art never at a loss to effect what thou wilt, command, I pray thee, deliverances for me; and be not far from me when trouble is so nigh unto me: but let me find thy help at hand, in this time of my extreme necessity.

O my God, thou hast been a shelter for me, and a strong tower of defence against the enemy. And though I walk in the midst of trouble, thou wilt revive me: thou wilt stretch forth thy hand against my enemy; and thy right hand shall save me. O my Saviour, I flee unto thee, to hide me. Be thou pleased to defend me from them that rise up against me. Consider the trouble that I suffer of them that hate me; and lead me in thy righteousness, because of my enemies: make thy way straight before my face. Deliver me, O

Lord, from the evil and violent man, and from my persecutors, that are stronger than I. O let not any that are my enemies wrongfully, rejoice over me. But show me some token for good, that they who hate me, may see it, and be ashamed, because thou, Lord, hast holpen me, and comforted me. O fortify me against that fear of man which bringeth a snare. Let me never be so awed by my fellow-creatures, as not to stand in awe of thee, my God. Let me never trespass against thee, to ingratiate myself with them; or decline thy service through fear of their displeasure. Thou hast been my help: O be thou pleased to come now to my succour, and to show thyself graciously and powerfully on my behalf. Hear me, Lord, for the glory of thy name; that I may see thy hand, and acknowledge thy power, and admire thy love, and adore thy goodness, while I have my being. *Amen*, and *Amen*.

A PRAYER UNDER SAD ACCIDENTS AND DISASTERS FALLING ON THE BODY.

O LORD, most high! the all-disposing God! who has taught us, that affliction rises not out of the dust, nor comes without thine appointment, but as thy messenger to fulfil thy will; thou hast good reason to do as thou hast done, though the reason may be hid from us. I know,

O Lord, that thy judgments are right, and that thou in faithfulness hast afflicted me. O why should a living man complain, a man for the punishment of his sins? Great God! I humbly submit to thy hand, and will bear the effects of thy displeasure, which I have brought down upon myself. O my Lord, give me patience, and strength, and grace, proportionable to this great trial; and enable me so to demean myself under it, that, after the affliction, I may find cause to say, it was good for me to be afflicted. Thou that hast torn and smitten, thou alone art able to heal the breaches thou hast made. Do thou remember me in my low estate, for the sake of that mercy of thine which endureth for ever: and help me to find out the cursed things that have provoked thee so to stretch out thy hand upon me. O that I may search and try my ways, and turn to the Lord, and bring forth fruits meet for repentance. And for his sake who was wounded for our transgressions, and bruised for our iniquities, Lord, forgive and heal my soul that has sinned against thee: and, in thy good time, restore my body too, if it seem good in thy sight: and make me to hear joy and gladness, that the bones which thou hast broken may rejoice.

If thou wilt, Lord, thou canst make me whole. O may it be thy good pleasure now to glorify thy power and mercy in my recovery: or, however thou shalt dispose of this vile body, grant me, O my God, an humble resignation to thy will, and satisfaction with thy dealings: and make this afflictive dispensation, which is so grievous at the present, to have a favourable and happy issue. O make it the messenger of thy love to my soul, and the means of sanctifying and preparing it for the Lord, and of fitting it to receive all the saving mercies of my God, in Jesus Christ. *Amen.*

A PRAYER UNDER CONFINEMENT AND LOSS OF LIBERTY.

O LORD my God, infinitely kind and good! I have, through thy gracious indulgence, long enjoyed my freedom in the world; and been permitted to go in and out, whither I would, at my pleasure. But now that I am under restraint, and confined to this place, O how much sorer affliction ought I with patience to endure, for turning my liberty into licentiousness, and for wandering (as I have done) from thee, and wearying myself in the ways of wickedness! This confinement I acknowledge to be but a light correction indeed, to one who deserves to be shut up in the eternal prison, from whence there is no redemption. But for thy dear Son, my blessed Saviour's sake, I beg, Lord, that this restraint may be, not in judgment, but in mercy to me: that it may bring me to timely consideration, and to a deep repentance for all those sinful liberties which I have taken, in living after my own foolish and hurtful lusts: let it remove me out of the way of temptations, and engage me more closely and dutifully to attend upon thee; that in thy service I may find a better freedom than that which I have lost. Let me obtain by means of it a freer access into thy presence, and power to tread down the enemies of my soul, whensoever they rise up against me.

O that now I am sequestered from the world, I may also be crucified unto it; and may leave it in affection, as I am shut out from its conversation. Let me in heart and mind ascend and dwell above, and have my conversation in heaven, and enjoy such fellowship with thee my God and Saviour, as shall be infinitely preferable to all the society and enjoyments of the world. If the Son of God shall make me free, I shall be free indeed. O pity me, tied as I am, and bound with the chain of my sins. Bring my soul out of prison, that I may give thanks unto thy name. Set my feet in a large room, that I may be at liberty to run the way of thy commandments. Then, however confined as to my body, even though I were to lie in a jail or a dungeon, I should be a prisoner of hope; looking for that blessed hope, to be delivered from the bondage of corruption, into the glorious liberty of the children of God. I ask this for the sake of him, who was apprehended and confined, and put to death for us, and now liveth and reigneth with thy eternal self, and Holy Spirit, over all, God blessed for evermore. **A*men*.**

A PRAYER UPON THE NEWS OF OTHERS' DEATH.

O THOU ever-living and all-disposing God, in whose hands our breath is, and whose summons we must all obey! What are we; what is man, even at his best estate, but altogether vanity! What man is he that liveth, and shall not see death? The great and the mean, the wise and the foolish, the evil and the good, all yield up the ghost, and go down to the grave. Thou art pleased, O my God, to spare me, whilst many of my neighbours and acquaintance are taken to their long home. Thou leavest me yet a living monument of thy goodness, long-suffering, and forbearance. O what am I better than others, that I should have further opportunities of working out my salvation, when others have the things which belong to their peace for ever hid from their eyes? Why have I not long since experienced the common lot of all men? Why have I not been called to give up unto thee an account of my stewardship? O let me not be as the brutes that have no understanding, without mindfulness of my mortality, or consideration of my latter end: but in the death of others, let me see, as in a glass, my own frail and uncertain

ON THE DEATH OF FRIENDS.

state. Let me see that there is but a step between me and death; and that, however my days may be prolonged on earth, I must at last go to the place appointed for all men living. O let me begin to answer the great end of life; and so live, as one that surely expects to die. And when my own turn shall come, may I depart in peace, and sleep in Jesus; having my soul safe in thy hands, and my body resting in hope of gloriously rising at the last day, through him who is the resurrection and the life, our blessed Saviour and Redeemer Jesus Christ. *Amen.*

A PRAYER UPON THE DEATH OF OUR DEAR FRIENDS.

GREAT God, the Lord of all; thou dost whatsoever thou pleasest in heaven and in earth; thou givest, and thou takest away: thou raisest up and thou castest down: nor can any stay thy hand, or say unto thee, What doest thou? But in all that thou doest, thou art wise, and righteous, and good. Thou art just in depriving us of those enjoyments which we have unworthily idolized, or ungratefully abused. Blessed be thy name, therefore, as well when thou takest away as when thou givest. Yet, O Lord, in mercy turn these losses to the advantage of my soul: and grant me such abundant supplies out of thine own fulness, that I may find in thee infinitely more than in all earthly friends and comforts. They were but the instruments and means of conveyance: thou, who art the eternal spring and fountain of all good, art still the same; and amidst all these changes, changest not. O let me find, though bereft of the creature, I am not forsaken of my God; and that, though I have nothing, I am really possessed of all things.

O my heavenly Father, take my eyes off from such poor dying comforts, to fix them upon the only satisfying good; in the enjoyment of which consists all my true life, and peace, and happiness. And let the frequent disappointments that I find in all the enjoyments of the world, teach me more wisdom than to place my affections upon them. Help me to disengage and loosen my heart from them: and raise up my desires and hopes to those glorious objects, which are so infinitely to be preferred before them. O let me be more crucified to the world, where is nothing but vanity and vexation of spirit: and may I have my conversation more in heaven; where my blessed Lord is, and all his happy followers, of whom the world was not worthy; and where there is every thing that the soul of man can want or wish. O God of the spirits of all flesh, and especially of the just made perfect, help me so to follow thy servants, who are departed in the Lord, that I, with them, may be counted worthy to live in thy presence, and to spend an eternity in the love and praises, the fellowship and enjoyment, of thee my God, who art blessed for evermore. *Amen.*

A PRAYER UPON THE REMEMBRANCE OF FORMER SINS.

O WHO can understand his errors? who can call to mind the innumerable offences of his past life? Since the time that I began to act, what alas! have I ever done that was free from sin? And, O the heinous offences, the presumptuous sins, the great transgressions, whereof I have been guilty; which stare me in the face, and alarm my conscience, and cast down my soul within me! When I consider the circumstances under which I have committed them, that they have been done against such light and love, such calls and warnings, such convictions and encouragements as I have experienced from the Lord, I am covered with confusion, O my God, and filled with bitter remorse and terrible apprehensions. O if they should rise up in judgment against me, they could not but utterly sink me into perdition. But, O Lord my God, help me so to remember them, that thou mayst blot them out of the book of thy remembrance; and so to humble myself for them, that thou mayst never lay them to my charge. For thine own mercy's sake hide thy face from my sins, and blot out all my iniquities, especially those which have taken such hold upon me, that I am not able to look up. And though thou hast kept me from my deserved shame in this world, O let not thy indulgence embolden me to repeat my sins; but let this thy goodness, O my God, work in me a more deep and serious repentance.

And thou, Lord Almighty, who alone canst bring good out of evil, be thou pleased to make my past falls an occasion of my surer standing for the future. O embitter the pleasures of sin to me, and hedge up the ways of wickedness (as with thorns and briers) before me; that I may loathe, as much as ever I have loved, my hateful ways, and never return again to such baseness and folly. And let the remembrance of all my former offences not only lead me to repentance, but stimulate me to more circumspection and watchfulness in future: that I may not live so far from thee as I have done; nor trespass against thee any more; but may pass the time of my sojourning here in fear: O grant it for the sake of him whom I have so impiously trodden under foot, and to whose Spirit I have done so great despite, even thy Son Jesus Christ, my only Mediator and Advocate. *Amen.*

THE CONVINCED SINNER'S PRAYER.

HEARKEN to the voice of my cry, my King, and my God! for unto thee will I pray. But wherewithal shall I appear before the Lord, and bow myself before the most high God, whose holy laws I have broken, and whose just displeasure I have incurred! I acknowledge my transgression, O Lord, and my sin is ever before me. My iniquities are gone over my head, as a sore burthen, they are too heavy for me to bear. When thou with rebukes dost chasten man for his iniquity, thou makest his beauty to consume away like a moth. My sin now has found me out; and that which once I thought too little to be repented of, seems now too great to be pardoned. I flattered myself in my own eyes, till my iniquity is found to be hateful. I thought I was rich, and increased with goods, and had need of nothing: but now I find that I am wretched, and miserable, and poor, and blind, and naked; so that there is nothing but disorder and ruin in my soul. I have undone myself: but to work my own recovery, I have no sufficiency. O how wicked have I been to harbour the mind, and allow myself in the way, which is enmity against God! How ignorant, yet how confident! How vile, yet how arrogant! In what need of mercy, yet how unmerciful! How sinful, yet how impenitent! How bold in the sins where conscience reproved me; but how indifferent in the cause where thy good Spirit encouraged me! Oh the spoils, and ruins, and desolations which my sins have made in my soul! How darkened has been my mind; how perverted my will; how sensualized my affections; how disordered my passions; how hardened my heart; and how mad have I been in cleaving unto things displeasing to my God, and destructive to my soul!

Vain would be the attempt to hide any thing from thee, who fillest heaven and earth. What shall I say unto thee, Lord? I scarcely know how to speak any thing bad enough of myself. O woe is me, that I have done so foolishly and wickedly! Whither shall I betake myself, seeing that against thee, O Lord, I have so sinned, and done such evil in thy sight! Thou art the offended Majesty, out of whose reach I cannot escape; and whose judgments I can never be able to endure. A guilty consciousness makes me afraid to come unto thee: yet I know there is nothing but certain destruction, if I keep away from thee. And though there is no peace to the wicked, whilst he continues in his sins, yet if the wicked forsake his way, and the unrighteous man his thoughts, and return to the Lord, thy promise, then, O God, is to have mercy upon him, and abundantly to pardon. I have none to look unto for deliverance from my sins, but unto the just and holy God, against whom I have so grievously sinned. And how shall I stand in thy sight, O Lord, who hatest and condemnest the works of darkness, and the workers of iniquity? whose wrath against sin burns as deep as hell, and as long as eternity.

I submit, great Lord, to thy offended majesty! and whithersoever I look, I have no hope but in thine almighty power, thy superabounding grace, and thine ever-enduring mercy. Nothing is too hard for thee to effect: the most wretched case is not past thy cure. Though our sins be as scarlet, thou canst make them as white as snow; though they be red like crimson, thou canst make them as wool. Yea, thou hast found a ransom, and laid help upon One that is mighty, even on thy dear Son, who is able to save to the uttermost all that come unto God through him. If I had not sinned, I had no need of such a Redeemer: but it was the sinful and the lost whom he came to seek and save. To the Lord Jesus therefore do I look, with the desire of my soul, to find healing through the precious blood of his cross. O merciful God! when my sins cry to thee for vengeance, be thou pleased to hear his blood and merits pleading and interceding for my soul; and speaking better things in my behalf than I am able to do for myself in all my prayers.

Behold, O merciful Lord, a miserable object on whom to glorify thy power and mercy! O look upon me, in my blood, and bid me live. Speak death to my sins; that my soul may live, and for ever bless thy name. Turn away thy face from my sins; and blot out all my iniquities. For thy name's sake, O Lord, pardon my sin, for it is great: too great for any, but a God of infinite goodness and mercy, to forgive. O magnify thyself in my deliverance. Make it seen, in thy work upon my soul, how great things, worthy of God, thou canst do: that where sin hath abounded, thy grace can much more abound. Return, O Lord, deliver my soul; O save me for thy mercy's sake. Save me from the guilt and punishment, from the power and pollution, of all my sins. And thou, Lord, who knowest how to deliver, make me some way to escape out of the perplexities into which my sins have cast me: that my iniquities may not be my ruin; but that they may be taken away and forgiven, and washed out with the blood of Jesus Christ. Turn thou me, O Lord God of my salvation, that I may be turned from my sins, and from this present evil world, unto thyself. O give me such conviction, as may end in sound conversion; and let me experience in myself that grace of God which bringeth salvation. I want thy grace, O Lord; and I shall want it to all eternity, if thou be not pleased to look graciously upon me in my blessed Redeemer. Thou wilt not have the less, how much soever thou bestowest: and thou canst not bestow thy grace upon any one that more needs it than myself. O God of all grace, that keepest mercy for thousands, hast thou not a blessing for me; a blessing for my perishing soul? For thy dear Son, my only Saviour's sake, let me find such grace in thy sight. O get thee everlasting glory, in so favouring the most unworthy of thy creatures. And whatever thou withholdest O deny me not thy saving grace, which, though so precious a treasure, is not too great or good for the God of infinite mercy to bestow. Do that work of thy grace thoroughly upon my heart, for which I may have cause to glorify thy name for evermore. *Amen.*

A PRAYER UNDER THE DREAD OF GOD'S WRATH AND EVERLASTING DAMNATION.

O LORD, the great and dreadful God, against whom I have greatly sinned! and who for my sins art justly displeased! when I consider the holiness of thy laws, and the strictness of thy justice; and when I reflect upon the heinous and innumerable sins of my heart and life; my flesh trembles for fear of thee, and I am afraid of thy judgments. O who may stand in thy sight, when once thou art angry? Who can bear up for ever under all the vials of thy wrath, when they shall be poured out to the uttermost: when thy mercy shall be clean gone, and thou shalt cast off, and be favourable no more? Yet would that be my woeful portion, if thou, O Lord, shouldst enter into judgment with me: I could then hope for no better but to be deprived of all the comforts of this life, and to be delivered into the bitter pains of eternal death. But though the just wages of my sins be death, yet the gift of God is eternal life, through Jesus Christ our Lord. O for his dear sake, who has satisfied thy justice, and appeased thy wrath, and suffered and died once, that we might not suffer and die for ever, even for thy Son's sake, O God and Father, have mercy upon me, a miserable sinner: from thy wrath, and from everlasting damnation, good Lord deliver me. And help me, in the fear of thee, my God, to flee from the wrath to come; and to rid my hands, and my heart, of every cursed thing, that provokes the eyes of thy glory, and kindles thine indignation against thy creatures.

O thou blessed Saviour of the world, save me from my sins, and from all their dismal effects: and reconcile me to God; and make my peace through the blood of thy cross. Thou tookest upon thee our mortal nature, that thou mightst, through death, destroy him who had the power of death; and deliver them, who, through fear of death, were all their life time subject to bondage. Have compassion, Lord, I beseech thee, on my infirmities; and suffer me not to fall a prey to my own fears. But be surety for thy servant for good: undertake for me to discharge that heavy load of debt which I have contracted; that, being justified by faith, I may have peace with God, through our Lord Jesus Christ. Hide not thy face from me, O my Lord, lest I be like to them that go down into the pit: but revive my soul with the sense of thy love, and the hopes of everlasting salvation; that I may give thee thanks from the ground of my heart; and tell with gladness what thou hast done for my soul; and keep myself ever in thy love, looking for the mercy of our Lord Jesus Christ unto eternal life. *Amen.*

A PRAYER UNDER FEARS AND DOUBTS OF OUR SPIRITUAL CONDITION.

O LORD my God, I hope thou hast, of thy rich mercy, changed and renewed me in some measure, and wrought a good work upon me, to bring me out of my natural and lost condition, into a state of grace and salvation. But yet the carnal nature is so predominant, and many sins are so lively and strong within me, and the good things of thy Spirit are still in so much weakness and imperfection, that I have just cause for fear: yea, the sorrows of my heart are enlarged, and my soul is disquieted within me. Alas! what cause have I to question, whether my spots are the spots of thy children; and whether I have known the grace of God in truth; or whether I do not deceive myself with vain hopes and expectations.

Mine eyes are unto thee, O Lord my God. Leave not my soul destitute. From the ends of the earth will I cry unto thee: when my heart is overwhelmed within me, lead me to the rock that is higher than I. O Lord, rebuke me not in thine anger, neither chasten me in thy sore displeasure. Forsake me not, O my God; be not far from me. Make haste to help me, O Lord, my salvation. Attend to my cry for I am brought very low: hear me speedily; my spirit fails. Save me, O God, for the waters are come in unto my soul: I sink in the deep mire, where is no standing. Bring my soul out of prison, that I may praise thy name.

O show me the true state of my soul; and make me to know the things that are freely given me of God. Deliver me, gracious Lord, from all those evils which provoke thee to hide thy face from me, and which make me so much a stranger to peace and comfort. O grant me clear and satisfactory evidences of my calling and election: and seal a comfortable assurance of thy blessed love in Christ Jesus upon my soul. O thou that didst say to the wind and waves, Be still, and they obeyed thee, compose my soul which is so disquieted within me: and bring me to see the light of thy countenance, and the joy of thy salvation. O thou that art of power to establish us, be pleased to establish my heart with grace; and let me be rooted and grounded in the faith, that I may not stagger through unbelief; but hold the beginning of my confidence steadfast to the end. Rejoice the soul of thy servant : for unto thee, O Lord, do I lift up my soul. And let the joy of the Lord be my strength; that I may be victorious over my sins, and abound in thy work; and never be so much pleased with any thing, as with doing the things which are pleasing to my God, through Jesus Christ. *Amen.*

A PRAYER UNDER STRONG TEMPTATIONS.

HOLY God! I desire to humble myself here before thee, for that continual proneness which is in me to sin against thee. After all the great things thou hast done for me, alas! how ready am I still to destroy myself! The malicious tempter is laying snares for me everywhere: and the world is distracting my attention both with its cares and pleasures. And O how prone is my sinful flesh to take part with my enemy against my own soul! Innumerable evils have compassed me about; my iniquities have taken hold upon me, so that I am not able to look up. They are more than the hairs of my head, therefore my heart faileth me. O the sin that still dwelleth in me, that is so nigh to me, that does so easily beset me, and is so apt to prevail against me; drawing me away from the path of duty, and leading me to things destructive to my soul! O wretched man that I am! who shall deliver me from the body of this death? Now that the custom of sinning has so increased my sinful inclinations, that the leopard may as soon change his spots, and the Ethiopian his skin, as I, who am accustomed to evil, can (of myself) cease from it; how shall I escape, if thou, O my God, do not stretch forth thine arm for my deliverance?

But with thee, the almighty God, all things

are possible: yea, thou canst as easily make me holy, as command me to be so. To thee all the powers of hell are weakness; nor can anything in the world resist thy will. O pity thy poor tempted creature, and give me not up to a reprobate sense, and to vile affections; nor to such blindness of mind, and hardness of heart, as will render me past feeling. Punish not my former sins, by giving me over to their sway and power; but let it be thy gracious pleasure, O Lord, that all my prevailing iniquities may flee and perish at thy presence. O speak powerfully to my filthy corruptions; say, Hitherto shall ye go, and no further. Stop and heal the diseases of my soul, that they may no more break out, as they have done, to the dishonour of thy name, the wounding of my conscience, and the hindering of my own and others' peace. Yea, so sanctify my nature, O Lord, and renew me in the spirit of my mind, that my heart may rise against these baneful evils; and that I may hate all iniquity, and every false way. Enable me so to resist the devil, that he may flee from me. Give me power from on high, to set me above all my sins: and give me grace sufficient for me; that I may not be false in thy covenant, nor regardless of my own best interests; but may manfully fight thy battles, and approve myself thy faithful soldier and servant, to my life's end. Make me faithful unto death, that thou mayst give me a crown of life: and take me in due time from this state of warfare, to reign with thee in glory for evermore, through Jesus Christ our Lord. *Amen.*

A PRAYER AFTER A RELAPSE INTO SIN.

O MY God! I am filled with confusion: I know not how to lift up my face unto thee, from whom I have so foolishly departed; and against whom I have so greatly sinned. I am ashamed to confess unto thee, what (alas!) I have not been afraid to commit against thee. Thou, Lord, hast made to know better; but I have held the truth in unrighteousness, and therefore deserve to be beaten with many stripes, seeing that I have known thy will, but have not done it. Alas! how oft have I been taught (as with briers and thorns) what an evil and bitter thing it is to trespass against the Lord! And yet I have repeatedly committed those very offences of which I have professed to repent, and of which I know I must repent. Nor have I only resisted the clearest light and conviction, but have trampled on the richest grace and love. Therefore I am inexcusable, O righteous Lord! and have nothing to say in my own defence. No, the guilt which I have contracted stops my mouth. O into what a depth am I fallen! and is there any hope now for one that has so wilfully, so heinously offended? O my Lord, the pardon and grace which I am necessitated to ask at thy hands are much greater

A PRAYER AFTER A RELAPSE.

than I have any reason to expect; yet not greater than thou, the God of all grace, canst give; nor greater than thou hast promised to bestow upon all repenting and returning sinners. To all who turn from their iniquities thou hast declared, that thou wilt have mercy upon them, and abundantly pardon; yea, thou hast made a way for their redemption by the death of thine own beloved Son. O then, let that blessed Saviour, whom thou hast sent into the world, exercise his power and pity towards me in this my woeful condition! make for me some way to escape, that I may not be thus taken captive by the devil at his will. Gracious God! there is nothing in me but sin and misery; but with thee there is mercy: have mercy, therefore, O Lord, have mercy on me for thy mercy's sake; spare me, good Lord, and withhold thine hand from inflicting upon me the vengeance I deserve: for thy own name's sake, pardon mine iniquity, which is so exceeding great: absolve me from the guilt of it, deliver me from its power, and cleanse me from the pollution of it. I confess with shame that I have gone astray like a sheep that is lost: but O! bring me back to thy fold; bring me back to the Shepherd and Bishop of my soul; and advance thine own glory in saving the chief of sinners.

O Lord of love, the God of my mercy, speak peace unto my soul; and let me no more return to folly. Give me grace to mortify this my besetting sin: I have indeed broken my vows repeatedly; yet once more would I determine, through thy grace, to resist this enemy of my soul: I will go forth in thy strength: O do thou confirm my resolutions, and enable me to perform my vows. Thou compassionate God, that succourest the tempted, lead me not into temptation; but let thy good Spirit guide me, and thine everlasting arms be underneath me: uphold me that I may not fall: cause'me to walk more circumspectly, and with full purpose of heart to cleave unto the Lord. O let these my repeated falls increase my hatred of sin, and my watchfulness in thy ways: and let me not only now, but at all times, have the fear of thee before my eyes, and be continually leaning on the arm of my beloved, that so I may walk worthy of my high calling, and be kept by thy power through faith unto salvation. *Amen* and *Amen*.

ANOTHER HUMBLING OFFICE UNDER ANY FOUL FALL.

O JUST and holy God! what shall I say unto thee, and how shall I show my face before thee, after I have so highly affronted thy glorious Majesty, and violated thy righteous commands! O that I should have such lamentable occasion again to confess and bewail the sin, which I have so often confessed and bewailed. Holy Lord! I am ashamed that I have such need to repeat these confessions; and afraid lest my sins should have so provoked thee, that thou wilt hear me no more. O what mercy, from the Father of mercies, do I experience, that the judgments, which I have merited, are not executed upon me! What patience, but that of the long-suffering God, would ever bear with such a wretch, who has continued to provoke him every day? Most justly mightst thou, Lord, refuse to hear me now crying to thee in the anguish of my soul, since I have so often refused to hear thee, calling upon me by the motions of thy Holy Spirit. O the havoc and desolation which sin has made in my soul! Surely the many aggravations of my sin do make it beyond measure sinful: such frequent falls do ruin my hopes: so that I am ready to fear, lest thou shouldst abandon me to my wretched self, and leave me to be filthy still; and to lie and perish in my sins, because I have revolted more and more.

Behold, I am vile in my own eyes; I abhor myself, and humble my soul in the dust before thee, O Lord: I acknowledge my transgressions, and am sorely afraid of thy judgments. My sins have taken such hold of me, that my heart fails me. Yet, Lord, if thou wilt, thou canst make me clean, and make me whole. I come therefore once more to implore mercy for my perishing soul. Thou who hast charged us to forgive an offending brother seventy times seven, (even as oft as he repents) wilt not thyself be less merciful to thine offending creatures, when they seek forgiveness at thy hands. Though we so often forget our duty, thou canst never forget to exercise mercy. A woman may sooner forget the fruit of her womb, than thou shut up thy compassions from the penitent and returning prodigal. Let that mercy, then, O my Lord, that has hitherto so wonderfully endured me, be yet further exercised towards me, to the full extent of my necessities.

In the day of my trouble I will call upon thee, for thou wilt answer me. I believe, Lord, thy power and thy readiness to relieve those who prostrate themselves before thee. For that end didst thou, O blessed Saviour, come into the world: for that end didst thou shed thy precious blood; even that thou mightst atone for our sins, and reconcile us to our offended God. O that I, who have the greatest need of that atonement, may feel the benefit of it; and that where sin has abounded, thy grace may much more abound! Look upon me. O Lord, as thou didst on thine offending disciple; to melt my heart into a kindly, relenting, and penitent concern for this great evil. Make me to look on him whom my sins have pierced; that I may mourn, and be in bitterness for the grievous offences which I have committed against thee, the Lord of love, and the God of all my mercies. What is past I cannot recall; but thou, my Lord and Saviour, canst remit it, and give me grace to repent of it. O give me such true repentance for it, that thou mayst blot it out of the book of thy remembrance, and be reconciled to my guilty soul.

And grant, O gracious Lord, that the custom of sinning may not render me insensible of my guilt, or ever lead me to commit these great sins with little remorse. Nor let it so increase my sinful inclinations, that I should become a slave of corruption, or be induced to harbour within my soul its greatest enemies. Be thou, O Lord, my strong tower of defence against them: and enable me to go on conquering and to conquer, till, in the name of the Lord, I have destroyed them. So often have I fallen by their hands, that I fear lest one day I should so fall by them as never to rise again. But thou, my strength and my Redeemer, art stronger than the strong one, and able to secure me from his most violent assaults. O blessed keeper of Israel! keep back thy servant from presumptuous sins: let them not have dominion over me: that I may be upright and innocent from the great transgression. Punish not my past sins by giving me up to commit iniquity with greediness: but subdue my iniquities that prevail against me; and pluck me out of the mire and the snare, for thy mercy's sake. O that the same mercy, which has hitherto so often spared me, may now be exercised in the renewal of my soul: let it so strengthen all the good things of thy grace within me, that I may be able to do all things conducive to thine honour, and necessary to my own salvation. O let me be found faithful unto death, that thou mayst give me the crown of life; not for any worthiness in me, but for the worthiness of thy dear Son, and for the sake of thy own tender mercies in Christ Jesus. *Amen.*

A PRAYER FOR TEMPORAL BLESSINGS.

O LORD our God, thou knowest that while we are in this life, we stand in need of continual supplies for the support and nourishment of our bodies: and thou hast promised to impart them unto all who seek first thy kingdom, and the righteousness thereof. Thou hast also commanded us to ask of thee our daily bread; and to cast our care upon thee, for all that is needful for us. I pray therefore to thee, my heavenly Father, for such a portion as thy wisdom sees to be suited to my condition. While I have a life to be nourished, let me not want the supports and comforts of it. Give me skill and ability to provide for myself; and add thy blessing to my endeavours. Where I cannot supply all my own necessities, O do thou raise up friends to help me; that I may never be destitute of food convenient for me. And having food and raiment, let me be therewith content. In prosperity, keep me from forgetting thee: and in adversity, keep me from thinking myself forgotten of thee. O keep me from all unnecessary cares, and unprofitable disquietudes. Teach me how to want, as well as how to abound. Add to me, O my Father, what at any time thou knowest me to need; and bless to me every thing which thou bestowest: that my bodily comforts may not be to me an occasion of falling, but rather an encouragement to my duty, and an incentive to me to abound in thy love and praise. And in the want of all other supplies and succours, be thou, O God, my all in all, in life and death, and for evermore, for Christ's sake. *Amen.*

A PRAYER IN PROSPERITY.

BLESSED God, rich in goodness and mercy: thou art the portion of my inheritance and of my cup: thou maintainest my lot. The lines are fallen to me in pleasant places; and I have a goodly heritage. I abound and am full of thy good things; and am surrounded on every side with thy mercies. Thou makest my affairs to succeed in such a manner, that I cannot but be pleased and satisfied with my condition; and desire with all my soul to acknowledge, and bless, and praise thee for all thy special favours, wherein thou hast made me to differ. Glory be to thee, O Lord, who hast dealt so well with thine unworthy servant, and signalized me with such great and manifold blessings. But when thou hast made my mountain to stand strong, I must not say in my prosperity I shall never be moved. I know not what shall be on the morrow, nor how soon the sun may be hid, that now shines upon me. O Lord, help me, in the time of my health, and peace, and prosperity, to remember and provide for the time of trouble, and sickness, and death : when the world's enjoyments will shrink away from me, and prove utterly unable to support and comfort me. Yea, because the prosperity of fools destroys them, and the gaining of the world is the loss of so many souls, grant, O heavenly Father, that this world may not be my portion ; that I may not abuse the world's good to thy dishonour and my own undoing ; nor turn the gifts of thy bounty into weapons of rebellion against thee. But enable me to use them in thy fear, and to do thee better service in proportion to the obligations thou layest upon me. O make me as willing, as thou hast made me able, to refresh the bowels of my poorer brethren : and to give to them as freely as I myself have received. Let not my riches be kept to my hurt; but rather be laid out to do myself and others the most substantial good. As I have opportunity, let me do good to all ; especially to them who are of the household of faith.

O gracious Lord ! take the snare out of my worldly enjoyments ; and preserve me from the danger and destruction that so commonly attend a full and prosperous condition. And rather deprive me of all my earthly possessions, than suffer them to impede my progress towards thy heavenly kingdom. O let me not want the affliction which thou knowest to be needful for my salvation. And though thou makest me poor, or givest me trouble, let me be contented, and bless thy name, as well when thou takest from me, as when thou givest to me. But whatever I have here to enjoy, O let me never set my heart upon it: nor trust in uncertain riches, but in the ever-living God, who alone can be a suitable portion for my immortal soul. O preserve me from pride and forgetfulness of God, from love of the world, and from all other vices and corruptions incident to a high and plentiful estate. And let none of my abundance or success in the world, ever puff me up with a proud conceit of myself, or a scornful disdain of others, or a wanton kicking against the Lord. O let it not turn me from thee: but with the cords of love do thou draw me nearer to thyself. And with all my other plenty, let me, O my God, enjoy the fulness of thy grace, and be rich in faith and good works. And with all my other successes, O that my soul may prosper, and be made glad with thy saving mercy, and thy favourable acceptance of me in Jesus Christ. *Amen.*

A PRAYER FOR A BLESSING ON OUR INTENDED MARRIAGE.

O MY God, thy bountiful favours have exceeded all my expectations, as well as my deserts: and though I have wretchedly abused thy kindness and love, yet still thou waitest to be gracious, and art not weary of showing mercy. Now thy good providence, O Lord, is opening a way for my future settlement in life: if thou knowest it to be for my good, O Lord of love, promote and bring it to pass. But grant that I may proceed in thy fear; and that while I 'am seeking to have my own designs accomplished, I may have a just regard to the glory of thy name; and desire nothing any further than it shall conduce to the eternal welfare of myself, and of thy servant, on whom my thoughts and affections are fixed. O give me such a partner of my fortunes, as may be a blessing to me, for this life and a better. And make us truly beneficial and comfortable to one another in all the best respects, pertaining to our chiefest good. Grant, Lord, that we may be helps meet for each other, in reference to both worlds; and that our love may be sincere without guile; pure without wantonness; and lasting without decay. O thou that fashionest all hearts, unite our affections upon truly Christian principles, that they may not speedily decline, but remain firm and durable to the end. Unite both of us to thy blessed self, as well as to each other: that our marriage may be in the Lord; and that it may not separate us from thee, but bring us nearer to thee. O grant us new supplies of thy grace, for this new estate of our lives: that we may fill up the relation into which we are entering, as becomes thy people. Let us not only be faithful in keeping the marriage-bed undefiled; but be mutual helps and comforts, both in our temporal and spiritual concerns; and ever conspire together, to promote our mutual edification and comfort. Above all, let us live to glorify and praise thee our God, through Jesus Christ. *Amen.*

A PRAYER FOR BLESSING,

DIRECTION, HELP, AND GOOD SUCCESS, IN ANY GREAT ENTERPRISE.

O LORD God, infinitely wise and good, who teachest man knowledge, and givest both the skill and power to accomplish our purposes, I know not what to do: but mine eyes are upon thee, and all my expectation is from thee; and I desire continually to wait, and call, and depend upon thee. It is a great work which I have now to do: but O how little strength to do it! All my sufficiency is of thee, who workest in us to will and to do of thy good pleasure. Thou that hast been my help, leave me not, neither forsake me, O God of my salvation: but let me be taught of God what I have to do: and let the gracious Lord make me to understand what is thy pleasure concerning me. O that my ways were directed to please thee; that so I might have the light of thy countenance ever shining upon me!

My Lord, and my God! leave me not in the hand of my own counsel; nor to the conduct of my own foolish and deceitful heart: but lead me by the way that I should go, and teach me thy paths; that discretion may preserve me, and understanding may keep me. O make my way prosperous; and give me thy blessing and good success. Bring all needful things to my remembrance: and where I have not the presence of mind, or the ability to perform thy will, O magnify thy power in my weakness; and let me go forth in thy strength, and speed and prosper by thy grace and blessing. Let thy good providence so be my defence and security, and thy Holy Spirit my guide and counsellor; that I may wisely choose, and rightly manage, and successfully accomplish, the things wherein I am engaged.

Thy will be done, O Lord, however I may be pleased or crossed: and let me ever design thy glory, whether it be for gain or loss in respect of this present life. O be thou still a gracious Father to me, and a merciful provider for me: and grant me now the comfortable sense of thy gracious acceptance of me, and of thy designs of mercy towards me. Be thou pleased to take me me under thy fatherly care and conduct, and preserve me from the evils into which I am prone to fall; and quicken me to the good which I am averse to perform: establish thou the work of my hands upon me; yea, the work of my hands establish thou it. My God and guide, my help and strength! if thou lead me not, I shall run into errors; if thou keep me not, I shall fall into dangers: but hold thou me up, and I shall be safe. And let me so experience thy power and presence with me, that I may manage this and all my other affairs to thy glory, and that in my dying reflections upon what has past, my soul may have peace, and thy name be glorified, through Jesus Christ. *Amen.*

A PRAYER WHEN GOING ABROAD.

O LORD! thou art the same God in all places and nowhere can I go, but thou art there. Both at home and abroad, on my way, and at the end, thou art ever with me, by thine universal presence. O let me also experience the presence of thy grace, and of thy good Spirit with me; to conduct and guide me continually, to protect and save me from all dangers and mischiefs, and to make my way prosperous, and all my affairs successful. Let the blessing of the Lord follow me, and rest upon me: and do thou preserve my going out, and my coming in; and never leave me, nor forksake me, O Lord, but be my God and guide this day, in all this journey, and all my life long. And make me to feel that my whole life is but a pilgrimage, and passage through this world; in which I am continually hastening home to the end of all my travels, and to the place where I must take up my everlasting abode.

O merciful God! make me continually mindful of that progress, and of that journey's end: and keep me from either wandering from thy way, or falling into sin of any kind; which would be the greatest evil that could come upon me. Take care of me, I beseech thee, and lead me, and keep me: and after all my journeyings here, O bring me safe at last to thy holy hill, and to thy heavenly rest; even to that blessed end of my faith, the everlasting salvation of my soul. I humbly ask this through the greatness of thy mercy to me in thy dear Son, my gracious Lord and only Saviour, Jesus Christ. *Amen.*

A PRAYER FOR ILLUMINATION AND KNOWLEDGE.

O LORD, thou eternal, uncreated light, thou hast not left thyself without witness amongst us; but in thy word and works before us, and in our souls and consciences within us, and in all thy creatures on every side of us, thou hast left traces of thy power, wisdom, and goodness. That I have, therefore, no better knowledge of thee, and of the things belonging to my peace, is my shame: it is owing to my sinful dulness and negligence in that which most nearly and eternally concerns me. Ah, Lord! I have not improved in knowledge answerable to the light which thou hast caused to shine upon me; nor according to the means of instruction wherewith thou hast blessed me. But I have need to be taught myself the things whereof I might have been a teacher of others. For this I desire, Lord, to humble myself before thee, and to implore thy pardon: and I now come to ask wisdom at thy hands, knowing that thou givest to all men liberally, and upbraidest not.

I cannot see or know thee, O Lord, but by the beams of thine own light, which thou art pleased to impart. O wilt thou vouchsafe yet further and more fully to manifest thyself to my soul? Teach me to know aright *Thee*, the only true God, and Jesus Christ whom thou hast sent. O blessed Sun of Righteousness, arise upon me with healing in thy wings, to scatter all the clouds of folly and ignorance, and error and prejudice, that overspread my soul. Open mine eyes, that I may behold wondrous things out of thy law. And open my understanding, that I may understand the scriptures; and not remain in darkness concerning anything that is needful for me to know, in order to my present peace and duty, and to my eternal safety and felicity. And whereinsoever I, or any whom I am concerned with, are otherwise minded than we ought to be, O God, reveal the same to us: and let us all be taught of thee, to know thee, from the greatest to the least; and not be unwise, but understanding what the will of the Lord is.

That the soul be without knowledge is not good: O incline our ears to wisdom, and our hearts to understanding; that we may follow on to know the Lord, and increase in the knowledge of God. Shew us thy ways, O Lord, and lead us in thy truth. And whatever else we are ignorant of, let it be given unto us to know the mysteries of the kingdom of God. O Lord, our light! give us understanding in the way of godliness: give us a spiritual discernment of the things of thy Spirit: and make us wise unto salvation. Give us the spirit of wisdom and revelation in the knowledge of thee, the eyes of our understanding being enlightened, that we may know what is the hope of thy calling, and what the riches of the glory of thine inheritance in the saints, and what is the mighty power of thy Spirit, which works in them that believe.

O put thy law in our inward parts, and write it in our hearts: that the scriptures may not be to us a book sealed, or a gospel hid; but a lamp to our feet, and a light to our paths. O that our ways were directed to keep thy statutes! Help us, O good Lord, so to do thy will, that we may know the scriptures to be of God, and may have the witness in ourselves; and may perceive the divinity of thy word, by the power and efficacy of it upon our lives. And though now we see but darkly as in a glass, and know but in part;

and cannot by searching find out the Almighty to perfection; yet help us still more and better to know our God, so as we can know, till hereafter we shall know as we are known, and see face to face, in that blessed presence of thine, where is fulness of joy for evermore. *Amen.*

A PRAYER FOR FAITH AND TRUST IN GOD.

WITHOUT faith, it is impossible to please thee, O God: and therefore I come to beg of thee that faith which is thy gift. Lord, help my unbelief; and increase my faith. Whatever thou hast revealed, let me take it upon the credit of thy word: an' where I have thy promise, let me not stagger through unbelief, but fully persuade myself that it shall be as thou hast said. O bless and enrich my soul with such a holy, lively, and unfeigned faith, as may enlighten my mind, and purify my heart, and influence my whole life; such a faith, as may enable me to receive Jesus Christ for my Saviour, and heartily to give up myself to him as my Lord: that, being ruled and sanctified by him in this life, I may be for ever saved and glorified by him in the life that is to come. O help me so to assent unto the truths, that I may also consent to the terms, of the gospel. And give me that effectual faith which shall work by love; that faith which shall enable me to overcome the world, and to fix my attention on those great and glorious things which are unseen and eternal.

In my greatest darkness and distress, O let me trust in the name of the Lord, and stay myself upon my God; committing my ways unto thee, and casting my burthen upon thee, and putting my trust in thee, though thou slay me. Let me trust in thine almighty power to help and save; in thy tender inclinations to pity and relieve; and in the sure promises which thy love hath made (and which thy faithfulness will certainly make good) unto all that wait and call upon thee. And though I am not presently answered in the wishes of my heart, O let me tarry and wait patiently for the salvation of the Lord; and have my eyes upon the Lord my God, till thou have mercy upon me. Yea, make so sound and strong in the faith, that my faith may never fail: but that it may be found to praise and honour and glory in every time of trial; and at the great appearing of our Lord and Saviour Jesus Christ. *Amen.*

A PRAYER FOR POWER TO LIVE BY FAITH
UPON CHRIST, AND THE DIVINE PROMISES.

IT is thy command, O my Lord and Saviour, that they who believe in God should believe also in thee, as their only Mediator with the Father: even in thee, who countest it no robbery to be equal with God ; yea, who thyself art over all, God blessed for ever. Thou hast told us, that it is life eternal to know thee ; and that, as none can come unto the Father but by thee, so none shall perish who believe in thee. O the riches of thy grace, and the wonders of thy mercy, that it should so be done to poor sinners! Blessed for ever be thy glorious name! and blessed be the God of all grace, who, of his abundant mercy, has provided such a remedy for us in our lost estate ; to save us through faith in him, when we could not be saved by any merits or performances of our own.

Great and holy Lord! in all that ever I do, I cannot but see my extreme need of a Saviour ; and that I am undone without thy free grace in Christ Jesus. And therefore I desire to go to him, and to be found in him ; not having my own righteousness, but that which is through the faith of him: and to sit down under the shadow of that tree of life, which yields the richest fruits, most sweet to all who have ever tasted of his grace. O that Christ, who is the end of the law for righteousness to every one that believeth, may be the Lord MY righteousness! that his righteousness may be imputed to me! and that with the heart I may believe unto righteousness : even so believe in Jesus Christ, that I may be justified by faith, and have peace with God through him!

The blessed Jesus is my life and strength, my wisdom and riches, my health and joy, my glory and my all : there is no healing for my soul, but in his precious blood: no peace for my conscience but in his reconciling me to God : no satisfaction to my mind, but in that most perfect atonement, which satisfies even the strictest justice of heaven. O none but Christ! none but Christ! Without this all-sufficient Redeemer, I am a lost creature. I beseech thee, therefore, O Lord, (whatever else I want) leave me not destitute of him: but give me an interest in Christ, or I die eternally. Though I have so long slighted all his love, and neglected his great salvation, yet, O my Father, I dare not add this to all my other offences, to despair of that mercy, which, in him, thou art pleased to hold forth even to the most sinful and unworthy. Seeing that thou art, in Christ Jesus, a God reconciling the world unto thyself, and hast given him to be the propitiation for our sins; and that he came to seek and to save even the lost, and to call sinners to repentance; and that he invites to him the labouring and heavy laden; yea, bids all that are athirst, to come and take the water of life freely; and that he promises, that such as come to him he will in no wise cast out; to him therefore will I look, and in him will I trust; and of thee, my gracious Father, I beg for help to do it as I ought. O be thou pleased to shine into my heart with thy heavenly light, to reveal thy Son in me, and to show me his all-sufficiency for my wants, yea, to show me also my own happy interest in him. Dear Lord! give me thy Son to save me; and give me thy Spirit to draw me to him; and enable me to take hold of him, to rely upon him, and to believe in him, to the saving of my soul. O make me more acquainted with the way of saving sinners by Jesus Christ; and help me humbly to acquiesce in it, and thankfully submit to the righteousness of God.

Seeing thou, O God of all grace, justifiest sinners freely by thy grace, not for any merit of their works, but for the worthiness of thy Son, through the redemption that is in Christ Jesus, O may it be given unto me to believe on him, and to repose all my trust in him; that, believing, I may have life through his name. And may I be still fully persuaded in my mind, that he is the true Messiah, the only Saviour of the world. Let me never distrust his power, or his love: never be faithless, but at all times believing and confident, that he is my Lord and my God, who loved me, and washed me from my sins in his own blood. And let the God of hope fill me with all joy and peace in believing, whilst I lie at the feet of Jesus, and cast my burthen upon the Lord, and lean on the beloved of my soul. Though there is nothing in me but pollution and disorder, O let me not keep aloof from my Saviour; but come to him at his call, and believe in his name, that through him I may be made clean and whole. None can more need his help, O Lord, than I do. O that it may not pass by me: but let the Saviour of the world be the Saviour of my soul; and let

Christ abide with my Spirit, and be ever at hand, to do me good. O that my Redeemer may look with an eye of favour upon me, and revive me with some tokens of his love, which is better than all the enjoyments and comforts of the world.

Help me, O thou great Author and Finisher of our faith, to pray in faith; believing that I shall receive the things which I ask in thy name. O my Lord and my God! make me to know and believe the love thou hast to me; yea, that thou hast loved me with an everlasting love. Make me to know whom I have believed; and, that Jesus Christ is my Strength and my Redeemer. And let this sweet assured hope comfort me under all troubles, fortify me against all temptations, and quicken me to the performance of all my duties. O that Christ may dwell in my heart by faith; and that the life which I now live, may be by the faith of the Son of God, who loved me and gave himself for me: and, though I now see him not, yet believing, let me rejoice in him with joy unspeakable and glorified.

It is thy gracious promise, Lord, to blot out thy people's transgressions, for thine own sake, and neither to remember their sins, nor to let sin have dominion over them. Thou hast promised to have mercy upon the wicked and unrighteous, and abundantly to pardon them, if only they forsake their wicked ways, and their unrighteous thoughts. Thou hast assured them, that thou wilt take away from them the heart of stone, and give them a heart of flesh; that thou wilt put thy Spirit within them, and cause them to walk in thy statutes, and to keep thy judgments, and do them; and that, when they unreservedly give up themselves to thee, thou wilt perform in them the good work of thy grace. Thou hast promised, that though they fall, thou wilt uphold them with thy hand, and so put thy fear in their hearts, that they shall not finally depart from thee. Thou hast assured them, that thou wilt preserve them to thy heavenly kingdom, and give unto them eternal life. O what exceeding great and precious promises! what cordials to fainting souls! for, great as they are, and almost beyond belief, they shall all be fulfilled in their season. Faithful is he that has promised, who also will do it. It is ratified in heaven: and not one jot or tittle of thy word, Lord, shall pass away, till all be fulfilled. O let me believe that I, even I, shall see it. What time I am afraid, let me trust in thee; and let me give glory to my God, in believing thy gracious promises, though I know how unworthy I am to have any part or lot in them. Let me lay up thy kind words of promise, O my Father, as the richest treasure, and confide in them as the surest tenure: counting nothing so firm, as what God hath said; and despising all the wealth, and honours, and pleasures of the world, in comparison of Thyself, and thy Son, and thy Spirit, and thy love, and thy grace and thy glory; all which

I earnestly beg of thy bountiful hands, for **Jesus** Christ his sake. *Amen.*

A PRAYER FOR REPENTANCE.

O MOST holy Lord God, against whom I have greatly sinned, and who for my sins art most justly displeased! thou hast revealed thy wrath from heaven against all ungodliness and unrighteousness of men; and hast declared, that except we repent, we shall all perish. Thou wilt not save any without repentance; though, upon our repentance, thou hast assured us of thy gracious pardon and acceptance. When we return unto thee, and humble ourselves before thee, thou wilt show us thy mercy, and grant us thy salvation. O gracious Lord! great indeed is thy mercy, to vouchsafe unto us this remedy. But O how averse am I to repent! yea, how unable am I to perform this necessary work! Thou searcher of hearts, thou seest that my heart is hardened through the deceitfulness of sin: I cannot, I cannot humble myself aright: my heart must for ever remain obdurate, if thou do not soften it by thy grace: I can no more turn to thee with all my heart, than I can turn the course of a river back to its fountain: unless thou draw me, I can never run after thee; if thou endue me not with power from on high, I must continue for ever a miserable captive to sin and Satan.

A PRAYER FOR REPENTANCE.

O thou that didst cause water to gush out of the stony rock, break and melt my rocky heart: thou that fashionest all the hearts of the sons of men, take away from me the heart of stone, and give me a heart of flesh: teach me to look on him whom my sins have pierced, and mourn: cause me to be in bitterness for all the offences that I have committed against thee, the Lord of love, and the God of all my mercies. O give me true repentance for them; such repentance as thy holy word requires, and such as thy gracious goodness in Christ Jesus will mercifully accept. give me that repentance unto life, which is never to be repented of. Thou knowest, Lord, I desire to have that brokenness of heart, and that deep contrition, which thou wilt not despise: O that thou wouldst vouchsafe it to me! O that I might so repent, and be converted, that my sins might be blotted out, and that a season of refreshing might come to me from thy presence! Turn thou me, O good Lord, and so shall I be turned; renew me in the spirit of my mind, that I may bring forth fruits meet for repentance: not only confessing and bewailing my sins, but also hating and forsaking them, yea loathing and abhorring them from my inmost soul. I cannot recall my sins, O Lord, thou knowest: but, O that I might never repeat them more! O that I might have such a sense of thy loving-kindness, as should effectually divorce me from all my former ways! Let me henceforth walk with all possible care and circumspection, and make it the great business of my life to keep myself in thy fear and love. Let the past time suffice to have wrought my own will: henceforth let me have grace determinately to forsake all evil ways and evil thoughts; that so thou mayst have mercy upon me, and abundantly pardon all my multiplied transgressions. Hear me, O God, and answer me, through the infinite richness of thy grace and goodness in Christ Jesus my only Saviour. *Amen.*

A PRAYER FOR HUMILITY.

O MOST high God, infinitely glorious above all our expressions, or our thoughts! Thou sittest on the circle of the earth, and the inhabitants thereof are as grasshoppers: yea, before thee, all nations are as nothing, and counted to thee less than nothing and vanity. O what is man, that thou shouldst be so mindful of him! yea, that he should be so unmindful of himself, as to overlook all his own vileness and sinfulness, and to swell with the conceit of his own worth and excellence! I desire, O Lord, to humble myself for the pride of my heart, and to confess with shame, that I have thought more highly of myself than I ought to think; and vain-gloriously set off myself before men, when I deserved nothing but shame and confusion. O thou that resisteth the proud, and givest grace to the humble, give me the grace of humility: and make me vile in my own eyes, that I may be accepted in thy sight. Make me, Lord, of the number of those poor in spirit, those humble and contrite ones, to whom thou wilt look, and with whom thou wilt dwell.

O set my sins in order before me, and make me to know my transgressions; that I may not flatter myself in my own eyes, but look upon myself as sinful dust and ashes; deserving only to be trodden under foot, and to be cast out as the off-scouring of all things. Let me never take anything but shame to myself; but at all times give thee the glory of whatever is good in me. Great and holy God! make me more studious to be thy favourite, than to be so accounted: and better pleased to do my duty, than to hear that I have done it. Neither let me seek glory of men, but the honour that cometh of God only. And the more I have received from thee, the more let me ascribe unto thee: and not be proudly opinionated of myself; but give all thanks and glory to thee for any good, wherein thou hast made me to differ. Let me not desire the praise of men, whilst I am doing the work of God; but let me perform all my offices, as one that would approve himself to thee, the heart-searching God.

O discover me so to myself, that I may still walk humbly with my God, and be clothed with humility; considering how frail I am, as a creature, and how vile, as a sinner. Let me ever hate and resist the pride that goeth before destruction;

and so humble myself under thy mighty hand, that thou mayst exalt me in due time. And for all the good that ever I have performed or enjoyed, not unto me, O Lord, not unto me, but to thy name, be all the praise and glory, humbly and heartily acknowledged and rendered, both now and evermore. *Amen.*

A PRAYER FOR TENDERNESS OF HEART.

ALMIGHTY Lord, the God of all grace, who speakest to the heart, and it obeys thee; and, when it is grown callous and hard, canst make it soft and relenting; and give sight and sense even to such as are blind and past feeling! O show the power of thy heavenly grace, in working upon this stupid, insensible heart of mine; that I may know the evil of my sins, and the things belonging to my peace. And be thou pleased to give me such a sight of my sins, such humiliation of soul, and brokenness of heart, as may prepare me for all the promised mercies of my God in Christ Jesus. O Father of mercies! punish not my past sins, by leaving me to commit sin with greediness; nor ever give me up to such blindness of mind, and hardness of heart, as shall render me senseless and incorrigible. But quicken and awaken my dull soul into a lively sense of sin, and tenderness of conscience, and due apprehension of my great, eternal concerns. O make me ever jealous over my heart, and watchful over my ways; continually fearing to offend, and endeavouring to please my God: enable me to keep my heart with all diligence, that it be not hardened through the deceitfulness of sin: and to stand at a distance from every evil and accursed thing, that is provoking in thy sight, and destructive to my soul.

O let me not continue in sin, that grace may abound; nor abuse that mercy which has so long borne with me, and been so abundantly good to me: but give me, O my God, such an abundant increase of spiritual life, as may produce in me a greater quickness of spiritual sense, and make my conscience quick of feeling, even as the apple of my eye; that I may so feel my sins here, as to prevent my feeling them for ever, when there shall be no remedy. From hardness of heart, and contempt of thy word and commandments, good Lord deliver me. Give me a heart so soft and tender as to smite and correct me for every, even the least evil. Impress it with such a fear of offending thee, that it may keep me back, not only from gross and scandalous offences, but from all that is suspicious, or that has a tendency to sin; even from the occasions of falling, and from the very appearance of evil. O let me so observe thee with a child-like tenderness, and awful regard, all the days of my life; that I may not slavishly dread thee now, or be consumed with thy terrors in the day of thy wrath: but may then receive the blessed portion of thy children, who looked for and hasted to the coming of the day of Christ. *Amen.*

A PRAYER FOR THE FEAR OF GOD.

O LORD, the great and dreadful God! in whose hands is my time, and at whose mercy is my soul, and all that concerns me both here and for ever; thou, even thou, art to be feared; and who may stand in thy sight, when once thou art angry? The fear of the Lord is the beginning of wisdom; and happy is the man that feareth always; but to harden our hearts against thy fear, is not only folly and impiety, but madness and ruin. I am afraid, O Lord, because I have feared thee no more: I am afraid, because I have thought so lightly of thee, who couldst, if it had pleased thee, have avenged thee of thine adversary, and cast me, at any moment, into the depths of hell. I am afraid, because I have been so fearless in the ways of sin, where I should not have dared to venture; and so timorous in the cause of God, where I should not have feared the face of any man. O absolve me, I beseech thee, good Lord, from all this guilt, that lies upon me: and put thy fear into my heart, that I may never experience what a fearful thing it is to fall into thy hands. O stir up my heart to fear thy name! and let thy fear be ever before my eyes to restrain me from the evil of my ways. Let me so stand in awe of thee, that I may not dare to provoke thee. Let me not be so much afraid of a man that shall die, as of the almighty, ever-living God; nor so fear any loss or suffering, (which can at most be only temporal,) as I fear the sin and wickedness, that would deprive me of the good everlasting. O let me fear the Lord, and depart from evil: let me have my God in such regard, that I may not wilfully violate thy holy laws: let me ever be afraid to dishonour thy name, or to rebel against thy word, or to rest short of what thou requirest at my hands. And O that thy fear may not only keep under some of my sins, but regulate my whole life, and sway my very heart: that I may do thy will entirely from the heart, and go on to perfect holiness in the fear of God.

May I fear thy name, and not dishonour it; fear thy wrath, and not provoke it; fear thy word, and not despise it; fear thy goodness, and not abuse it; fear thy omniscience, and not make bold with secret sins; fear thy omnipotence, and not strive with my Maker in any case. And give me, O my God, the right mixture of fear and faith; that I may not incline either to presumption or despair; that, in the event of crosses or evils coming upon me, I may not sink down into such consternations as shall unfit me for my duty: and that no successes, or prospects of this world's good, may harden my heart, or lift me up into wantonness and stubbornness against thee: but that I may keep up an awful regard of thy glorious Majesty, and a dutiful respect to all thy holy commands, to the latest hour of my life. *Amen.*

A PRAYER FOR THE LOVE OF GOD

O THOU infinite goodness and love, who art most sweet and amiable in thyself; and most attractive on account of thy glorious excellences and perfections; and also for all the wonders of thy mercy and bounty! What rich mercy is it, that thou hast made us capable of loving thee; (beyond which the highest angels know no greater bliss:) yea, that thou hast not only given us capacities for it, but the greatest obligations, to engage our hearts to it! Yet after all the reasons and motives which we have to love our God, O how poor and defective has been my love! Yea, in what strangeness and enmity to thee, O Lord, have I lived! It is my sin and shame and misery, to be so listless and backward to thy love. O my God, I have done foolishly and wickedly, in forsaking the fountain of living waters, to hew to myself broken cisterns, that can hold no water: shutting my heart against the love of my chiefest good; and preferring any trifles and vanities of this present time, yea, and the satisfaction of my own foolish and hurtful lusts, above thee and thy love, which is better than life.

O gracious God! be thou pleased to pardon all the defects of my love to thee, and all the excesses of my love to earthly things: and turn my inclinations and affections from all vain objects, to thy blessed self, who art most worthy of all my love: and (to conquer all my prejudice, and for ever win my heart) O show thyself to me as a pardoning God, full of compassion, ready to forgive, and willing to save. Yea, make me to know so much of the love wherewith thou hast loved me, that I may make better returns of love to the gracious giver of all my good. Touch my heart with such a powerful sense of thy loveliness and thy lovingkindness, that I may experience stronger desires and inclinations after thee, and greater complacence and delight in thee; and may love all other things, in comparison of my best and dearest Lord, as if I loved them not.

The Lord direct my heart into the love of God: and shed abroad, and increase, thy love in my heart: that I may love the Lord my God with all my heart and soul, and mind and strength. O show me the vanity of all those tempting things, which would draw away my love from thyself: and so discover thyself to my soul, that my heart may be unalterably fixed on thee: yea, make this heart of mine, which has been so cold and insensible to thy love, to feel henceforth its mighty warmth and power; that, from complaining of the want, I may come to rejoice in the abundance of it. O my life, my hope, and joy, that hast so much and eternally obliged me! give me the grace and the power to love thee; let me be ever longing to appear before thee, and delighting in the duties that bring me nigh to thee, and that help me to communion with thee. Increase my love to thy word, and to all the things of thy Spirit and grace. And let me take more satisfaction and pleasure in the light of thy countenance, than in any increase of corn and wine, and all the most desired enjoyments of this life. O let me not rest in the gifts, forgetting the bountiful giver of every good thing: but draw me, and join my heart, dear Lord, still nearer to thyself, with the cords of love. And together with all my enjoyments in the world, O let me enjoy still more of thee, my God; in the enjoyment of whom consists all my true life, and peace, and happiness, here and for ever. Engage to thyself, O my Lord, the chief and choicest affections of my heart; and take it the willing captive of thy love. And help me at all times to manifest my love to thee, by hating evil, and keeping thy commands, and delighting to do thy will, O my God. Let the desire of my soul, the care of my heart, and the endeavour of my life, be to observe and please thee. And so secure my heart, Lord, to thyself, that I may not go a whoring from thee; but may be rooted and grounded in thy love, and through thy good help and grace, may keep myself in the love of God; looking for the mercy of our Lord Jesus Christ unto eternal life. *Amen.*

A PRAYER FOR HOPE.

O LORD God of hope, the blessed Founder of all our great and glorious expectations! thou hast promised thy people such bliss and glory, as is not only above our deserts to enjoy, but above all our very thoughts to conceive. Yet inconceivable as it is, it is not too great for thine almighty hand, and thy boundless love to give. And, because thou hast made such preparations for thy people, answerable to thine own infinite greatness and goodness, thou art not ashamed to be called their God. None has seen, nor can tell or think, the things which thou, O God, hast laid up for them that love thee. But it is good to hope, and quietly wait for the salvation of the Lord. Even in dark days, and perilous times, when thou makest us to know adversity, and threatenest us with still increasing judgments, yet is it our duty patiently to wait for thee, till thou return unto us in mercy, and cause the light of thy countenance to shine upon us.

O my God! give me such hope as may lift up my head, and strengthen my heart, and embolden my spirit, against all temptations and discouragements of the present time: that I may never yield to any consternations, so as to destroy my faith and hope, or unfit me for thy work and service. O give me for a helmet, the hope of salvation; that hope which may be as an anchor to my soul, both sure and steadfast. O let me hope, and praise thee more and more, and rejoice in the hope that maketh not ashamed; yea, and hold fast the rejoicing of my hope firm unto the end.

Though I am sinful and unworthy, yet let me hope in the Lord, with whom there is mercy and plenteous redemption, to redeem his people from all their iniquities. O gracious God, infinitely good! I could have no hope but in thy tender mercies, and in thine exceeding great and precious promises, which gave assurance of pardon and acceptance to all that humbly seek thee, through the mediation of thy Son, Jesus Christ. But I beseech thee, O Lord, remember thy word unto thy servant, on which thou hast caused me to hope. O seal me with that Holy Spirit of promise, which is the earnest of our inheritance; that I may abound in hope, through the power of the Holy Ghost. Let Christ in me be my hope of glory: and having this hope in me, help me to purify myself, as my Lord is pure: that my hopes may be rational and well-founded; and that I may be counted worthy to enjoy thee in thy kingdom and glory, through the name and merits of Jesus Christ, my only Mediator and Redeemer. *Amen.*

A PRAYER FOR CHARITY.

O MOST gracious and merciful Lord our God, who art goodness and love itself, thou hast commanded that he who loveth thee, should love his brother also; yea, that we should love our neighbour as ourselves. Father of mercies, forgive me all my sins of uncharitableness: and give me a heart to abound with loving-kindness to all who are partakers of my nature, and objects of thy fatherly compassion. Let me not despise any for their low estate; nor hate any for their abusive carriage; nor cast off any as reprobate for their scandalous wickedness; but be kindly affectioned to all; desirous of their holiness and happiness, and contributing what lieth in me to promote it: showing the mercy, which thou knowest I need; and forgiving others, as I myself desire to be forgiven. Make me ready to distribute, and willing to communicate: and, as I should be glad to find favour, and to receive a supply of my own wants, give me, O gracious God, a large heart, and (according to my ability) an open hand: that I may give cheerfully, and sow plentifully, while I have time; doing good unto all men, especially to them that are of the household of faith: yea, loving the opportunities of such well-doing; and blessing thy name, for disposing me to seek refreshment to my own bowels in gladdening the hearts of thy poor.

And O that we may all approve ourselves the disciples of our Lord, by the love we have one to another; and show that we are passed from death to life, because we love the brethren. May we ever esteem them above all; and regard those as dearest unto us, who most distinguish themselves in performing thy blessed will. O let our love be without dissimulation; not only in word and in tongue, but in deed and in truth. May we love one another with a pure heart fervently: may we seek the good of all, however undeserving they may be in themselves, or however hostile to us: and let our delight be in the saints, and in the righteous, that are more excellent than their neighbours. Make us to love them for thy holy image appearing in them; and to set our hearts upon them, because thou art with them, and hast a favour unto them, and hast loved them with an everlasting love. O Lord of love, keep me from censoriousness, and rash judging of any: that I may think and hope the best of all, which their case will admit; and love every one for *his* sake, who has showed the greatest love to us all, even our dearest Lord, and only Saviour, Jesus Christ. *Amen.*

A PRAYER FOR CHASTITY.

O GOD of infinite purity: thou hast called us not to uncleanness, but to holiness. Thou hast commanded us to be holy, as thou art holy;

A PRAYER FOR CHASTITY.

and hast promised to none but the pure in heart, that they shall see thee here in the beauties of holiness, and partake of thy joys above. O how shall I, a polluted wretch, show myself before thee, who art perfect purity; and in whose sight even heaven itself is not clean! O most gracious Lord! look not upon me, as I am in myself; for through my sins I have made myself so vile, that, unless thou hide thy face from my sins, thou canst not but abhor my soul, and pour out all thy wrath upon me. In thy tender mercy, wash me thoroughly from my iniquity: cleanse me from all my sin and guilt, in that fountain opened for sin and uncleanness, even in the precious blood of the Lamb of God, who was slain to take away the sins of the world. Lord, if thou wilt, thou canst make me clean: O create in me a clean heart; and say to my defiled soul, as thou didst to the leper, "I will, be thou clean." O my God! cast the unclean spirit out of thy temple: and if he will not go out, but by prayer and fasting, let me add such abstinence to my prayers as may help to mortify the fleshly lusts that war against my soul. And by any means, help me, O my Strength and my Redeemer, to possess my vessel in sanctification and honour; not in the lusts of concupiscence, as those that know not God. Holy Lord! chase away the birds of prey, that would devour thy sacrifice; and drive out these unclean beasts, that would trample down the plantation of thy grace in my soul. O let me not live after the flesh, lest I die eternally : but enable me by thy Spirit to mortify the deeds of the body, that I may live for ever. Instead of doing the works of the flesh, let me hate the very garment spotted with it ; and not, without utter detestation, so much as name the things which are practised by many without remorse. Help me, my God, to avoid every occasion of falling; and to abstain from all appearance of evil : help me so to delight in purity, and to keep myself from my iniquity, that I may walk as becomes a child of my heavenly Father; not grieving thy Holy Spirit, but doing the things which are pleasing in thy sight, through Jesus Christ, our Lord. *Amen.*

A PRAYER FOR MEEKNESS AND PEACEABLENESS.

O ALMIGHTY God, who alone canst order the unruly wills and affections of sinful men ! wilt thou be pleased to subdue my exorbitant passions, and suppress in me that pride from whence cometh contention ; and root out every thought that is inconsistent with gentleness and meekness of spirit. O help me to put away all bitterness, and wrath, and anger, and clamour, and evil speaking, with all malice. And however I am tempted and provoked, O that I may possess my soul in patience; and not be overcome of evil, but overcome evil with good. And enable us, O

God of patience, to bear one another's burdens, and to forbear one another in love: that we may not contend, but for the faith of Christ; nor strive, but to enter in at the strait gate; nor provoke one another, but unto love and to good works.

If thou, the great God, shouldst enter into judgment with me, and break out in fury upon me, as I have been ready to take fire at affronts, and to fall with rage upon my antagonists, how soon should I be consumed, and sink under the load of my numerous transgressions! O may I ever dread to be rigid towards others, knowing how much I myself stand in need of mercy! And do thou, the God of peace and love, forgive me, I beseech thee, all the sins that ever I have committed against peace and love. O let the peace of God rule in my heart; and thy wonderful long-suffering towards me be ever an engagement to show all meekness to all men! Let me bear the ignorance and wickedness, the follies and mistakes, the wrongs and indignities of my fellow-creatures, seeing that I myself am undone without the forbearance of God; and have nothing to hope for, or to comfort myself in, but the finding of such favour at thy hands.

O teach and help us all to live in peace, and to love in truth, following peace with all men, and walking in love as Christ has loved us; that we may be united and knit together as fellow-members of the same body, whereof he is the glorious head. Teach me to look at the example of him, who, though grievously wronged and provoked, yet did not cry, nor lift up, nor cause his voice to be heard in the streets; and *of* him let me learn meekness and lowliness of heart, that *in* him I may find rest to my soul. O my God! suppress all bitter resentments in my mind; and let the law of kindness be ever in my tongue; and a meek and quiet spirit showing itself in all the conduct of my life. And, Lord, make us all so gentle and peaceable, and easy to be intreated, and hard to be provoked, that we may be followers of God as dear children; and that thou, the God of peace mayst be with us, and delight to dwell amongst us, and rejoice over us, to do us good: for thy mercy's sake in Christ Jesus. *Amen.*

A PRAYER FOR PATIENCE

O MY God! thou knowest what an evil world we live in; and how much I myself have contributed to make it still worse by my sins: and shall I, who have done so little good, and so much evil, expect nothing but good at thy hands? In the world, thou hast told us, we shall have tribulation: and O that tribulation may work patience; and that I may be contented to bear whatever thou art pleased to lay upon me. Enable me to possess my soul in patience, however tried by corrections from thy hand, or by injuries

A PRAYER FOR PATIENCE.

from the hands of men. To blame the instrument, or complain of thy providence, under the pressures lying upon me, will but torment myself, and still add to that which I count so grievous to endure. O let me better provide for my own ease as well as duty, than so to disquiet myself in vain. And, whatever thou doest with me, O Lord, let me be dumb, and not open my mouth to reply or murmur, because it is thy doing. Make me to acquiesce and rest satisfied even in the bitterest dispensations of thy good providence; contented with such things as I have, and patient in the want of such comforts as I have not. And since nothing but trouble and sorrow is my deserved portion, O let me not be querulous and froward; forasmuch as thou dealest not with me after my sins, nor rewardest me according to my iniquities. May I patiently encounter all difficulties and grievances in my passage through this troublesome world: knowing that the same afflictions are accomplished in my brethren that are in the world, and that it is but the common lot of all sinful mortals upon earth. O make me patient until the coming of the Lord; enduring all things with a meek and quiet spirit; and thoroughly convinced that they are happy that endure; and that such as endure unto the end shall be saved. O my Lord, let not any pains or sufferings ever drive me from thee; but rather be the means of bringing me nearer to thee. And let the remembrance of the great day of the Lord, and of the eternal state that is approaching, work in me a contempt of this world, a mortification of my lusts, and a patient abiding of the cross. Make me to feel that it is of very little importance what we enjoy, or what we suffer here for a short season, provided we be delivered from the wrath to come, and be made happy in thy kingdom for evermore. O let me, by patient continuance in well-doing, seek for glory and honour and immortality; and count nothing in this world either dear to possess, or difficult to suffer; so that I may but finish my course with joy, and at the last rest from all my labours and troubles, with the redeemed and blessed of the Lord. All this I wait and beg for at thy good hands, O my gracious Father, for the sake of Jesus Christ. *Amen.*

A PRAYER FOR THE MORTIFICATION OF ALL FLESHLY LUSTS.

I HAVE vowed and promised unto thee, my God, to renounce all the sinful lusts of the flesh: and I am devoted, as one holy to the Lord: that, having put on Jesus Christ, I should no more make provision for the flesh, to fulfil the lusts thereof: but should cleanse myself from all filthiness of flesh and spirit, perfecting holiness in the fear of God. But though I have some delight in the law of God, after the inner man, yet I find

FOR MORTIFICATION OF SIN. 195

another law in my members, warring against the law of my mind, and bringing me into captivity to the law of sin which is in my members. And this I acknowledge and bewail before thee, O Lord, my God; who alone canst set me free from the lusts that are too hard for me. O help me, thou God of my salvation, against the power of these prevailing iniquities; and purge away my sins, for the glory of thy name. May the time past suffice to have served my own lusts and pleasures. O let not sin any longer reign in my mortal body, that I should obey it in the lusts thereof. But help me, Lord, to cut off the right hand, and to pluck out the right eye; to keep under my body, and to bring it into subjection, that I may have the mastery of my lusts, and overcome the sins that have so often overcome me. O mortify and destroy in me every vicious inclination that exalts itself against the authority of my Lord, and that gives Satan an advantage over me.

Preserve me, Lord most holy! from all those sinful pleasures that would rob me of the pleasures which are at thy right hand for evermore. O let me not lead a sensual life, minding the things of the flesh, as if they were worthy of my esteem; but make me spiritually-minded, that I may above all things savour and relish the things of the Spirit of God. Let not any sinful appetite, but thy heavenly Spirit and grace, have the predominance in my soul: do thou and thou alone, govern my heart and life. Especially, let the sins to which I am most strongly tempted, be effectually subdued. O let me not yield myself a miserable slave to my lusts; but demean myself as a wise and faithful follower of my Lord and Saviour. And as thou, who hast called me, art holy, so make me holy in disposition, and in all my conversation; that, being a lover and follower of holiness, I may be counted worthy to see and enjoy my Lord. O gird with might to that spiritual conflict wherein I am engaged: enable me to fight not only against flesh and blood, but against those infernal foes, who are too strong for me to deal with; that (through Christ strengthening me) I may vanquish all that withstands thy glory, and my salvation; and go on conquering and to conquer, till Satan be for ever bruised under my feet. Fight for me, and fight with me, O my God, that nothing may ever separate me from the love of God, which is in Christ Jesus my Lord. *Amen.*

A PRAYER FOR SINCERITY.

O MY Lord, the only wise God, whose understanding is infinite, and from whom no thought can be withheld! Thou fillest the whole world with thy presence, and hast all things ever naked and open before thine eyes. Thou that teachest man knowledge, shalt not thou know? Thou searchest the heart, and hast even our most secret sins in the light of thy countenance. And thou chiefly callest for our hearts; and requirest truth in the inward parts; and wilt bring every work into judgment, and every secret thing, whether good or evil. My God, I acknowledge and bewail before thee, the guile and deceitfulness of my heart: I lament that I have been so unmindful of thy presence, and so regardless of thy glorious Majesty. I confess, O Lord, that for these things thou mightst long since have cut me off, and appointed me a portion with the hypocrites. But, as thou hast spared me thus long, humble me, I beseech thee, and pardon me, for all the hypocrisy and treacherous dealing, whereof I have been guilty. And as thou canst speak to the heart, and order it even as thou wilt, O make my heart right with thee, and without any allowed guile in thy sight: that so I may not be found wanting in that day, when thou shalt come to judge the world.

O let thine all-seeing eye, and not the eye of the world, restrain and regulate my conduct. And let thy blessed favour, more than the approbation of sinful men, be ever my study and delight. Search me, O God, and try me; and whatever unpardoned guilt or unrepented wickedness, whatever unknown error or countenanced lust, lies in my soul, O help me to see it; and, of thy mercy, deliver me from it: and let me not regard iniquity in my heart. Let no presumptuous sins have dominion over me. Let me not allow myself in any way of wickedness; nor go on in formality and hypocrisy to serve thee: but enable me to walk before thee with an upright heart, and to do all things sincerely and heartily, as unto the Lord. O let me not be only almost, but altogether a Christian; obeying from the heart all thy holy will; and not so much concerned to seem religious, as to be so in deed and in truth. Make me willing to part with the dearest sins, and to perform the hardest duties, for the sake of that adorable Saviour, who left the highest glory, and endured the sorest misery, for the sake of my soul. O make me true to my own convictions, and faithful in exerting my own endeavours: yea, make me ever jealous over my heart, and conscientious in all my thoughts, and words, and ways: that my praise may not be of men, but of God; and that I may have continual rejoicing in the testimony of my own conscience, and in that peace of God, which passeth all understanding. O my Father, who seest in secret! let the performing of thy holy will, and the honouring of thy blessed name, and the enjoying of thy gracious favour, be the great end which I design and aim at, in all my actions and undertakings: that thou, the great and good God, mayst in all things be glorified by me, through Jesus Christ. *Amen.*

A PRAYER FOR INCREASE OF GRACE.

O GOD of all grace, who quickenest the dead, and art both the Author and Finisher of thy people's faith! thou hast told us that the path of the just is as the shining light, that shineth more and more unto the perfect day; and that they go from strength to strength, growing in grace, till they appear before thee in glory. But, O Lord, how barren and unfruitful have I been among the trees of righteousness! and how little have I made my profiting to appear under all the means of grace which thou hast mercifully vouchsafed unto me; how weak and low am I still in my spiritual estate! how weak is my will, and small my strength, to that which is good! how much am I behind many of thy servants, who have not had the helps and advantages which I have so long enjoyed; and how little is it to be seen in my life what great things the Lord has done for my soul! O my God, I have not well improved the talents which thou hast put into my hands, nor answered the care and kindness of heaven, which I have so long experienced. Thou hast not been wanting to me, O good Lord! but I have been exceedingly wanting to myself, and to that duty which I owe to thee, my God. I am ashamed that it is no better with me, that so many mercies have been lost upon me. Forgive me, O my Father, and renew me after thy blessed image. O help me still more and more to put off the old man, which is corrupt according to the deceitful lusts; and to put on the new man, which after God is created in righteousness and true holiness. Whatever else I want, Lord, deny me not thy grace! but increase it in me, and discover it still more and more upon me. Yea, let the graces of thy Spirit that accompany salvation, so flourish in my soul, that the peace of God, which passeth all understanding, may keep my heart and mind through Christ Jesus.

Blessed Saviour! who camest into the world that we might have life, and have it more abundantly, let me receive out of thy fulness grace sufficient for me; that I may be strong in the Lord, and ready to every good work. My Life, my Strength, and my Redeemer! leave me not under the curse of barrenness, to halt or decline in my spiritual estate: but, as thou hast wrought all my works in me, stablish, I beseech thee, that which thou hast wrought for me; and strengthen the things which remain, that are ready to die. Let the seeds of grace which thou hast sown in my heart be watered by thy good Spirit; that my soul may prosper and increase with the increase of God, even as a watered garden, or as a spring whose waters fail not. Make me to grow in knowledge and in grace; and to abound in all those fruits of righteousness, which are by Jesus Christ, to the glory and praise of God; so that I may have the witness in myself, that I am thy servant. O my Lord, carry on with power the work of faith and holiness in my soul; that my sinful corruption may grow weaker and weaker; and thy grace in me may grow stronger and stronger; till, from groaning under the body of sin and death, I come to triumph over all the enemies of my soul. And as thou art pleased to afford me the means of grace, O grant me the increase of thy grace, that they may not be lost upon me; but that in the use of them I may be made still wiser, and holier, and better, and fitter for thy blessed acceptance in Jesus Christ my only Saviour. *Amen.*

A PRAYER FOR QUICKENING GRACE.

I ACKNOWLEDGE and bewail before thee, O thou living and all-seeing God, my sinful dulness, and backwardness to the duties of thy holy service. When I should delight in the law of God, and serve thee with gladness, and make it my meat and drink to do the will of my heavenly Father, O how cold and listless am I in the performance of that which is best for me, and which most nearly and eternally concerns me! I am alive to the world, and very apt to be transported with the objects of sense; but O how heavy and dead in those offices of attendance on my Lord, which are the joy and glory of all the hosts of heaven! My soul cleaveth to the dust; quicken me, O Lord, according to thy word; according to thy precept, which commands us to be spiritually-minded, and to be fervent in spirit, serving the Lord. And quicken me, O my God, according to the word of thy promise, that sin shall not have dominion over thy servants; and that thou wilt perfect that which concerneth them. Dear Lord! be thou pleased to perfect that which concerns my soul. And engage the love of my heart to thy service. Let it be my delight to do thy will, O God; and with an enlarged heart to run the way of thy commands. O help me to put forth myself with vigour and activity in thy holy ways: and to apply myself to the performance of thy blessed will, not only because I must, but because it is the desire of my soul, and the joy of my heart, to be so engaged: let nothing in the world give me so much pleasure and satisfaction as to approve my heart unto thee, my God, and to have all my works acceptable in thy sight, through Jesus Christ, my only Mediator and Advocate. *Amen.*

A PRAYER FOR THE DIVINE ASSISTANCE.

O LORD God Almighty, who givest power to the faint, and increasest strength to them that have no might! without thee I can do nothing; I am unable even to will or think anything that is good, or to keep myself from anything that is evil: but my help is in the name of the Lord, who made heaven and earth. Thou, O my God, art able to keep me from falling, and to make me perfect in every good work, and to work in me that which is well-pleasing in thy sight, through Christ Jesus. And thou hast encouraged me to come boldly to the throne of grace, that I may obtain mercy, and find grace to help me in time of need. Lord of all power and grace! I come, trusting in thine almighty strength, thine infinite goodness, and thy gracious promises; I come to ask of thee whatsoever is wanting in myself; and to obtain grace sufficient for me. Let thy good Spirit help my infirmities, and strengthen me with might in the inner man; that so I may be strong in the Lord, and in the power of his might; and do all things as I ought, through Christ strengthening me.

O thou that hast shown thyself graciously on my behalf, and hast brought me hitherto, I beseech thee, cast me not off, nor abandon me to myself, who am a reed shaken with the wind, a leaf driven to and fro: but let me still experience thy help at hand, and find thee to be an all-sufficient God, performing all things for me. I will go forth in the strength of the Lord God, and trust in the Lord Jehovah, in whom is everlasting strength. O my Lord! come to my succour, and be thou my helper: carry me on in thy holy ways; and make all that I think, and speak, and do, acceptable in thy sight. O may I both put forth myself, to stir up the grace of God that is in me; and let me find such fresh supplies of grace, that I may see my desires accomplished, and my endeavours brought to good effect, through Jesus Christ, our Strength and our Redeemer. *Amen.*

A PRAYER BEFORE THE HEARING OF GOD'S WORD.

O MOST blessed Lord, the God of all grace! who art pleased to send out thy light and thy truth among us; both to discover our sins unto us, and also to make the way of life and salvation plain before us: be thou pleased also to send the Spirit of thy Son into our hearts, to make it plain to our understanding, and to render it the savour of life unto our souls. O Lord, open our ears, and quicken our attention to the instructions that shall be given us, that we may receive thy word with all carefulness and meekness, yea, with all readiness and gladness, with an unfeigned delight in it, and a hearty desire to live and grow by it. And strengthen our memories, that we may treasure up and retain what we hear; that we may not let it slip, but may derive substantial benefit from, and be to all eternity the better for it. O gracious God! teach us to profit; and make our improvement more answerable to those means of grace, which through thy mercy we enjoy. Let the word which shall sound in our ears, sink down also into our hearts, and take root within us, and produce in our lives the fruits of righteousness. Let us not be forgetful hearers, but faithful doers of thy word. O let the immortal seed of this heavenly word beget such principles of grace and holiness in our hearts, as may be in us a well of water springing up to everlasting life. Make us so obedient to thy holy precepts, that we may also inherit the glorious promises of thy word. O let our teachers be taught of God, and direct the stewards of thy mysteries to give unto every one his portion in due season. And whilst thy servants are planting and watering, do thou, O God, bestow thy blessing, and send an abundant increase. Make the waters of thy sanctuary healing to our souls. Yea, make thy word as fire in the mouths of thy messengers: and make it to come home to our souls in demonstration of the Spirit and of power. Let it be mighty through God, to the pulling down of strongholds, and subduing all opposition to the obedience of Christ. Come down in the midst of us, O God of our salvation, and cause thy word to do thy great and glorious work upon all our hearts; that we may have reason to praise and glorify thee to all eternity. *Amen.*

A PRAYER AFTER HEARING OF THE WORD.

WE bless thee, O Lord, the living God, who holdest our souls in life, and providest for us that heavenly food by which we are to live for ever. It has now been delivered and received; but the blessing is in thy hands, O gracious God, to make it prosperous and successful to the gaining and saving of immortal souls. O wilt thou be pleased to send it home to the heart; and there make it to abide, till it has done thy will, and wrought thy work effectually. Make use of it now to build us up in the faith of Christ, and to help us forward in all holiness of life: let every hearer become a doer of thy word, that we may all, in this world, be blessed in our deeds, and hereafter be for ever blessed in the joy of our Lord.

O that all who have been convinced of their sins, may also be converted to thyself: that they may not only think of the holy change that is to be wrought in them, but seek incessantly the attainment of it. And let thy blessed Spirit so prevail with them, that their good impressions may not be lost, till they have effected the work of thy grace within them. O make thy word mighty through God, to plant thy grace where it is not; to increase it where it is; and to bring us all into a state of greater nearness to thee, and more entire conformity to thine image. Let us find our knowledge more clear and spiritual; our faith more firm and operative; and all our graces continually increasing in strength and activity. Let us so hear, that our souls may live before thee, both now and evermore. *Amen.*

A PRAYER FOR MINDFULNESS OF GOD'S PRESENCE.

O LORD, the infinite, incomprehensible God! thou art the high and holy One, who inhabitest eternity, and dwellest in the light which no man can approach unto; and from thy glorious throne in heaven, thou lookest down upon all the inhabitants of the earth, to give unto every one according to his ways, and according to the fruit of his doings. Though no mortal eye can see thee, no finite understanding comprehend thee, yet thou art here, and everywhere present; and now and evermore thou seest us, and understandest our thoughts afar off, and art thoroughly acquainted with all our ways. Yea, thou art so universally observant as to have a particular concern for every person and action in the whole world. Great God! thou fillest heaven and earth with thy presence; O fill my heart with thy grace, and with a mindfulness of thy presence with me: that I may set the Lord always before me; and evermore remember thee in all my ways.

O that ever I should forget the God that made me; the God who quickens everything that lives, concurs with everything that moves, and upholds everything that has a being, throughout the world! O that I should have been, as it were, without thee in the world, and forgetful of thee, in whom I ever live, and move, and am; and who hast been watchful over me for good all my days! Holy God! because I have regarded thee no more thou mightst make me sensible of thy presence in judgments worthy of thyself. But, O Lord, in mercy pardon all such my sinful neglect and inadvertence. And as I am ever exposed to thine all-seeing eye, make me to walk as in thine immediate presence. Let the remembrance of thy presence sway and guide me, in secret and in company, at all times, in all places, and in all my actions: let me demean myself as ever under the awful eyes of the great God of heaven and earth: and fear thee above all other powers, love thee above all other gods, serve thee before all other lords, and trust in thee more than in any other refuge. Yea, let me rejoice, under the shadow of thy wings, and herein solace myself, that thou art my right hand, and ever with me. O let not the remembrance of my Lord be grievous to me: but let my meditations of God be sweet, as well as frequent; that delighting myself in the Lord, thou mayst give unto me the desires of my heart. And so guide me with thine eye, that I may not err from thy statutes, but be ever accepted in thy sight, through Jesus Christ. *Amen.*

A PRAYER FOR DEVOTION,

AND A RIGHT FRAME OF SPIRIT IN THE WORSHIP OF GOD.

O MOST high and holy Lord God! thou wilt be sanctified in them that come nigh unto thee: thou art greatly to be feared, and to be had in reverence of all that are about thee. Be pleased to sanctify me with thy grace; and help me so to draw nigh unto thee in prayer, that thou mayst draw nigh unto me in the communications of thy love and mercy.

I desire, O my God, to meet thee in thy ways, and (in compliance with thy gracious appointment) I fall down and worship here at thy footstool in the name and through the mediation of thy dear Son. I am indeed most unworthy to come into thy holy presence, and utterly unable (of myself) to perform any service meet to be presented to thy heavenly Majesty! but O let thy great mercy overlook my unworthiness; and keep me from every thing that would make my prayers an abomination to the Lord. And, as thou hast made me sensible of my duty, and of my own insufficiency to discharge it as I ought, O let thy good Spirit help my infirmities; let thine almighty power keep me from sinful dulness and distractions, that I may worship thee in spirit and in truth, and offer thee a sacrifice that shall be well-pleasing in thy sight, through Jesus Christ our Lord. *Amen.*

A PRAYER FOR THE ENJOYMENT
OF GOD'S GRACIOUS PRESENCE AND DIVINE COMMUNION.

O THOU infinite Majesty of heaven and earth, who canst nowhere be absent, but fillest all things! no place is so desolate as to be without thee; no men so bad, but they live and move, and have their being in thee: yea, the very devils are not out of thy reach; but are aware of thy presence, though to their cost: even in hell, thou art there: but to thy people, that bear thine image, and know thy voice, and prize thy love, to them thou art pleased to communicate thyself in a more especial manner; and to go in and out among them, as the children of thy family. And thou hast promised, that thou wilt not leave them comfortless; but will come to them and dwell in them, and be their God, and make them thy people. Thus thou dost manifest thyself to them, as thou dost not unto the world. Yes, Lord, our sins do make a wall of separation between thee and us; and for them thou mightst justly forsake us, and cast us off in displeasure. How justly mightst thou hide thy face from me especially, and abandon me to my wretched self!

But though my ill desert may well provoke such indignation against me, yet let my wretchedness move thy compassion towards me; and where thou canst not take pleasure in me, yet, Father of mercies, have pity on me; and cast me not away from thy presence, neither abhor me, for thy name's sake; but for the sake of that mercy which has moved thee to do so much for me already, O come to me, and make thine abode with me, and rejoice over me, to do me good. My soul is as a desolate wilderness, yea, even the very image of hell, without thee, my God; but, O Emmanuel, God with us, for thy mercy's sake, for thy promise sake, see me lying afar off; and bring me nigh through the blood of thy cross. O bring me out of my present state of alienation from thee; and make me safe under the shadow of thy wings, and happy in the comforts of thy love.

If thou reject me, O my God! what in the world can then avail, or make any recompence for the loss of thy favour? in thy favour is life; without it, I am dead while I live, and shall be for ever accursed when I die: but if thou be with me, and lift up the light of thy countenance upon me, I shall overflow with joy unspeakable. Even in the absence of all other friends and comforts, I shall not need, I shall not desire them: if only I can go to God, my exceeding joy, and be taken up with my blessed Lord, I *shall* want nothing, I *can* want nothing; for in thy presence is fulness of joy for evermore. O blessed are they whom thou choosest, and causest to approach so nigh unto thee, and who are so highly favoured by thee: for thy presence can make the poorest cottage better than the stateliest palace; and fill the hearts of thy servants with divine delights, to which the greatest men of the world are strangers. O what manner of love is this, that the great God of heaven should vouchsafe to visit and reside with poor mortals on earth! But, Lord, how unworthy am I, that thou shouldst come under my roof! O blessed Jesus! be thou pleased to regard my undone state without thee, and my restless longings after thee, and be pleased to come unto me, dear Lord, not because I deserve, but because I need thee; not for my merits, but for thine own. My Lord and my God! whom have I in heaven but thee? and there is none upon earth that I desire besides thee. O be not as a stranger to the soul in which thou hast planted an inclination to serve thee: but bless and honour me with that divine fellowship of which thou hast made me capable, and which my soul panteth after. O give me the satisfaction to find that thou hast given me a heart to seek. Yea, give me grace, O my Lord, to go on seeking, till I find thee, whom my soul desires above all to love. Let me endure any thing rather than thine absence and displeasure; and desire nothing so much as thy presence and favour.

And be not thou far from me, O my God; but let me experience thy gracious presence with me and behold thy goodness passing before me. Lord Jesus, thou hast promised to be with thy people even to the end of the world: O come, be with my spirit, and dwell in my heart by faith. Be with me, O my Saviour, everywhere, and at all times, in health and in sickness, in prosperity and trouble, in all estates, and in all events and circumstances of my life; let thy presence sanctify and sweeten to me whatever befalls me. Never leave nor forsake me in my present pilgrimage, but abide with me till thou hast brought me safe, through all trials and dangers, to thy heavenly kingdom; that I may there dwell in thy sight, and enjoy thy love, and inherit thy glory for evermore. *Amen.*

A PRAYER FOR HEAVENLY COMFORTS.

O MOST blessed Lord, the God all consolation, who comfortest those that are cast down, and givest such peace and joy as the world can neither give nor take away! I confess myself unworthy of one gracious look from thee, or of one glimpse of the light of thy countenance to be lifted up upon my soul. I deserve to be in heaviness for my sins; to groan under the oppressive burden all my days; and at last to go down in sorrow to my grave. But because thou knowest Lord, that our spirits fail when we are under the hidings of thy face; and that we cannot hope to go on with fidelity and alacrity in thy way, unless we possess that joy in the Lord which is our strength; I beseech thee, O Lord of love, to speak peace to my conscience, and to say to my soul, that thou art my salvation. Let thy heavenly consolations fortify me against the desire of all sinful pleasures, and engage my heart to faithfulness in the covenant of my God. O give me some tokens of thy love, some discoveries of the light of thy countenance, some experience of that joy with which the stranger intermeddleth not. My soul thirsteth for thee my God, to see thy power, and thy glory, so as I have seen thee in the sanctuary. How long wilt thou forget me, O Lord? for ever? how long wilt thou hide thy face from me? how long shall I take counsel in my soul, having sorrow in my heart daily? O cause thy face to shine upon me: and let my heart rejoice in thee, because I have trusted in thy holy name. Let my mouth be filled with thy praise, and with thine honour, all the day long. And let my soul be satisfied, as with marrow and fatness, when I praise thee with joyful lips.

Whatever be my lot as to those common favours, which thou distributest indifferently amongst all sorts of men, O remember me, Lord, with the favour which thou bearest to thy people, and visit me with thy salvation: let me see the good of thy chosen, and rejoice in the gladness of thy nation, and glory with thine inheritance. O that, renouncing all confidence in the flesh, I may rejoice in Christ Jesus, and count thy love better than wine, and prefer it above my chief joy. And since the work of righteousness is peace, and the effect of it is quietness and assurance for ever, O make me a true and faithful subject of that spiritual kingdom, wherein dwell righteousness, and peace, and joy in the Holy Ghost. Let me taste and see that thou art gracious: and let me have such manifest tokens of a divine influence upon my soul, and such an evident witness of thy Spirit within me, as shall assure my heart of thy love and favour to me in Christ Jesus; that my soul may bless thee, O Lord, and all that is within me may praise thy holy name. And let the comfort, wherewith thou comfortest me, be the means of comforting others, and of encouraging them to devote themselves to thy service: that so thou, the blessed giver of all joy and comfort, mayst in all things be glorified, through Jesus Christ. *Amen.*

A PRAYER AGAINST WORLDLINESS, AND FOR A HEAVENLY MIND.

THOU, O blessed God, art the only satisfying portion and happiness of our souls; in whom alone the desires of our hearts may find that rest and repose, which all the world besides can never give. But, alas, this world, and the things of it, have had too much of my thoughts, and too much of my heart; so that I have grown remiss in my affections, and cold in my regards to thee, my God, and to those things which are most worthy of my love. I have been eager in the pursuit of vanities, and of the trifling concerns of this present time; but O how slack and listless in that which does most nearly and eternally concern me! I have been intent upon this world, as if it would never end; and forgetful of the next, as if it should never begin! I have forsaken the fountain of living waters to hew out to myself broken cisterns that can hold no water: I have disquieted myself in vain, seeking rest, and finding none: because I have sought it where the precious treasure was not to be found. How justly mightst thou, O Lord, leave me to inherit my own wretched choice, to eat of the fruit of my own way, and to be filled with my own devices; how justly mightst thou give me all my portion in this life, which I have so foolishly preferred, and shut me out of that heavenly kingdom, which I have so madly despised.

But, O thou Father of mercies! forgive me all the defects of my love to thee, and all the excesses of my love to earthly things: and so moderate my desires after these inferior goods, that, instead of doting upon the world, I may covet earnestly the best gifts; and seek first thy kingdom, and its righteousness; esteeming godliness the greatest gain, and all else but as loss and dung, for the love of Christ and the glories of heaven. O show me so much of those great and glorious things of the world to come, as may deaden my affections to the things of this present world: crucify the world to me, and me unto the world; that being more disengaged and loosened from it, I may be more enamoured with, and intent upon, the things above, where Christ sitteth at the right hand of God. O let me not debase my heavenly soul, by grovelling in the earth, as if I had nothing to do but to serve this vile body. Enable me to despise the most tempting enjoyments of this world, and to find my happiness in the service of my Lord, and in the prospect of his glory. May my heart be with my treasure in the heavens: and let me be ever looking for that blessed hope, and the glorious appearance of the great God, and our Saviour Jesus Christ: not coveting great things in the world, nor desiring to continue long in it; but rather seeking to get safe out of it, and desirous to be dissolved, and to be ever with the Lord. Even so, come Lord Jesus. *Amen,* and *Amen.*

A PRAYER FOR GREATER CONCERNMENT FOR THE SOUL,

AND THE THINGS OF ANOTHER WORLD.

O LORD God, to whom I am indebted for all that I am, or have! thou hast given me my being, together with many opportunities and advantages for working out my salvation. And O, what have I to do upon earth, but to prepare myself for heaven? when I am placed here between an eternity of happiness and of misery; in a capacity for the one, and in danger of the other. O what should be my care and constant endeavour, but to flee from the wrath to come, and to lay hold on eternal life! to provide well for my everlasting condition, and to make sure work for my immortal soul, in this only time of preparation! But O how negligent and careless have I been in that which most of all concerns me: doing everything rather than the great work which thou didst send me into the world to do; so that thou mightst justly come upon me, Lord, to call me to my last account in a day unlooked for, and at an hour that I should not be aware of. But for the sake of that mercy of thine in Christ Jesus, which has prevailed with thee to spare me so long, go on, I beseech thee, O my God, to be merciful to me, in forgiving me all my past sloth and negligence, and in quickening me to a greater concernment and assiduity: that I may redeem the time that I have lost, and improve every present enjoyment to my soul's eternal advantage. O preserve me from all the distracting cares, and the sinful pleasures of this life. And let me look less upon the temporal things that are seen; and turn my eyes more towards the invisible and eternal things that are before me. O make me more concerned for my everlasting state, and more careful to do that work, which, above all things in the world, is most needful to be done. O let me dread the doom of the slothful servant; and not be listless in the business that is of greatest importance. Lord, show me the truth and reality of things to come: and give me such a view and apprehension of my supreme good, as may raise my desires after it, in proportion to its worth and excellency; and make me so dissatisfied without it, that I may count nothing too much to do, nothing too hard to endure, so that I may at last attain the blessed enjoyment of it.

O let the meditation of hell be a preservative to deter me from all the ways leading to that dreadful end: and may I so look to the joy set before me, that with all vigour and alacrity, I may exert myself to attain the possession of it. O my God, give me the spirit of wisdom from above, to discern the vast disproportion between the short moment of this present time, and the infinite duration of immortality; and between the pleasures of sin that are but for a season, and those heavenly pleasures that are at thy right hand for evermore. Seeing that all these things must be dissolved, O make me such a manner of person as I ought to be in all holy conversation and godliness, looking for and hasting to the coming of the day of God. Quicken me, O Lord, in my dulness, and hasten me out of my delays; that I may not prolong the time of doing what I am convinced is necessary to be done, to save me from the second death, and to bring me to eternal life. O to what purpose am I troubled and careful about many things, when I neglect the one thing needful! help me, my God, to use the reason and understanding which thou hast given me, and dispassionately to consider what will promote my true happiness; give me also resolution and faithfulness to choose and follow it, whatever difficulties at present may obstruct my way. Help me, O Lord, to remember and consider all the powerful inducements which may quicken me into a greater care for my eternal state: that my being may not last longer than the good of my being; but that it may go well with me elsewhere for ever, when all that is here shall fail me. O that I may now give diligence to make my calling and election sure; and strive to enter in at the strait gate; and labour for that meat which endures to everlasting life. Teach me, O my God, by patient continuance in well-doing, to seek for glory, honour, and immortality: that I may not fall short of that rest which remains for the people of God; but so labour here in thy work, that hereafter I may rest from my labours in thy kingdom; not for the merit of my works, but for thy mercy's sake in Christ Jesus. *Amen.*

A PRAYER FOR FAITHFULNESS

AND CONSTANCY IN THE PROFESSION OF OUR RELIGION.

O MY Lord and my God, who hast called me to the knowledge of thine eternal truth, and by the light of the gospel shining upon me hast made the way of life and salvation plain before

A PRAYER FOR FAITHFULNESS.

me! be thou pleased to give me courage still to confess thee before men; and to own thy holy religion, even in the face of an evil and adulterous generation. O let me not be tossed to and fro, and carried away with every wind of doctrine, by the sleight of men, and cunning craftiness, whereby they lie in wait to deceive. My God and guide! suffer me not to be led away with the error of the wicked, and to fall from my own steadfastness: but may I ever hold fast the profession of my faith without wavering, and hold the beginning of my confidence steadfast to the end. O give me such an experimental knowledge and love of thy holy truth, as may make me ever faithful in the profession of it: that my mind may not be corrupted from the simplicity that is in Christ; and that I may never be turned away from that religion, in which I have found so much comfort and advantage. And grant me, good Lord, to feel still more and more the powerful efficacy of it upon my heart: that I may be rooted and grounded in the faith; and take so much pleasure in the way into which thy grace has brought me, that I may never turn from it, nor prove false to it: but, notwithstanding all temptations to seduce or affright me from it, may openly declare for it, and faithfully persist in it till my life's end. *Amen.*

A PRAYER FOR ZEAL AND ACTIVITY IN THE PRACTICE OF OUR RELIGION.

O LORD, the holy jealous God! thou hast declared how loathsome to thee are the lukewarm; and hast pronounced him cursed that doeth the work of the Lord deceitfully; and hast told us the dreadful doom of the slothful servant, who was condemned, not for committing gross evils, but for neglecting to improve his talents; thou didst send us into this world, to provide for the next: and we are a people devoted to the Lord; having vowed and promised to serve our God with all the powers and faculties we possess. This is the one thing needful, that we were made for, and that we are all most strictly bound to, and must follow with our whole hearts, if ever we would escape the damnation of hell, and enter into the joy of our Lord. But I am ashamed, O my God, that I have loitered so long in thy vineyard, and trifled so much in thy work; that I have occupied myself about vanities, and slighted my greatest business. And well may I now tremble for fear of thy judgments, when I have so little approved myself, as one of thy redeemed, zealous of good works.

O merciful Lord! forgive me all my sinful omissions, and all my careless performances of the duties of thy service. And quicken me into a greater zeal and diligence to promote thy glory and to work out my salvation. And let me not contend merely for the *faith* and doctrine of the gospel, but be zealous for the *practice* of all its duties: that by my good conversation I may win others, and by the light which I cause to shine before them, may constrain them to glorify my heavenly Father.

To glorify thy name, and save our souls, is the greatest of all our concerns in the world: nothing can deserve so much of our care, and zeal, and diligence, as to obtain deliverance from thy wrath, and to secure the possession of thy heavenly kingdom. O how much are we concerned to be active in this work, and to give ourselves wholly to it, when upon this moment depends an eternity to come; and all that concerns us for ever, hangs upon this short life, that is so quickly gone, and will never return! O my God! imprint these considerations so deep upon my heart, that I may no more trifle with the weighty things of eternity, nor show a cold indifference about that which is of such absolute necessity. Make me to act as one that must be a blessed or a damned creature for ever: make me as zealous for my God, as ever I have been eager for the world; and as active in the pursuit of things eternal, as ever I have been in those which relate to this present world. Let me give up myself wholly unto thee; and show the sincerity of my professions by that zeal and fervency which are the very life and soul of Christianity. O thou great rewarder of them that

A PRAYER FOR ZEAL.

diligently seek thee! help me seriously to engage in thy service, and unweariedly to go through with it; not slothful in business, but fervent in spirit, serving the Lord; exercising myself unto godliness; continuing watchful in prayer; keeping my heart with all diligence; ordering my conversation with all usefulness: and running the race set before me with all cheerfulness. O let me be full of life and spirit in thy work, and full of good deeds and fruits to thine honour; ever labouring to be accepted here to thy favour, and hereafter to thy glory.

Yea, make me more zealous for thine honour, O Lord, than for my own. And whatever is injurious and reproachful to thee, O let me hate it perfectly, and oppose it strenuously: and yet with such prudence, and kindness towards men, that I may not betray my own shame, in defending thy glory; nor let my zeal consume, but inflame my charity, and put me upon doing all the good that ever I am able in my generation; that I may serve the interests of my Lord, and help forward the salvation of souls. O make me valiant for thy truth, and discreet in my conduct: that I may neither betray thy holy cause by my fear, nor become a reproach to it by my folly. O let me spend my zeal and spirits not for earthly, but for heavenly things; not for my own desires and honour, but for thy blessed will and pleasure; not in frivolous contentions about the little appendages and circumstantials of religion, but in pressing after the vital and substantial part, and in a concernment about the great unquestionable duties that are necessary to the saving of the soul. And grant me thy grace, O Lord, to live now so zealously to the glory of thy name, that I may come to live blessedly for ever in the glories of thy kingdom, not for the sake of my services, but of thy mercies, whose gift is eternal life through Jesus Christ our Lord. *Amen.*

A PRAYER FOR GRACE TO SERVE THE LORD WITH GLADNESS.

O MY God! thou art a Lord that hast pleasure in the prosperity of thy servants; and thy servants have the greatest reason to be pleased in the performance of thy commands. It is good for me to draw nigh to God, in whose presence is fulness of joy. Well may the hearts of them rejoice that seek the Lord! For thou dost not employ us, but to oblige us: not for any advantage to thyself, but only for our greatest good, that it may go well with us, both here and for ever. O my Lord, I am full of trouble and confusion that ever I should be so backward as I have been to thy blessed work; so lifeless in it, and so soon weary of it; to the dishonour of thy name, and the reproach of thy service; as if I had a hard master, and a hateful work. O that I should bear as a burden that which should be the solace of my life, and the rejoicing of my heart! Forgive me, I beseech thee, good Lord, all this which I bewail before thee; and heal that indisposition of mind which makes thy service a weariness unto me. And so renew my spirit, and draw my heart to thy blessed self, that I may not serve thee as from necessity, but inclination; not as forcing myself, but as delighting in thy work. O rid my mind of that tormenting dread which makes me uneasy in the service of my Lord. And give me a heavenly heart, and such a love to thy law as may sweeten all my obedience; that I may not account it grievous or tedious, but my soul's satisfaction and exceeding joy. O let me not serve thee, my God, with the spirit of bondage, as a slave; but with the cheerfulness and gladness of an ingenuous child: sitting down with delight under thy shadow, and so pleased with thy work, that my services may also be pleasing in thy sight, through Jesus Christ. *Amen.*

A PRAYER FOR ABILITY
TO ACQUIT OURSELVES AS WE OUGHT
IN OUR SEVERAL PLACES.

O LORD our Lord! thy word enjoins us, whereinsoever we are called, therein to abide with God. Thou hast commanded us not only to study quietness in that station, and to do our own

FOR ABILITY FOR OUR PLACES. 227

business, but to provide for ourselves and for our dependents, and to render unto all their due; and not to be burthensome to any, but rather to be helpful to those around us. O thou that givest skill and ability for the performance of those offices to which thou callest us, teach and enable me (I beseech thee) for the work of my place, and for all the duties of my calling. Good Lord! pardon all my past unfaithfulness and negligence therein: and direct and assist me in discharging it for the time to come. O make me so contented with what I get by honest means, that I may never offer to go beyond or defraud my neighbours in any matter; but be punctually just in all my dealings, and may conscientiously perform my duty in all my relations; carrying myself as I ought towards every one with whom I am in any way concerned in the world, whether superior, equal, or inferior; being offensive to none, but (as I have power and opportunity for it) kind and useful unto all. O let me not walk disorderly, neglecting my own proper calling, and busying myself in other men's matters; but may I keep in my own station, and with quietness work and eat my own bread, and provide things honest in the sight of all men: following after that which is lovely and of good report, and exercising myself to have always a conscience void of offence towards God and man. Yea, whatever any may justly expect from me, help me, O my God, to discharge it faithfully and acceptably. And command a blessing, Lord, upon all my honest labours and endeavours, and make them successful to promote my own and others' real and eternal good, and to glorify thy blessed name, through Jesus Christ. *Amen.*

A PRAYER

FOR SKILL TO BEHAVE OURSELVES ARIGHT

TO ALL WITH WHOM WE ARE CONCERNED IN THE WORLD.

O LORD my God! I desire to humble myself in thy sight for all the folly and disorder of my conduct: that I have so frequently failed in it, and so shamefully miscarried in my intercourse with my neighbours: that my example has too often tended more to the hardening than to the converting of sinners; and that I have lain as a stumbling-block and rock of offence in the way of my brethren: not only prone to be tempted with evil and to be overcome myself, but also becoming a temptation and a snare to others, so as to draw them into sin, or to embolden them in it. Though thou hast showed me what is good, and made me to know better things, and laid the greatest engagement upon me to be faithful in thy covenant, yet O how apt have I been to lose my relish of the things of God! how apt to be carried into folly with the stream of evil company, to fall into base compliance, and to consent with sinners and follow a multitude to do evil!

O my God! give me repentance and pardon for all my own sins, and for all the guilt which I have contracted in being accessory to the sins of others. And so fortify me with thy grace that I may not be awed or seduced from the path of duty; that I may never be ashamed of Christ before men, but boldly appear for thy truth, even in the face of an evil and faithless generation. O teach me to walk in wisdom towards them that are without, and in all kindness towards them that are within, and without offence (in prudence and usefulness) to all. Make me wise in the choice and in the enjoyment of my company; that they may not be to me, nor I to them, an occasion of falling; but that we may be mutual helps to each other, and examples of all that is good, and imitable, and praise-worthy. O gracious Lord! make me so faithful to thee and to my own conscience, that my conversation with the world may never discompose the religious frame of my soul. Let me not be startled at any bold censure of thy ways; nor ever be turned aside from thee through the contradiction of sinners. Make me to cease from man, whose breath is in his nostrils: (for wherein is he to be accounted of?) O turn my fear of men's faces into love for their souls! let me esteem them as my fellow-servants in thy work, and fellow-travellers to our long home: and, where I cannot promote their duty and felicity, grant, O Lord, that they may not hinder mine: and that when I am not edified, I may not be corrupted by them.

O my God, may thy presence ever sway me more than the presence of men; let me count it a small thing to be judged of them; and instead of being determined by their way or humour, let me regard my own conscience more than their opinion; and do all in the sight of God, heartily as unto the Lord. Let it not be my aim to ingratiate myself with men, but to please the great Judge of all. Yet keep thy servant, O Lord, from giving scandal and offence to any; that I may not, by pride and passion, by vanity and indiscretion, or by moroseness and uncharitableness, dishonour my profession, or make the way of truth to be evil spoken of. But help me, O my God and guide, to walk circumspectly, and to speak and act with due consideration of all times and places, persons and circumstances: enable me to behave myself wisely, and guide my affairs with discretion; and so to go in and out among my fellow-creatures upon earth as to preserve my integrity in thy sight, and have my conversation in heaven, and still enjoy friendship with thee and with thy dear Son, my only Lord and Saviour. *Amen.*

A PRAYER FOR GRACE TO USE OUR SPEECH ARIGHT.

O LORD our gracious God! who hast given us reason and speech to express our minds to one another, and to converse comfortably together, what great cause have we to praise thee that we are so fearfully and wonderfully made! and our tongues, that are our glory, are most of all so when with them we set forth thy glory. But alas! that I have so much cause to humble myself for all the abuses of my tongue; and that I have so many ways perverted the happy privilege of speaking: either holding my peace where I should have spoken to thine honour and the good of my neighbour; or else pouring out words to dishonour thy name, to wrong my own soul, and to offend and injure others! Forgive me, O merciful God, I beseech thee, all my sinful silence, my vain and idle words, and my evil, corrupt communications. And help me so to speak as to manifest thy grace in my heart, and to minister the same to my hearers. Set a watch, O Lord, before my mouth, and keep the door of my lips, that nothing may proceed thence, but what shall be in some way or other good for the use of edifying. Help me to keep my mouth as with a bridle, when I am provoked to speak unadvisedly with my lips. And let no profane or filthy speeches proceed out of my mouth; nor any thing be said by me that ought not to be named among Christians.

O Lord, open thou my lips, that my mouth may show forth thy praise. Make me forward to speak for thee, and for the service of thy truth, and the glory of thy name; but slow to speak any evil whereby I may defile myself, or hurt my neighbour. Give me, Lord, a considerate mind, to weigh what is fit to be said: and make me wise and serious, sober and modest, pious and charitable in what I speak: that it may be without offence, but not without profit to those who hear it. O fill my heart with such grace that, out of the good treasure, I may be ever producing somewhat to benefit the company and to advance thy glory. And put such thoughts into my mind, and such words into my mouth, that my tongue may be as the pen of a ready writer to utter things seasonable and acceptable for the good of my associates. Let me never turn my liberty of speaking into the licentiousness of vain or evil speaking; but employ it to the wise and noble ends for which it was given: speaking of and for thy testimonies, even before the greatest, without being ashamed.

O Lord, restrain the blasphemous and brutish generation that set their mouths against heaven, and (out of those open sepulchres) send forth impieties and impurities to dishonour him that made them, to grieve the souls of thy servants, and to spread the contagion of their ungodliness.

O fill their face with shame for what they have done, and their hearts with dread, to stop them from proceeding any farther. Confound the generation of vipers, that hiss and spit their venom against thy holy ways; and give them other tongues, that they may use thy gifts to better purpose. O let the lying lips be put to silence, that speak grievous things proudly and contemptuously against the righteous. And let such as fear thee and think upon thy name speak often to one another, so as to promote their common edification and the eternal salvation of their souls, through thy gracious goodness to them in Jesus Christ. *Amen.*

A PRAYER FOR PERSEVERANCE AND GRACE
TO ENDURE TO THE END.

ETERNAL God, with whom is everlasting strength! thou art able to keep us from falling, and to perform the good work begun in us till the day of Jesus Christ. But, Lord, thou knowest how weak and frail I am; how wavering and bent to backsliding; how apt to decline and fall, after all the great things which thou hast done for my soul. O Lord of love, have pity on my infirmities, and strengthen me in my weakness. Preserve me, thou blessed guardian of thy people, who keepest the feet of thy saints. O preserve me from the danger of apostacy, and

FOR PERSEVERANCE.

keep me that I fall not away from any good beginnings to which thy grace has ever brought me. And put thy fear in my heart, that I may not depart from thee. Make me so firmly thine, that nothing which befalls me in the world may ever separate betwixt thee and my soul, or turn me from that way of life which is above to the wise to depart from hell beneath. O let me not be of the number of those that draw back unto perdition, but of those who believe to the saving of the soul.

O Lord God, thou hast begun to show thy servant thy greatness, and thy mighty hand; go on, I pray thee, to work for the glory of thy name, and perfect that which concerns me. Thou hast been my help; leave me not nor forsake me, O God of my salvation: but hold thou me up, and I shall be safe, and shall have respect to thy statutes continually. Help me, O my God; yea, stablish, strengthen, settle me: and leave me neither will nor power to resist the gracious designs of thy love and mercy for the saving of my soul. And as (by my frailty) I still too often renew my sins, gracious Lord, (through thy mercy) renew me to repentance: and though I fall, let me not be utterly cast down; but uphold me with thine almighty hand, and keep me by thy power through faith unto salvation. O make me faithful until death, that thou mayst give to me the crown of life: make me so to endure unto the end that I may be saved, and receive the glorious consummation of all my hopes, even that blessed end of my faith, the eternal salvation of my soul. *Amen, Amen.*

A PRAYER FOR PREPARATION AND READINESS TO DIE.

LORD, what is our life but a vapour, that appears for a little time, and then vanisheth away! Even at the longest, how short! and at the strongest, how frail! and when we think ourselves most secure, yet we know not what a day may bring forth, nor how soon thou mayst come to call us to our last account. Quickly shall we be as water spilt on the ground, that cannot be gathered up again; quickly snatched away from hence, and our place here shall know us no more for ever. Our days, one after another, are spent apace : and we know not how near to us is our last day, when our bodies shall be laid in the grave, and our souls be called to appear at the tribunal of God, to receive their eternal doom. Yet how have I lived in this world, as if I should never leave it; how unmindful of my latter end! how improvident of my time! how careless of my soul! how negligent in my preparation for my everlasting condition! so that thou mayst justly bring my last hour as a snare upon me, to surprise me in my sins, and to cut me off in my iniquities. But, O Father of mercies, remember not my sins against me; but remember thy own tender mercies and thy lovingkindnesses, which have been ever of old. O remember how short my time is; and spare me, that I may recover my strength before I go hence and be no more seen. Make me so wise as to consider my latter end: and teach me so to number my days that I may apply my heart to true wisdom. Lord, what have I to do in this world, but to make ready for the world to come! O that I may be mindful of it, and be careful to finish my work before I finish my course!

In the days of my health and prosperity, O that I may remember and provide for the time of trouble, and sickness, and death, when the world's enjoyments will shrink away from me, and prove utterly unable to support and comfort me. Let me never allow myself in any course of living wherein I would be loath or afraid to die. But let me see my corruptions mortified and subdued, that they may never rise up in judgment against me. Enable me so to die unto sin daily that I may not die for sin eternally. Instruct me, good Lord, and assist me in my preparation for a dying hour: that I may not then be fearfully surprised; but may meet it with comfort and composure. Quicken me to a serious concern about that great work; and help me to perform it acceptably and with good success. O that I may be fitted for heaven ere I leave this earth, and may have peace with God through Jesus Christ, before I depart hence into that state in which I must abide for ever! O my Lord, make me so ready to meet thee at thy coming, that thine appearance may be the matter of my hopes, and desires, and joyful expectations: that I may look and long for that blessed time when thou wilt put an everlasting period to all my troubles and temptations, and exchange my present state of infirmity and sin for a state of endless happiness and glory. O thou who art my life and my strength, help me so to live as, at the hour of death, I shall wish I had lived; and so to make ready for death all my days that, at my last day, I may have nothing to do but to die, and cheerfully to resign my spirit into thy gracious hands. O my Father, hear and answer my humble petitions; and let me find a merciful admission to thy favour and thy kingdom, for the sake of my only Saviour Jesus Christ. *Amen.*

THE AUTHOR'S PRAYER FOR HIMSELF
AS A MINISTER.

O BLESSED Jesus, my Lord and my God, what high honour hast thou done me in calling me to the office which thou wast pleased to take upon thyself! who camest not to be ministered unto, but to minister, and to preach the gospel of the kingdom, and teach the way of salvation. All glory be to thee, who hast been pleased to dignify me with so high an office. But as thou thyself (the head of the corner) art to some a stone of stumbling, and a rock of offence; so thy messengers are to some indeed a savour of life unto life, but to others a savour of death unto death. And if thy wise and holy servant asked, Who is sufficient for these things? well may I (a weak and sinful creature) tremble, lest those amongst whom I minister should perish through my insufficiency or neglect, and their blood be required at my hands: yea, well may I fear lest when I have shown others the way to heaven, I myself should be shut out. But, O Lord, my life, my strength, and my Redeemer, thou hast appointed me to this station: to thee, therefore, do I look to qualify me for it. O thou that ordainest strength out of the mouths of babes and sucklings, magnify thy power in my weakness, that I may do all things as I ought, through Christ strengthening me. O let me learn from thee what I shall teach concerning thee. Open my understanding, O Lord, that I may understand the scriptures; and enable me rightly to divide the word of truth, and (by sound doctrine) both to exhort and convince the gainsayers. O put such thoughts into my mind, and such words into my mouth, that out of the abundance of my heart my mouth may speak, to the glory of thy name, and to the edification of those that hear me. O make me wise to win souls; and watchful over them, as one that must give an account of them not entangling myself with the affairs of this life, but waiting on my ministry; taking heed to myself and to my doctrine, studying to show myself approved unto God, and thoroughly furnished to every good work. Give me skill and conduct prudently to steer my course through all difficulties in my way, and give me patience and courage to withstand all assaults and opposition which I may have to encounter. O my Lord! be with me, and guide and help me, and strengthen and succour me, now and always, in the great work lying upon me. Open to me a door of utterance, that I may speak thy word as I ought to speak: and make me faithful, and diligent, and successful in my sacred calling; doing thy work as a workman that needs not to be ashamed; not preaching myself, but Christ Jesus the Lord; nor seeking the praise of men, but the honour of my God. Yea, make me an example of all the holy duties which I inculcate on others; that I may not lay upon them burthens which I refuse to bear myself; but may go before them in the ways which they are to follow; holding forth the word of life in my conversation, as well as in my doctrine. Let me shine with a convincing light before them, and never lay a stumbling-block in their way. Let me never make the heart of the righteous sad, nor strengthen the hands of the wicked, nor give just offence to any; but let me approve myself, as far as I am able, useful and beneficial unto all; keeping under my body, and bringing it into subjection: lest by any means, when I have preached to others, I myself should be a cast-away.

And, O thou that givest the increase, command a blessing (I pray thee) upon all my studies and endeavours; that I may not spend my strength for nought, nor labour in vain; but may make full proof of my ministry, and be instrumental (through thy grace) to convert sinners from the error of their ways. Teach me also to build up them that are in any measure sanctified; that so I may both save myself and them that hear me, and when I have finished my course, may give an account of my stewardship with joy, and not with grief; and receive a crown of righteousness at thy hands, not for my merits, but for thy mercies' sake. *Amen, Amen.*

THE MAGISTRATE'S PRAYER.

O THOU great and supreme Ruler of all the world, by whom all the governors on earth are set up to restrain the unruly and to favour thy people! though thou needst not the services of men or angels to assist thee, but canst immediately (by thyself) do whatever thou pleasest in heaven and in earth, with the least word of thy mouth, or motion of thy will! yet thou art pleased to honour some of thy creatures as thy vicegerents, and to order and govern the sons of men by

THE MAGISTRATE'S PRAYER. 241

the instrumentality of their fellow-worms, exalting some chosen out of the people to preside and rule over the rest. Me hast thou called, Lord, to this honour, and hast been pleased to set me above the common lot of men as one of the little representatives of thy blessed self. O King of glory! I will exalt thee, who hast vouchsafed to raise me to this dignity. And as thou hast made to differ from others in this, so make me to excel others in every thing that is excellent and praise-worthy. O that I may represent not only thy power and majesty, but thy wisdom and holiness, thy truth and goodness, thy justice and mercy! O that I may retain a lowly mind in my high station; and not forget or lift up myself, nor insult over my poor inferiors; but like the great God, who despises not any, may I condescend to men of low estate, and without respect of persons judge according to every man's work: yea, may I delight to succour the injured and oppressed; to deliver the needy when he cries, the poor also, and him that hath no helper.

O! may I rather fear my responsibility than be proud of my office; and, in the fear of the Lord, let me ever be careful to execute that which is righteous in thy sight. Let me have grace to discharge my trust with all faithfulness, as one that must be judged myself, and find the same measure which I mete to others. And, seeing that the eyes of all are upon me, and that my place exposes me more to common notice, and my example has a greater influence than that of private men, O make me, Lord, the more vigilant in the inspection of myself, and more careful in ordering my conversation aright: that I may not embolden others to commit such wickedness as I ought to punish, nor lead the people into the sin and ruin which I should help to save them from; nor be a scandal and grief of heart to the holy followers of Jesus, whom I am set up to patronise and comfort. But let my conversation be such as shall put to confusion the dissolute and abandoned, while my justice strikes terror into them. O make me a hearty lover of all good men, and let me honour them who fear the Lord. Make me ever ready and forward to defend and countenance and encourage the generation of thy children, who live godly in Christ Jesus. And let me with courage exert my authority in a zealous vindication of thine honour; and in asserting thy rights, and promoting the growth and advancement of thy true and holy religion. O that the glory of thy name, and the interests of thy kingdom, and the welfare of thy church, may be ever near my heart; that above all things I may seek the things of Jesus Christ, and truly and indifferently minister justice to the punishment of wickedness and vice, and to the maintenance of true religion and virtue. And whatever power and interest I have in the world, O may I so lay it out for the service of thy holy truth, and the enlargement of the kingdom of thy dear Son, that, after my advancement here, I may not be thrown down hereafter, nor receive the doom of an unfaithful servant for betraying my trust and abusing my authority. But let me appear with comfort and joy before my Judge in that great and solemn day, having a testimony from him that I did not hide my talent in a napkin, but improved it to his glory. And may I now be so jealous for thy cause, so careful of thine interests, and so studious of the welfare of thy people, that, at the last, I may be raised up with them to that highest of all bliss and glory which shall endure for evermore. *Amen.*

THE HUSBAND'S PRAYER.

ACCEPT my humble thanks, O Lord my God, who hast provided a help-meet for me, to be my partner in the nearest of all relations. O teach and enable me in all things to demean myself towards her as it becomes me in this station. May I be enabled to cherish her as my own flesh. Let me never on any account despise her, or be bitter against her; but may I bear with her infirmities, and forbear her in love and all gentleness. Nor let me insult over her as an inferior, but mildly use my authority in treating her as my dear yoke-fellow and companion. Let me not be rigid in opposing her, but ready to comply with her in all her reasonable desires and expectations. O make me meek and patient, faithful and kind, respectful and tender in all my conduct towards her: and may I show myself on all occasions well-pleased and satisfied with her, that she may find comfort in fellowship with me, and never have reason to regret that she has forsaken all others for my sake. O blessed Lord, espouse my dear friend to thyself in loving-kindness, and faithfulness, and tender mercies. Bless her and love her, and make her lovely in thy sight and in the eyes of all. Especially make her like the king's daughter, all glorious within: that she may not only appear to advantage in this world, but be blessed for ever in the world to come. And grant, O Lord our God, that we may be lovers of one another's souls, and promoters of each other's salvation; so that after a short season of fellowship here, we may meet again with rejoicing there, where we shall never part, even in that fulness of joy which is in thy presence; where, though there be no marrying nor giving in marriage, yet is there greater festivity and gladness than in any day of espousals, and where those who are united together in thy fear and love shall be blessed together in everlasting fellowship with thee, and with thy dear Son Jesus Christ. *Amen.*

THE WIFE'S PRAYER.

O MY God, thou hast called me to this state of life; and it is the disposal of thy providence that I should be joined in wedlock with thy servant. I bless thee, Lord, that thou hast dealt well with me, and provided graciously for me. O continue thy goodness to me, in giving me knowledge and grace to demean myself aright in this relation; that I may honour and obey the Lord in reverencing and obeying my husband. Enable me to submit cheerfully to him in all things not forbidden by thee; and to speak of him, and to him, with such words as shall mark the high esteem and fervent love of my heart towards him. Enable me so to demean myself on all occasions, as to give him satisfaction; that so his love towards me may be confirmed, and our mutual happiness increased. If at any time occasions of offence arise, teach me with silence, or with soft obliging words, to quench the flames, and to keep the unity of the spirit in the bonds of peace. O give me that ornament of a meek and quiet spirit, which in thy sight is of great price. Make me humble and modest, discreet and considerate, careful and diligent, faithful and constant, mild and patient: remembering not only the duties and comforts, but also the temptations and crosses, of the married state; and taking the worse with the better, as a part of my portion; showing myself herein a follower of wise and godly matrons. Bless my dear partner, O Lord, with the best of thy blessings: and love him, and keep him in thy continual care, till thou bring him to thy heavenly kingdom. O bind us both in faithfulness unto thee, as well as to one another. And as we are one flesh, so make us of one heart, and of one soul; that nothing but death may ever make a separation between us. And let our union be cemented, not merely by the considerations of honour and interest, but chiefly by an ardent longing for each other's spiritual and eternal welfare: that so we may admire, and love, and serve thee together in this world, and glorify thee together in the world to come, through Jesus Christ our Lord. *Amen.*

THE WIDOW'S PRAYER.

O EVER-LIVING and all-disposing God! thou hast taken from me the friend of my bosom, that was even as my own soul; and by the *want*, hast now taught me the *worth*, of that blessing which I once enjoyed. I submit to thy righteous dispensations; and notwithstanding thy hand is heavy upon me, I confess that thou hast chastised me far less than my iniquities have deserved. I lament that I have provoked thee to anger: but, whatever has been the cause of thy judgments, deliver me from it, I most humbly beseech thee. Whereinsoever I have failed, either towards thee, or towards my dear partner, O forgive it for thy mercy's sake in Christ Jesus. I bless thee for having brought me into an union with him. He was thy gift; and it was thy goodness that I enjoyed, and thy help and comfort that I found, in him. And now thou canst supply to me, by thyself, what I received from thee by his hands. Thou art still the same fountain of goodness, whatever means of conveyance thou cuttest off from us. O pity me, Lord, under the breach which thou hast been pleased to make upon me; and support me in the dejection of my heart; and guide and comfort me in all the perplexity of my thoughts. Withdraw not thou thyself from me, O my God, now that trouble is upon me; but make use of this bitter dispensation as the means of bringing me nearer to thyself, and of raising this heart of mine from the present world, to that better place, where I hope my dear friend is now in thine immediate presence. And now that I am a widow indeed, and desolate, enable me to trust in thee, my God, and to continue in supplications and prayers night and day. O thou that hast a peculiar care, and tender regard for the widows, be pleased to espouse my cause, and direct my path, and show me what I have to do, and fit me for every duty now incumbent upon me. O let my Maker be my husband, to teach and help, to defend and comfort me, to deal graciously with me, and to be all in all to me. And bring me safe, O my God, through this vale of misery, to the blessed kingdom of thy glory; for the sake of thy beloved Son, my only Saviour Jesus Christ. *Amen.*

THE ORPHAN'S PRAYER.

O LORD my God! thou art he that took me out of my mother's womb: and art pleased to style thyself, in a peculiar manner, the father of the fatherless. Now that I am left unto thee, mine eyes are upon thee, O my father, and I desire to pour out my soul before thee, and to entreat thy gracious favour. Have compassion on me, and leave me not desolate. Expose me not helpless and unprotected to the wants and dangers of this wicked world: but now that my father and mother have forsaken me, O Lord, do thou take me up; and be a father (and the best of fathers) to me, and still a gracious provider for me. Guide me, O my heavenly Father, and direct my friends also, who are concerned in the disposing of me and my affairs. O be thou pleased to choose my inheritance for me; and order all that concerns me, for the promoting of thy glory, and the advancing of my present and everlasting happiness. Direct my designs, that they may be agreeable to thy blessed will; and bless and prosper my endeavours, that they may succeed according to my desire, and furnish me with continual occasions of praise and thanksgiving. My Lord, I commit myself to thee: O be thou my God and guide, even unto death. Be ever watchful over me for good, and preserve and keep me, and conduct and lead me, in all the variety of estates and affairs of this life, till thou hast brought me to inherit the blessed portion of thy children, in that most sweet and glorious life, which shall never fail. Grant this, O merciful Father, for thy dear Son's sake, my only Saviour, Jesus Christ. *Amen.*

THE AGED'S PRAYER.

O LORD of my life: thou art my God from the womb; my hope and trust from my youth. By thee I was brought into the world; and upon thee have I lived all my days. O with what patience and long-suffering hast thou endured me! and with what loving-kindness and tender mercies hast thou still prevented and followed me! how many have I seen snatched out of this life (as I fear) miserably unprovided for their death; whereas thou prolongest my days, and, together with more days, still addest new mercies to my life. O that the lengthening of my days may be a real benefit; and that, as my life is prolonged, so the whole work which God has given me to do, may be finished! may I redeem the time, and improve all the opportunities and means of grace which thou art pleased to put into my hands, for the everlasting advantage of my soul! And let my age be the good old age; and the remaining time of my sojourning here, be the best of all my time.

Though my sight is dim to the world, let my eyes be ever towards the Lord, and open to see the things belonging to my peace. Though my ears are dull of hearing, let my heart be attentive to thy calls, and let me hear thy voice, while it is called to-day. Though I cannot (as formerly) relish the pleasures of meat and drink, yet let me taste the goodness of the Lord, and savour the things of the Spirit of God, and hunger and thirst after righteousness, and long for those pleasures which are at thy right hand for evermore. And though my limbs are weak, and my strength will not serve me to travel abroad as I have done; yet make me strong in the Lord, to do thy work, and to walk in thy ways, and to perform my great journey homeward, to my house eternal in the heavens. And, seeing there is no man that liveth and shall not see death, and the longer I have escaped it, the nearer I am now to it, and shall one day certainly fall by it, and must every day reckon upon it, and know not but that my soul may this night be required of me, O let not my length of days tempt me to forget their end, or to put my last day far from me: but let me keep it ever in my prospect, as drawing nigh to me; that I may order all my concerns, not only like a stranger and sojourner, but as a dying man, who is ready to drop into the grave, and as waiting, watching, and preparing for the coming of his Lord. O that at thy coming, thou mayst find me so doing!

And, because I am old in sins, as well as in years; weighed down with iniquity, as well as with age; O my gracious Lord, give me that godly sorrow for my sins, which shall work repentance not to be repented of. Thou hast saved many old sinners; O God, be so merciful to me a sinner. Put all my sins to the account of thy dear Son: and wash me thoroughly from them in the fountain of his precious blood. Especially, O merciful Lord, acquit and discharge me from the sins that lie heaviest upon me, and that make the thoughts of death and judgment most painful to me. O give me, Lord, some token for good, that I may have an evidence of my having found mercy at thy hands, and that I may depart in peace, and finish my course with joy; and, in the end of my life, be numbered among the redeemed and blessed of the Lord, through the tender mercies of my God, and through the all-sufficient merits of my only Saviour Jesus Christ. *Amen.*

THE CHILD'S PRAYER.

O MY God and Father, who hast made me, have mercy upon me, and teach me to know thee: and incline my heart to love thee; and enable me in all my life to do thy will, as I ought to do. Thou hast formed me for thyself; and in the church I have been devoted, and offered up unto thee, as thy child. O thou adorable Saviour, who hast ordered children to be brought unto thee, and hast declared, that of such is the kingdom of heaven, give me thy grace, that I may understand and seek after God; yea, that I may seek thee early, and with my whole heart. Dispose me to remember thee, my Creator and Redeemer, in the days of my youth, and to take upon me *now* thy light and easy yoke; that thou mayst not be unmindful of me *in the time of age*, or leave me comfortless in my latter days. As I grow in years and stature, so help me, Lord, to grow in wisdom and grace, and in favour with God and men. O keep me from the evil of this world; and carry me safely through it to thy heavenly kingdom. Make me obedient to my parents and teachers; and lowly and respectful unto all. And bless to me all the means that are used for my instruction: teach me to profit by them, and to acquire such learning, as shall qualify me to discharge with advantage the duties of any station which I shall hereafter be called to fill. O my heavenly Father! take care of me, and provide for me; and so dispose of me in the world, that I may be useful in my generation, and a blessing to the place where thy providence shall fix my abode. Preserve me, O my Lord, from the infection of bad examples: let me never be led away and enticed to follow the despisers of thy laws; but make me a lover and follower of such as are truly good, and a pattern to others of all that is lovely and of good report. O God, thou knowest my foolishness, and seest how weak I am: O look not upon my follies, nor be extreme to mark what is done amiss; but have pity on my infirmities, and forgive my sins. Out of the mouths of babes and sucklings thou hast ordained strength: O magnify thy power in my weakness, and make me a profitable member of society, and an instrument to promote thy glory. Leave me not, O Lord, to myself, or to my own foolish counsels; but let me be taught of God how to behave myself, and what to do. And take thou the gracious charge and government of me; and keep my heart ever in thy fear and love; and direct all my ways to please thee, my God, through Jesus Christ. *Amen.*

A PRAYER TO BE USED BY THE RICH AND GREAT.

O LORD, the gracious giver of all our good things! thou hast opened thine hand to me in a bountiful manner, and given me all things plenteously to enjoy: thou hast made me to be full and to abound, whilst multitudes around me are poor and indigent. O that this plenty, which

I have for my body, may not prove a snare to my soul! Let me never trust in uncertain riches, nor rest in thy gifts, forgetful of the giver. Better were it that I had been altogether destitute of this world's good, than that I should make it my idol, or be satisfied with it as my only portion. It is indeed too often found, that the prosperity of fools destroys them. O merciful God, grant that this fatal consequence may not ever arise from the wealth bestowed on me! Let me never be suffered to abuse thy bounties, or to make them an occasion of sinning against thee. I am thy steward, O Lord; grant, I beseech thee, that I may be found faithful in what is committed to my trust: that I may honour thee with my substance, and improve my talents agreeably to thy mind and will. O that with the fulness put into my hands, leanness may not be sent into my soul! That I may not wax proud and wanton, and indifferent about a better world, when I am so well provided for in this! O let not my riches choke thy grace, or damp my zeal in thy service. But the more thou hast done for me, O my God, make me the more careful to approve myself to thee, more anxious to please thee, more fearful to offend thee. And, seeing that thou hast pronounced it so hard for the rich to enter into thy kingdom, O keep me continually vigilant to escape the temptations and dangers to which I am exposed.

Suffer me not, O my God, to trust in uncertain riches, or to value myself upon my worldly possessions: but make me to covet earnestly the true riches, even the treasures of thy heavenly grace and love. Enable me to count all things but loss and dung, that I may win Christ, and be rich in good works, and abound in the fruits of righteousness. As thou fillest me with thy good things, so fill my heart with thy love and grace, that I may use every gift aright to thy glory. O let me not despise any above whom thy distinguished kindness has raised me. But give me a heart to condescend to them of low estate; and, amidst all my plenty, let me be clothed with humility. Make me forward to all the offices of charity; ready to communicate, willing to distribute; laying up in store a good foundation against the time to come, that I may lay hold on eternal life. Let it be my delight to make to myself friends with the unrighteous mammon, that, when I fail, they may receive me into everlasting habitations. Whatsoever I have in the world, O that I may have it sanctified to me by the word of God, and prayer! and may be enabled, by a right use and conscientious improvement of it, to honour thy name, from whom every good and perfect gift proceeds! Let me so use the world, as not to abuse it. Let me rather be deprived of all that I possess, than be retarded by it in my spiritual progress. Let me rather cast off the thick clay, with which my feet are loaded, than not run my race with patience, and so run as to obtain the treasures which are eternal in the heavens. *Amen.*

A PRAYER TO BE USED BY SUCH AS ARE POOR AND LOW IN THE WORLD.

O LORD, the great disposer of all our estates and concerns! thy providence appoints to all their several stations; and it is thy will that there should be poor and low, as well as rich and high, in the world. One thing is needful; and it is not the wealth of this world, but the riches of thy grace, that will do us good, and make us happy. If thou shower not down plenty upon me, yet, Lord, give me what is needful and convenient for me. And, however thou dealest with me as to the things of this life, O deny me not thy saving grace, which is the portion of thy chosen, and better than thousands of gold and silver. Teach me, O my God, to suffer need, without repining at my lot, or coveting what I do not possess, or envying those who are in better circumstances than myself. O make me contented with my portion, and not grieved on account of my meanness and obscurity in the world, but desirous only to be known in heaven, and to be accepted of my God in Christ Jesus. Let me never stretch out my hand to iniquity; nor seek to help myself, by any dishonest ways: but choose rather to be poor than wicked; and to want my daily bread, rather than be destitute of thy heavenly grace. Enable me to cast all my care upon thee, and to trust in thee for all needful provision. Let me labour, working with my hands the thing which is good, that I may have sufficient for my necessities: and may thy blessing succeed and prosper all my honest designs and poor endeavours.

And the less I have of this world, O let me be more concerned to labour for a better! And as I have no inheritance upon earth, make me determined, through thy grace, to be a partaker of the inheritance of thy saints in light. Let me not lose both worlds; nor pass from a destitute condition here to want even a drop of water in the eternal world; but let me have treasure in heaven, even thy blessed self, O Lord, to be my portion for ever. Let me be found among those poor of this world, whom thou hast chosen to be rich in faith, and heirs of the kingdom which thou hast promised to them that love thee.

And blessed be thy name, O righteous God, that with thee there is no respect of persons, but the poor are as acceptable to thee as the rich: yea, thou hast dealt exceedingly graciously with me, in that thou hast put out of my way many of the snares and temptations that hinder others. The riches of the opulent render it extremely difficult for them to enter into thy kingdom; but my poverty lays no obstacle in my way to the obtaining of thy glory. If only I am poor in spirit, as well as low in the world, I have thy promise that the kingdom of heaven shall be mine. My God! grant me that poverty of spirit, with all other things that accompany salvation. And then, however destitute I am in this life, thy will be done: though I have nothing to depend upon in the world, yet I will rejoice in the Lord, I will joy in the God of my salvation. Having thee for my God, I can want nothing that is good. O Lord, give me thyself, and then I have all: and for that best of gifts, I will bless thy name for evermore. *Amen.*

A PRAYER FOR THE MASTER OF A FAMILY.

O MOST high God, the great Lord of all, whose providence disposes the several ranks of men in the world, and whose word instructs masters, as well as servants, how to demean themselves in their respective places, thou hast made me the head of this house. O that I may walk in it with an upright heart, and not shelter any evil thing under my roof! may I ever countenance the pious, and correct the vicious, and yield myself a pattern of all that is virtuous and praiseworthy: and let me so command my children and my household after me, that they also may keep the way of the Lord. Let this be my determination, through grace, that, as for me and my house, we will serve the Lord. O that there may not be a hypocrite, or an unrenewed profane person amongst us! let not me, who am called a master, myself be a servant of sin: let me not be enslaved by my own passions and lusts; but have the dominion over myself; and keep my eyes ever waiting upon the Lord my God, even as the eyes of servants are to the hands of their masters.

O that my wife may be the spouse of Christ; my children the children of God; my servants the servants of the Lord; and all the members of my family the true members of thy church, and the constant followers of all that is laudable and good. Let me not carry myself with rigour amongst them, nor despise the cause even of my servants; but with patience and candour attend to their complaints, and give unto them that which is just and equal; knowing that I also have a Master in heaven. Let me not insult over any that are under the yoke: nor be severe and cruel to them; nor oppress or defraud them in their wages; nor withhold any rewards or encouragements which they may justly expect from me. But let my dealings with them be upright and candid, merciful and kind. Let me take care of their bodies and their souls, and of all that concerns them, as their benign patron and their faithful friend. Let me ever treat them with all due regard, as my brethren and fellow-servants before God, with whom is no respect of persons. O give me, Lord, an understanding heart, and such a spirit of wisdom, that I may go in and out before my people, as one that is taught of God; and in whatsoever I enjoin to them, let me have respect to thy will, and seek the advancement of thy glory.

Bless my house, O Lord, and preserve it from all diseases and from all dangers. Keep it also from vice and ungodliness; and make it a nursery of virtue and piety, and of all that is exemplary and of good report. Direct, O God. and help every every one of us in the discharge of our respective duties. Enable us to employ ourselves as we ought, and with quietness do our own business, never forgetting the great work for which we were sent into the world. O keep us evermore in thy fear and love: and enable us not only to begin well, but to hold on our way even to the end; that we may meet again around thy throne, and be partakers together of thy heavenly kingdom, through Jesus Christ, our common Lord and Saviour. *Amen.*

THE SERVANT'S PRAYER.

O GOD, the Father Almighty, Maker of heaven and earth! it is the appointment of thy good providence, that there should be various ranks and degrees of men, and that I should be placed in the station where I now am. Wherefore, I submit, Lord, to thy most wise and gracious disposal, and desire (with content and thankfulness)

THE SERVANT'S PRAYER.

to accept of my portion, how low soever in the world. If my blessed Redeemer, who is Lord of all, would take upon him the form of a servant, and condescend even to the meanest offices for the service of our souls, O why should it be grievous to me to be a servant under the yoke? In serving man as I ought, I do also serve the Lord: and though bound to man, I may be the Lord's freeman: yea, in faithfully discharging the duties of my place, I shall be as acceptable to my God as any that enjoy the highest station. I leave it to thee, therefore, O Lord of all, to choose my inheritance for me. Only I beg at thy hands that my lot may fall where my soul may prosper, though my work be less easy, my provision less delicate, my accommodation less convenient. If my soul do well, I shall be for ever happy: if my heart be right with God, I shall be blessed with his countenance and love: and if I be found in the way of righteousness, I shall be exalted in due time, however abased at present. O my supreme Lord and Master, who art King of kings, and Lord of lords, let me prefer thy favour, (wherein is life,) and thy loving-kindness, (which is better than life itself,) to all the ease, or profit, or honour, that the world can give me: and let it be more my concern to glorify thee by a quiet, faithful, and diligent discharge of the duties of my place, than to serve myself by a restless desire of continually advancing my temporal interests.

O let me not be the servant of sin; but let me

enjoy the blessed liberty wherewith Christ has made us free: even liberty from sinful bondage, and liberty to follow my Lord fully, and to run the way of thy commandments with an enlarged heart. And, Lord, be thou pleased to fit me for the service to which I am called; that I may perform it to the glory of thy name, to the satisfaction and comfort of those whom I serve, and to my own everlasting advantage. O make me true and faithful, careful and diligent, humble and obedient, meek and patient, kind and peaceable. Enable me to do the business of my place, not with eye-service as a man-pleaser, but in singleness of heart, as unto God. Let me not be cross in my temper, or froward in my conduct, but ready on all occasions to bear with others and deny myself. Let me not be hasty to answer again, and thereby to stir up wrath; but enable me, with silence and submission, to follow the things that make for peace. Let me never lower my master's character, in order to set off my own; or consult my own gain or pleasure at the expense of his interests: but enable me in all things to consult his will and pleasure, his credit and interest, as far as will consist with my duty to thee. Let it be my ambition to act worthy of my God unto all pleasing, and to be found faithful in the sight of him who searcheth the heart, and trieth the reins. Give me thy grace, O most merciful God and Father, that I may so acquit myself towards my earthly master, as to have my person and services accepted of thee through the mediation of thy beloved Son, my blessed Saviour and Redeemer, Jesus Christ. *Amen.*

THE SOLDIER'S PRAYER.

O LORD God of hosts! who hast all the creatures, in heaven and in earth, ever ready to fight thy battles, and to execute thy commands! thou didst not sow any seeds of enmity in our nature; but didst create man in thine own image, endued with all the principles of love, and dispositions to peace. It is from our lusts alone, the wars and fightings have come amongst us. We first, by transgression, made ourselves enemies to thee; and have therefore been justly left by thee to cherish enmity against our fellow-creatures, and to bite and devour one another. O my God, I lament the sad necessity that exists for learning and exercising the art of war. But, now that I am in a line which binds me to the performance of military duties, instruct me, O Lord, and enable me to behave myself as a truly Christian soldier ought to do. Above all things incline me, O Lord, to enlist under thy banners, and enable me to become a good soldier of Jesus Christ. Let me war a good warfare, and never cease to fight against those enemies that war against my soul. And that I may have peace with thee my God, let me have no peace with my sins; nor ever take part with those that rebel against thee. Let me never be carried away by the influence of ungodly examples, or be led to commit any wickedness, against which thou, O God, hast declared thy wrath from heaven. O grant that I may never strive with my Maker; nor allow myself in such a habit of mind, and course of life, as are enmity against God; but let me dread more to fall into thy hands, than into the hands of those who can only kill the body; and ever show myself the more zealous for thee, the more I see others set themselves against thee. O Lord most high! make me valiant for thy cause as well as for my queen and country. And preserve me, O my God, from the profaneness and blasphemy, the lewdness and debauchery, the rudeness and violence that are so common amongst men of my profession: let me not be infected with their contagion; but preserve my integrity, amidst all the temptations wherewith I am surrounded.

Though the sword is in my hand, let the peace of God rule in my heart. And though I am a soldier, let me not be a man of blood, delighting in war, but a ready servant of my country, a faithful instrument for our common defence and safety, and a dutiful subject to the powers ordained of God, for the Lord's sake. O my Strength and my Redeemer, strengthen my heart and hands for the service to which I am called. And make me successful and victorious, through

THE SOLDIER'S PRAYER.

thy blessing and power from on high. It is thou, Lord, only, that makest us to dwell in safety: O cover my head in the day of battle: and in all times of danger, be thou my shield and buckler. Keep me, if it may please thee, from the calamities to which I am exposed, or over-rule them for my spiritual and eternal good; that wounds in my body may be the health of my soul, and temporal death prove to me the gate of everlasting life. And seeing that I go with my life in my hands, and am more exposed than other men to dangers and death, O make me more careful of my soul, more mindful of my latter end, and more diligent to maintain a constant readiness to meet my God. And whether I prosper or miscarry in the attempts and enterprises wherein I am now concerned, O let my soul be ever precious in thy sight, and safe in thy hands. Help me, O thou, my Leader and Commander, thou great Captain of my salvation, so to live that I may find it the greatest gain to die: and let me go on (as Christ's faithful soldier) so conquering and to conquer, that, having overcome all the enemies of my soul, I may sit down in thy kingdom, and participate thy glory, and triumph in thy praise for ever and ever. *Amen.*

THE SAILOR'S PRAYER.

ALMIGHTY and ever-blessed God, whose eyes are in every place beholding the evil and the good; look down, I beseech thee, on thine unworthy servant that desires now to obtain mercy at thy hands. Thou seest that my lot is cast in a situation where my temptations are manifold, and my advantages for religious improvement but few. Alas! O Lord, how baneful have I found the influence of evil company; and how often have I myself proved a snare to my companions! but pardon, I pray thee, all the guilt which I have contracted; and lay not to my charge my multiplied iniquities. Wash me in the fountain opened for sin and for uncleanness; and let the blood of Christ, which cleanseth from all sin, purge my conscience from dead works to serve the living God.

Let me not, O Lord, be any longer regardless of my eternal interests. Surely in a peculiar manner it becomes *me* to stand ready for death and judgment. Exposed as I am to continual dangers, and not knowing what an hour may bring forth, O let me be mindful of my latter end; and live every day, as if I knew that it would be my last. And if, by reason of stormy winds and tempests, I be lifted up to the heavens, and go down again into the depths, and the hearts of all around me melt because of their trouble, let me know in whom I have believed, and be enabled with composure to commit my soul into thy hands: let me have the comfort of knowing that thou art reconciled to me in the Son of thy love, and that death will be to me a door of entrance into thy heavenly kingdom.

Let me not be afraid to confess thee before men, or be ashamed of having it known that I am thy servant. Let me rather be emboldened to let my light shine before men, and to be a witness for thee amongst those with whom I live. Let me be deeply grieved at all the evil which I behold, and labour to the utmost of my power to turn my fellow-sinners from the error of their ways.

Blessed God! infinite are my obligations to thee for the many kind interpositions of thy providence which I have experienced, and for that measure of grace which, of thine own love and mercy, thou hast seen fit to bestow upon me. O that thou wouldst fill my heart with a grateful sense of thy mercies, and dispose me to render unto thee according to the benefits conferred upon me. Let me especially live nigh to thee in secret prayer. Let me delight in reading thy blessed word, and in meditating on the great things of thy law. Make up to me the want of public instruction by the special assistance of thy good Spirit. Open my understanding that I may understand thy word; and incline my heart to obey it with all cheerfulness. Enable me in the most unreserved manner to devote myself to thee, and to glorify thee with my body and my spirit which are thine.

This, O my God, I would regard as my chief happiness on earth; and this I humbly ask at thy hands, through the merits and mediation of Jesus Christ, my blessed Lord and Saviour. *Amen.*

THE CONDEMNED MALEFACTOR'S PRAYER.

OUT of the depths do I cry to thee, O Lord! Lord, hear my voice: let thine ears be attentive to the voice of my supplication. If thou, O Lord, shouldst mark iniquities, O Lord, who should stand! But there is forgiveness with thee, that thou mayst be feared. Therefore I wait for the Lord; my soul does wait; and in thy word do I hope. Though my sins have found me out, and brought me to shame, and they are heinous beyond expression, and the thought and remembrance of them fills me with horror and confusion; yet I believe (Lord, help my unbelief) they are not greater than can be forgiven: they do not exceed the value of that atonement which thine only dear Son has made, or the merits of that perfect obedience which he has rendered to thy holy law. No, Lord; neither do they exceed thy boundless mercies, nor the great and precious promises which thou hast given us in the gospel of thy Son. Vile indeed, and inexpressibly wretched is my guilty soul: but it is not past thy help and care, O Lord God Almighty, who, at the lowest, canst raise, and, at the worst, art able to relieve us. Except we repent, thou hast told us that we shall perish: but upon our repentance, thou hast promised thy gracious forgiveness. And though sin has abounded, yet when we forsake our wicked ways and thoughts, and return to the Lord our God, thou hast promised to have mercy upon us, and abundantly to pardon. It is thine own most true and faithful word, O Lord, that whosoever believeth in Christ shall not perish, but have everlasting life; and, that he who confesseth and forsaketh his sins shall have mercy. Though therefore I cannot find such mercy now at man's tribunal, yet I may, and will, ask it of thee, the Father of all mercies, who dost not reject the cry even of the vilest, in their distress, but rememberest us in our lowest estate, and encouragest us to trust in that mercy of thine which endureth for ever. O thou that hast promised to forgive every penitent sinner, make me, Lord, I beseech thee, one of that number. O touch my heart with true remorse, that it may melt and bleed for my sins, and become such a broken, contrite heart, as thou wilt not despise.

O that the distressing circumstances which I am in, may be turned (through the riches of thy grace) into a happy occasion of converting my soul, and of furthering my everlasting salvation!

This is a time of shame and sorrow with me; but help me, gracious God, so to repent and be converted, that my sins may be blotted out, and that a time of refreshing may come to me from the presence of the Lord. For thy name's sake, O Lord, pardon my sin, for it is great; too great for any but the God of infinite goodness and love, to pardon. And, that thou mayst have the glory, and my soul the blessed fruit of thy mercy, O Lord, prepare me for it by such a deep and serious repentance as thy holy word requires, and such as thy goodness in Christ Jesus will mercifully accept. What is past I cannot recall; but thou, Lord, canst remit it, and give me grace to repent of it. O strike my rocky heart, that the tears of penitence may flow down like a river; and enable me so to humble myself for my sins, that they may be blotted out from the book of thy remembrance. O blot them out as a morning cloud: blot them in the blood of thy beloved Son, who came to seek and to save that which was lost; and who suffered and died once. that we might not suffer and die eternally. Wash me thoroughly from my iniquity, and cleanse me from my sin: wash me in that fountain that was opened for sin and uncleanness, even in the precious blood of that Lamb of God, that was slain to take away the sins of the world.

My soul is exceeding sorrowful, even unto death: O most gracious Lord! grant that my sorrow may be a godly sorrow. Let me not merely sorrow for the bitter consequences of my sin, but for my sin itself, and for all the offences which I have ever committed against thy divine Majesty. O blessed Jesus, who camest to call sinners to repentance, and thyself didst hang upon the cross, and show compassion to the poor malefactor, who suffered with thee, remember me now in my last hours, and show mercy unto me for thy own mercy's sake. O Son of David, have mercy upon me. Both now and ever vouchsafe to hear me, O Christ; graciously hear me, O Lord Christ. And let thy mercy be showed upon me, as I do put my trust in thee. O glorify thy mercy in my salvation, and not thy justice in my destruction.

Though confusion is now my portion, yet help me, Lord, to bear thine indignation, as it becomes me; and so to improve the humiliating circumstances into which my sins have brought me, that I may not hereafter awake to shame and everlasting contempt. And though I am now under the sentence of a temporal death; yet spare my soul, O most merciful Lord, and deliver me not into the bitter pains of eternal death. O that I may have all my shame, and sorrow, and evil things, in this life; and not be removed from this dungeon to that infinitely more tremendous prison, where I shall want even a drop of water to cool my tongue, and be confined in chains of everlasting darkness to the judgment of the great day. Be merciful unto me, O merciful Lord

272   FOR THE PROSPERITY OF THE CHURCH.

God: and show forth in me all the wonders of thy grace, and power, and mercy, to prepare me for, and support me under, the deserved punishment, which I am about to suffer; and to give me hope in my death, (even in this infamous death;) and after death, a happy mansion (the least and lowest mansion) in the house of my God. I humbly ask this, for the sake of thine own tender mercies, and for the infinite merits of the great Redeemer of the world, my only Lord and Saviour, Jesus Christ. *Amen, Amen.*

A PRAYER FOR THE ENLARGEMENT AND PROSPERITY OF THE CHURCH.

O GOD of all grace, who hast called out of this present evil world, a chosen generation, to know thy will, to seek thy face, to follow thy ways, and to inherit thy glory, pour out thy blessings upon those who are yet in darkness and the shadow of death: make bare thine arm and exert thy power, that all the ends of the earth may remember themselves, and turn to the Lord, and that all flesh may see the salvation of God. Call home to thee again thy once favoured people the Jews; and take the veil from their hearts, that they may see and own their Messias. Let that blood of Christ, which they so profanely imprecated upon their own heads, cleanse them from the guilt of shedding it: yea, let it cleanse them

FOR THE PROSPERITY OF THE CHURCH. 273

from all their sins. Bring in, O God, the fulness of the Gentiles: and give thy Son the heathen for his inheritance, and the utmost parts of the earth for his possession. O give thy gospel a free and effectual course throughout the world; let it be propagated where it has not yet reached; and let the joyful sound be heard even where Christ is not yet named. Give success to it, where it shines already; let all who have received it, sincerely obey it; cause every one that names the name of Christ, to depart from iniquity; and grant that all who make a profession of godliness may be constrained by the love of Christ to live unto thee, and to adorn the doctrine of God our Saviour in all things.

Convince and convert both the avowed enemies of Christ, and also the enemies of his own house. Beat down all antichristian powers, both in the false church, where Christianity is so foully corrupted; and also beyond the borders of Christendom, where it is openly opposed. Show unto all of them the light of thy truth; that they may know it, as it is in Jesus: expel their prejudices, together with their darkness; and bring them to receive thy truth in the love of it, that they may be saved. O that the true religion of our Lord Jesus may prevail powerfully, and gain more proselytes daily throughout the world. O that Jerusalem may soon become the joy and praise of the whole earth: and that we may see the good of it all the days of our life! O thou Father of lights, grant that all errors in doctrine, and all ungodliness in practice, may be more and more exposed and suppressed, till they be utterly abolished! Let the wickedness of the wicked come to an end; but let truth and holiness increase in credit and authority till they reign and flourish even to the ends of the earth: grant this, we most humbly beseech thee, through the abundant grace of our Lord Jesus Christ. *Amen.*

A PRAYER FOR THE REFORMED CHURCHES ABROAD.

BLESS, O Lord, in an especial manner, all the churches that profess thy holy and eternal truth. Protect them from the enemies that have evil will at Sion: preserve them in the faith; and restore peace unto them, wherever they be in trouble. And wherever they enjoy peace, O cause them to know the day of their visitation, and so to improve this mercy that they may be edified and multiplied. Thou hast showed thy people hard things! thou hast made them to drink the wine of astonishment: O how long shall thine anger smoke against the sheep of thy pasture! make them glad according to the time wherein thou hast afflicted them, and wherein they have suffered adversity. Lord, how long shall the wicked triumph! how long shall they utter and speak hard things, and take crafty counsel against thy people, and consult against thy hidden ones! Arise, O God, plead thine own cause: remember how the foolish man blasphemeth thee daily. Help, Lord, for the godly man ceaseth, for the faithful fail from among the children of men. O that thou wouldst arise and have mercy upon Sion; and that the time to favour her, the set time, were come! Thou art our King, God; command deliverances for Jacob. Arise for thy servants' help; and redeem them for thy mercy's sake. Let not the rod of the wicked rest upon the lot of the righteous: but give a check and stop to the persecuting spirit, that breaks in pieces thy people, O Lord, and afflicts thine heritage. When their enemies come to eat them up, let them stumble and fall; and let thy people never be ashamed. Yea, not only restrain the remainder of that wrath, but so turn it, (as thou didst in the persecuting Saul,) that the enemies and opposers of thy truth may become lovers and followers of the same.

O hear the sighs, support the spirits, and hasten the deliverance of those, who, for thy sake, are killed all the day long, and counted as sheep for the slaughter. Make thy face to shine upon thy servants; and redeem Israel out of all his troubles. Be thou, Lord, a refuge for the oppressed; a refuge in times of trouble: and come in to their succour; and make them a way to escape out of the hands of such unreasonable men, whose very mercies are cruel. O break thou the arm of the wicked and evil man: and judge the oppressed, that the man of the earth may no more oppress. Show thy marvellous loving-kindness, thou that savest by thy right hand them that trust in thee, from those that rise up against them. When their power is gone, then manifest thine own: and when there is none to help, then let thine own arm bring salvation. Pity such as are banished for righteousness' sake, and driven to seek their bread in strange countries; grant them to find favour with those among whom they are scattered: let thy fatherly care provide for them; and in thy good time, restore them to their possessions, and to sure habitations, and to quiet resting-places. Or, if thou seest not good to abate their troubles on earth, enable them to glorify thee in the fires, and, in due season, bring them forth, as gold purified from its dross. Fill them even now with peace and joy in the Holy Ghost: and lead them to seek more earnestly those heavenly mansions, where they shall not only rest from their labours, but shall behold thy glory and sing thy praise for evermore. *Amen.*

A PRAYER FOR OUR CHURCH.

BLESSED be thy name, O Lord our God, who hast called us to be thy people; and caused the day-spring from on high to visit us, and the light of thy gospel to shine upon us. Thou hast sent to us the word of salvation: and made thy holy religion to be our birthright, and the professed religion of our nation. Thou hast not been deficient in kindness to us, O gracious Lord, but O how grievously have we failed in our duty to thee! Great things hast thou done in our behalf: but O how little have we done in thy service; and how much against thy holy, good, and righteous laws! We have long experienced thy care and kindness, as the vineyard of the Lord which thy right hand hath planted: thou hast hedged us about with thy providence; digged and pruned us with thy judgments; watered and refreshed us with thy mercies; and justly mightst thou expect to find in us fruits answerable to all thy care. But alas! we have brought forth wild grapes; and have been overgrown with the briars and thorns of contention. Our works have (too often) been no better than the unfruitful works of darkness. We confess, O Lord, that we have walked unworthy of our holy vocation, and that thou mightst justly take away the gospel of the kingdom from us, and give it to another people, that should bring forth fruits more worthy of it.

'But, O gracious, long-suffering God, who in judgment hast ever remembered mercy towards us! enter not into judgment with us for our unmindfulness of thee: lay not to our charge the numberless evils of which our own consciences accuse us; our barrenness under all the means of grace, our ingratitude for thy most precious benefits, and our abuses of the innumerable favours which we so long have enjoyed. Remember not our sins against us; but remember thy own tender mercies and loving-kindnesses, which have been ever of old. O say not of this land, thou hast no pleasure in it; but return, we beseech thee, O God of hosts: look down from heaven, behold and visit this vineyard, and the branch which thou madest strong for thyself. Be thou as a wall of fire about our church, to protect it against all that would invade its peace, corrupt its purity, or destroy its prosperity. And be thou as a refiner's fire, and like fuller's soap, in the midst of us; to purge away our dross, and to purify us yet more from all remaining errors and corruptions. Let thy church be established in the midst of us: let righteousness be the foundation of her walls, and peace the ornament of her palaces.

O may that right hand of thine which doeth valiantly, work wonders for our safety. Especially be thou pleased, O Lord, to work such a holy reformation amongst us, that we may not be nominally, but really, a reformed people, even a peculiar people, zealous of good works. Make us eminent for that righteousness which exalteth a nation; that thou, the righteous Lord, who lovest righteousness, mayst bless us, and compass us with thy favour as with a shield. Thou hast seen how much we have resisted hitherto the means thou hast used for our good: but be merciful unto us; and cause thine anger towards us to cease; and rejoice over us to do us good; and do for us what thou knowest will be effectual to reclaim and save us. Give us grace that shall be sufficient for us, and that shall constrain us to walk worthy of the calling wherewith we are called. Cast not out our prayer; but hear, and answer us, O God of our salvation, for the sake of Jesus Christ, thy Son, our Lord. *Amen.*

A PRAYER FOR UNITY.

O GOD of the spirits of all flesh, who hast made of one blood all nations of men, to dwell on the face of the whole earth! Wilt thou make us to agree in mind and affection, as we do in nature and constitution; and give to all nations unity, peace, and concord? And, as thou hast called the faithful throughout the world, into one body, so make the multitude of believers (as once they were) of one heart and of one soul. O let not the seamless coat of Christ be rent in pieces; nor thy church be divided by schisms and contentions: but make us one fold and one flock, under Jesus Christ, the great Shepherd and Bishop of our souls. Heal the wounds which our mutual jealousies and animosities have made: let not those invidious names that tend only to exasperate and to widen our breaches, be kept up; but take away from the midst of us that perverse spirit which makes us a nation void of counsel, and disposes us to bite and devour one another. O God of peace! incline our hearts to hearken to all peaceable counsels, and to comply with all healing designs. And so allay the heats which our dissensions have raised, that amidst the variety of sentiments which obtain amongst us, we may yet keep the unity of the spirit in the bond of peace, and evidence our relation to the Prince of Peace, by following after those things that make for peace.

O Lord, rebuke the storms which our unhallowed passions have raised: say to the winds and to the waves, be still; and they shall obey thee. O heal our breaches; and give us peace with thee, our God, as the foundation for a firm and lasting peace with each other. Let the uniting Spirit of Christ Jesus draw and knit us together in the blessed communion of thy saints; and let us all, with one heart and one mind, exert ourselves to advance thy glory, and the public good, and the common salvation of all our souls, through thy rich mercy to us in our blessed peace-maker, Jesus Christ. *Amen.*

A PRAYER FOR THE QUEEN AND ALL OUR RULERS AND MAGISTRATES.

ALMIGHTY Lord, the most high God, by whom kings reign and princes decree justice! Thou puttest down one, and settest up another; and there are no powers but of thee; the powers that be are ordained of God. Thy word directs us to pray for kings, and for all that are in authority. And, both in duty and inclination, I become a petitioner to thy heavenly Majesty for thy chosen servant, Queen *Victoria*, and for all our governors both in church and state. Give thy judgments, O God, to the Queen, that she may judge thy people righteously, and break in pieces their oppressors. Give her the spirit of government, and make her wise as an angel of God, to discern between good and evil: a ruler after thine own heart, and a follower of wise and pious princes in things excellent and praiseworthy. O make her obedient to thee; and make her subjects obedient to her for thy sake. Rule her heart in thy fear and love, that she may rule her people to thy honour and glory. In her days let the righteous flourish and enjoy abundance of peace, with the liberty of thy gospel, and the free profession of thy true and holy religion. Protect her, Lord, that she may protect us. Bless her arms with good success and victory: and her government with all happiness and prosperity. O keep her as the apple of thine eye: hide her under the shadow of thy wings; that no mischief may befall her, nor any son of Belial come near to touch thine anointed, or to do her any harm. And may she long continue to rule and reign for thee in her earthly kingdom, till she come to live and reign with thee above in thy kingdom of glory.

Give, Lord, unto all our rulers a mind and spirit suitable to their situations. Make them a terror only to evil-doers, and a praise to them that do well. O that they may use for thee all the power which they have received from thee, not bearing the sword in vain; but curbing and suppressing all vice and ungodliness; and defending and encouraging whatever is holy, just, and good. O give them wisdom to understand, and hearts to consider, and abilities to redress, the grievances of thy people: that under their protection we may lead quiet and peaceable lives, in all godliness and honesty.

And grant, O Lord, that I, and all my fellow-subjects, may submit to every ordinance of man for thy sake; and in conscience towards God, yield obedience to the powers which thou hast ordained. Let the fear of God teach us to honour the queen: and a sense of our duty to thee keep us within the bounds of our duty to them; that we may not bring an evil report upon our holy profession; but put to silence the ignorance of foolish men, by well-doing. And may all rulers so rule, and subjects so obey; and every one of us, from the highest to the lowest, understand and seek after God (seeking thee, Lord, whilst thou mayst be found, and calling upon thee while thou art near) that thou mayst not root us out from being a people, (as we have justly merited;)

but be still our God, and do us good in the accustomed ways of thy loving-kindness to us, through the Son of thy love, our blessed Lord and Saviour, Jesus Christ. *Amen.*

A PRAYER FOR ALL OUR BISHOPS, PASTORS, AND MINISTERS.

O LORD most high, thou glorious head of all the church! who hast appointed various offices in it, for the perfecting of the saints, for the work of the ministry, for the edifying of the body of Christ: bless in an especial manner all those whom thou hast sent to bless the people in thy name; and make all our spiritual fathers careful and tender nursing fathers of thy church. Grant them knowledge and grace, that they may order their conversation aright; enable them to watch for souls, to feed the flock of God, and to take the oversight thereof, not by constraint, but willingly; not for filthy lucre, but of a ready mind: may they care for all committed to their charge, and give to every one his portion in due season: enable them rightly to divide thy word, and to speak it as they ought to speak, that they may be useful in their generation, and approve themselves to thee as workmen that need not to be ashamed. Make them skilful and faithful in their sacred callings: and in all their endeavours to promote the knowledge and love of thy truth,

O give them good success. And let both their example and their doctrine be such as shall help to save themselves and those that hear them. O that they may speak as the oracles of God, in demonstration of the Spirit and of power; and that they may show themselves patterns of all the good things which they preach to others; not prostituting their holy calling to serve the interests and lusts of men; but conscientiously discharging it, to the glory of their Lord! Let them not walk in craftiness, nor handle the word of God deceitfully; but by manifestation of the truth, may they commend themselves to every man's conscience in the sight of God. Let them be such ensamples to the flock, that having preached to others, they themselves may not be cast-aways, but may experience the joy of that salvation which they preach: and when the chief Shepherd shall appear, may they be counted worthy to receive the crown of glory that fadeth not away.

Though the world hates, and the devil opposes them; and even many that should encourage their labours, do but strive to weaken their hands, and afflict their hearts; O great and good Lord, do thou show thine own strength, to accomplish thine own work. Open a wide door to the gospel; and defeat all opposition. Stop the mouths of false prophets; and drive away ravenous wolves from the flock; and give them faithful pastors after thine own heart. And, Lord, crown the endeavours of thy messengers with thy heavenly blessing: that they may be mighty through God, to pull down the strong-holds of sin; and to edify and build up thy church in the true fear and love of God, and in the right knowledge and faith of our Lord Jesus Christ. And because wise men die, and cannot bequeath their learning and talents unto others, do thou interpose to supply the breaches made upon us by their mortality. Bless both our universities, and all the schools and seminaries of good learning and true religion in the land: that they may send forth men able and fit to serve thee in church and state; who may successively do good in their generations, and show thy people the way of happiness and salvation. *Amen.*

A PRAYER FOR SOCIETIES,

CONFEDERATE TO PROMOTE REFORMATION OF MANNERS.

O RIGHTEOUS Lord! thou lovest righteousness, and thy countenance doth behold the upright. Thou favourest them that espouse thy righteous cause; and wilt for ever glorify such as turn many to righteousness. Thou hast commanded us not only to be holy, and to walk circumspectly ourselves; but also to show our concern for the souls of others. Thou hast appointed us to contend for thy most holy faith; yea, to contend also with the wicked, and not to suffer sin upon our brother. Thou hast enjoined us, at the peril of our own souls, to use our utmost endeavours to convert sinners from the errors of their ways: and to recover out of the snare of the devil, those who have been taken captive by him at his will.

Help, Lord; for the godly man ceaseth, and the faithful fail from among the children of men. Wherever we turn our eyes, how many are there who seek their own things, and how few who seek the things that are Jesus Christ's! Arise, O God, and plead thine own cause: and be with them that rise up against the evil-doers; and that strive, by executing judgment, to stay the plague and wrath that are gone out from the Lord against us. Plead *their* cause, O Lord, with them that strive with them, and stand up for *their* help; and stop the way against them that persecute them: and make them successful in promoting the honour of thy great name, and the interests of thy holy religion.

O that none of the correctors of others may deserve like censure themselves! but that they may all be blameless and harmless, the sons of God, without rebuke, in the midst of a crooked and perverse nation, among whom they should shine as lights in the world. O give them a tender love to the souls of men, a zeal according to knowledge, and prudence to walk in wisdom towards them that are without. And give them courage to endure the contradiction of sinners: let them account it a small thing to be judged of man's judgment: and help them in patience to possess their souls, and in meekness to instruct those that oppose themselves. Make the weapons of their warfare mighty through God to the pulling down of strongholds. And so speed them with thy heavenly blessing, that, how small soever their beginning was, their latter end may greatly increase. O let them go forth in thy strength, and prevail and prosper, as the blessed of the Lord.

Though we live in an age when iniquity abounds, and almost all abominations are shamefully committed, yet thou, Lord, who dost marvellous things, canst bring light out of darkness: and when thou pleasest, canst change the face of evil times. Yea, thou hast taught us to expect glorious things in the latter day, even such a holy and happy state of things as this wretched sinful world has never yet enjoyed.

O when shall it be, Lord, that judgment shall return unto righteousness, and that all the upright in heart follow it? O when shall the wickedness of the wicked come to an end; and profaneness and lewdness, intemperance and extravagance, be put to confusion! when shall iniquity stop her mouth, and the righteous flourish, and Jerusalem be the joy and praise of the whole earth?

The Lord hasten it in his time! In the mean while, speak, O Lord, from heaven, and restrain the floods of ungodliness that have lifted up their voice and their waves; and say to those proud waters, hitherto shall ye go, and no further.

O cherish and prosper all good beginnings, and all hopeful proceedings, for the furtherance of piety, and for the advancement of thy glory. Make magistrates and ministers, and all orders of men, vigilant in keeping their own hearts, and ordering their own conversation aright; that they may more successfully promote the edification of their neighbours. Make them all to account it, not their duty, but their honour and pleasure, to advance this blessed work: make them to do it heartily, as to the Lord; to the reforming of the world, and to the rejoicing of all that love our Lord Jesus Christ in sincerity. *Amen.*

AN ADDITION IN TIME OF WAR.

O LORD, the great and dreadful God! against thee we have so greatly sinned, that thou mayst justly use our enemies as thy scourge to correct us; and if thou shouldst give us over to their power, it is meet that we should patiently bear thine indignation. But, however thou mayst be pleased to express thine anger against us, O let us not fall into their hands, whose very mercies are cruel. Arise, O God, let not man prevail, nor those that hate us swallow us up: but scatter them by thy power, and bring them down, O Lord, our defender. Thou that makest the wrath of man to praise thee, O bring glory to thyself even from the fury of our enemies : yea, restrain the remainder of their wrath ; and put a stop to the effusion of blood ; that wars may cease, and our land have rest, and thy people be blest with peace. Our eyes are upon thee, our great Saviour and mighty Deliverer, to give us help from trouble: for vain is the help of man. In times of danger, O be thou our shield and buckler. And when our sins lay us open to the malice of enemies, gracious God, be thou our hiding-place, to preserve us from the evils we dread, and from the judgments we deserve. O, for thy truth's sake, for thy beloved Son, our blessed Saviour's sake, spare us, good Lord, and give us not up a reproach to our enemies ; nor let them ever have cause to rejoice in our ruin.

O go forth with our armies, thou Almighty Lord of hosts; and bless and prosper both our land and naval forces. And that we may not be in rebellion against heaven, while others are warring against us, O save us from our provoking sins ; and so direct our ways to please thee, that thou mayst make even our enemies to be at peace with us. Purge the camp of every cursed thing, which would incapacitate them for standing before their enemies; and turn them from all the provocations which weaken our hopes of receiving good by their hands. Cover thou their heads in the day of battle ; and preserve them in the time of danger. O let them be as the sun when it goeth forth in its strength; let them return with safety, honour, and victory; and bless them, O God, with good success. O hear the prayers and cries of thy servants, who stand in the gap, interceding in the anguish of their souls for this sinful nation, which has so long abused thy mercy: spare us, good Lord, and save us by the kind hand of thine omnipotence: let us be plucked as a brand out of the fire; that we may see the good out of thy chosen, and rejoice in the gladness of thy nation, and glory with thine inheritance: vouchsafe it to us, we beseech thee, according to the riches of thy grace and goodness in Christ Jesus our Lord. *Amen.*

A PRAYER IN PUBLIC COMMOTIONS AND DISTRACTIONS.

ALMIGHTY Lord, the righteous God! thy judgments are in all the earth: and it is no wonder that a world which has so trampled on thy laws, should experience thy heavy displeasure. Behold, O Lord, we hear of wars and rumours of wars, and that the sword is making havock among the nations. And though we have hitherto been kept from such wasting calamities as have swept away multitudes of our brethren, yet thou, for our sins, hast now visited the nation, and made it tremble. O heal the breaches of it, for it shaketh. We have no sanctuary to flee unto, but that mercy of thine, which we have so often abused; nor any help from trouble, but what we seek at thy hands, who, for our sins, art justly displeased. O thou that waitest to be gracious, and whose mercy endureth for ever, have compassion on us, and save us. Spare us, good Lord; spare thy people, whom thou hast redeemed with thy precious blood, and distinguished with thy peculiar favour. Turn us again, O Lord God of hosts; cause thy face to shine, and we shall be saved. O make a way for us to escape out of those fears and dangers, wherein our sins have involved us; that peace may be restored to us, and the gospel of peace be continued to us and our posterity, as long as the world endures. O that we may learn righteousness by thy judgments; and not dare to go on in our trespasses and rebellions against thee, when thou hast a controversy with us, and art making inquisition for blood! but let us so turn to thee, in the way of our duty, that thou mayst turn to us in a way of saving mercy. And, seeing that this is not our rest, and that little but alarms and commotions are to be expected in this tumultuous world, O that we may have our eyes continually lifted up to thee, from whom cometh our help; and lay up our treasure in that kingdom which cannot be moved! Make us to choose that good part which shall not be taken away from us; that so we may have comfort in our life, and hope in our death, even the hope of that eternal life, which is thy promise and gift, O blessed God, through Jesus Christ. *Amen.*

IN TIME OF INFECTION.

O LORD God, the giver of our health, which is the blessing that sweetens all the other blessings of our lives; it is only of thy mercy that we have any measure of health continued to us. And, O how just were it with thee, utterly to take away from us that health, which we have so greatly abused to a forgetfulness of thee, and to wantonness against thee! How justly mightst thou smite us with the most sharp and noisome diseases, and hurry us out of the land of the living, by signal and desolating judgments! Our flesh trembles for fear of thee, and we are afraid of thy judgments; lest thou shouldst pierce us with the arrows of the Almighty, and sweep us away with the besom of destruction. But, O thou hope of Israel, the Saviour thereof in time of trouble, regard not our ill deserts; but remember thy own tender mercies, and gracious promises: and have pity on us: and turn away this plague from us. Put a stop to the raging infection, and say to the destroying angel, it is enough; that we may no longer be afraid of the terror by night, or of the arrow that flieth by day, or of the pestilence that walketh in darkness, or of the destruction that wasteth at noon-day; but may, with ease in our minds and gladness in our hearts, serve thee, the only true God, and devote to thee the life and health which thou hast spared. O hear us in this hour of our necessity, and let our cry come unto thee, through the merits and intercession of thy dear Son, our most compassionate and prevailing Mediator, Jesus Christ. *Amen.*

A PRAYER FOR RAIN.

WE confess, O Lord, that we have so greatly abused the comforts of thy good creatures, that thou mightst justly withdraw them from us, and make the heavens over us as brass, and the land itself to mourn, and all that grows upon it to wither. But, O thou Father of mercies, who in judgment rememberest mercy, consult not now our merits, but thy own mercies. Thou that hast the bottles and treasures of heaven at thy command, be pleased now to open the windows of heaven, and cause the rain to come down in its season; making grass to grow for the cattle, and herbs and fruits for the service of men. And, however thou art pleased to deal with us, O suppress all our repinings at any of thy dispensations; and let them all be sanctified unto us; that we may be prepared to receive the mercies which we want, or to wait thy time for them with meekness and resignation. We ask it for the sake of Jesus Christ our Saviour. *Amen.*

FOR FAIR WEATHER.

LORD, if thou shouldst turn our fruitful land into barrenness for the wickedness of them that dwell therein, thou wouldst be righteous; and just would be thy judgments. We could not open our mouths to reply against thee, but must bear the indignation of the Lord which our sins have so much deserved. But, O Father of mercies, spare us, and forgive us, for thy own mercy's sake; and put a stop to the calamity that threatens destruction to the work of thy hands. Let not the rain, which is thy blessing, be turned into a curse. Put a stop to the overflowing showers, which injure the fruits of the earth, and endanger the loss of our blessings. And as thou hast given us plenty, and caused our land to yield its increase, so give us (we pray thee) a seasonable time to gather in the fruits, which thy bounty has provided for us; that, in the use of them, we may joyfully serve thee, and live to thy glory, as we do upon thy bounty. And when thy judgments are in the land, O that we who inhabit it, may learn righteousness! Nor let our concern be so great for our bodies as for our souls: that however we fare here, it may go well with us for ever. O let us not labour for the meat that perisheth, so much as for that which endures to everlasting life; which thou hast promised to give, and which above all we beg at thy hands,

O Lord God our Father, for the sake of Jesus Christ our only Saviour. *Amen.*

A PRAYER IN TIME OF FAMINE.

O LORD Most High, the Creator of every comfort! thou hast long dealt out thy blessings to us with a plentiful hand; and we have freely enjoyed all the abundance of good things which thou hast heaped upon us. But when thou hast fed us to the full, how have we kicked against our blessed owner, and most bountiful benefactor! how have we abused the provisions for our bodies, in pampering the lusts that war against our souls! Most righteous, therefore, we confess, would be thy judgments, O Lord, if thou shouldst stretch out upon us the line of confusion, and the stones of emptiness; and break the staff of our bread; and curse us in all our store, and in all the endeavours of our hands to help ourselves.

But, O thou blessed Father of mercies! in mercy avert from us the hunger, and thirst, and nakedness, and want of all things, which is the due desert of our sins. Let not the husbandman be ashamed, sowing much, and gathering little; let not the land mourn, and all the inhabitants, with the beasts of the field, and the fowls of heaven: but humble us, O Lord, for all our abuse of thy past mercies; and deliver us from those sins which have turned our land into barrenness.

Be pleased to command a blessing upon us; and abundantly to bless our provision, and to satisfy our poor with bread: and give us fruitful seasons, filling our hearts with food and gladness; that we may see thy hand, and praise thy power, and adore thy mercy and bounty, and, in the strength and refreshment of our restored comforts, may joyfully devote ourselves to thy holy service all the days of our lives. *Amen.*

DEVOUT APPLICATION TO THE LORD
IN TIME OF THUNDER, OR SOME TERRIBLE TEMPEST.

O LORD God, most high and almighty! who lookest upon the earth, and it trembles; and touchest the mountains, and they smoke; how wonderful art thou in thy works, and terrible in thy doings! Thou hast all the creatures at thy command, and employest them (when thou wilt) as the executioners of thy wrath! even the devouring fire, and stormy winds, ungovernable as they appear to us, do yet fulfil thy will. In these astonishing flames, these roaring noises, and dreadful commotions, thou showest the power of thy hand, which no creature is able to resist. When thou, O God of glory, thunderest, and causest thy voice to be heard from heaven, thou makest us to know the terrors of the Lord; and how fearful a thing it is to fall into the hands of the living God. And we must own it, Lord, to be only of thy mercies that we are not consumed, even because thy compassions fail not. O let these thy compassions now be extended to us, and showed upon us. And in tender mercy cause the threatening destruction to pass over us.

O despise not the prayers of thy poor creatures, crying to thee in their extreme distress: but now and evermore vouchsafe to hear us, O Christ; graciously hear us, O Christ; graciously hear us, O Lord Christ. And let us not only find mercy from thee now, but more especially in that great day of the Lord; wherein the heavens, being on fire, shall be dissolved, and the elements shall melt with fervent heat, and the earth, with all its works, shall be burnt up. O Lord of all mercy, save us now from our sins; for it is our sins that make us afraid; and fearfulness surprises us, because we have been false in thy covenant, and rebellious against thy word, and have provoked the Holy One of Israel to anger. O forgive us all the guilt which we have contracted; and which fills us with fearful expectation of thy wrath and fiery indignation. And let the all-sufficient merits of our Redeemer's death, (that death which made the earth to quake, and the rocks to rend,) atone for every wickedness, whereby we have offended thy divine Majesty.

And, O that we may not only be filled with awe at present, whilst thou art shaking thy rod over us, but be awakened permanently from all carnal security, all hardness of heart, and forgetfulness of thee our God, who art a consuming fire. And let the fear of thy judgments humble us: let thy terrors soften our hearts, and leave such deep and lasting impressions on our minds, that we may never disregard the works of the Lord, nor the operation of his hands; but with all awfulness revere and adore thee, the supreme Ruler of all the world. O Lord our governor, keep us in thy fear, not only through this day, but to the latest hour of our lives. Keep us from every thing that may provoke the eyes of thy glory: and enable us to walk before thee in such a humble, godly, circumspect manner, that thy name may be glorified in us, and that we may be glorified in and with thee for evermore. *Amen.*

IN TIME OF ANY SORE AND GRIEVOUS CALAMITY.

O MOST high and glorious Lord God, thou supreme governor of the universe, how unsearchable are thy judgments, and thy ways past finding out! Thy path is in the great deep, and thy footsteps are not known. Clouds and darkness are round about thee, yet righteousness and judgment are at all times the basis of thy throne. Thou canst never do injury to any; but art righteous in all thy ways, and holy in all thy works. Who would not stand in awe of thy glorious majesty, O Lord? Thou canst consume us by thine own immediate stroke, or arm any of thy creatures in heaven or earth against us. Thou canst make the vilest of them the executioners of thy just indignation; or turn the very things wherein we have offended into the instruments of our punishment. Thou canst plague us even in our comforts: making the choicest blessings of our lives to become the heaviest of our crosses, and the keenest of our torments. Thou canst in a moment take away life from us, or make it less desirable to us than death itself.

We fall down and kneel before the Lord our Maker, in humble submission to thy correction, acknowledging the heavy desert of our sins, and the perfect justice of thy judgments. Humble us, O good Lord, under thy hand: and forgive the iniquities that have provoked thee so to stretch it out against us. Thou that takest away the sins of the world, have mercy upon us, and turn us from our sins; and deliver us from evil, and take away thy plagues from us. O let thy boundless compassion cover the multitude of our transgressions: remember thy poor unworthy creatures in mercy: relieve and help us in our need and distress: and save and free us from our fears and dangers, and from our griefs and pressures: that we may comfortably spend our few remaining days, and glorify thy name for evermore. *Amen.*

A PRAYER FOR OUR BENEFACTORS.

I DESIRE with all thankfulness to acknowledge thy loving-kindness, O Lord, my God: that thou hast given me so many comforts, and raised me up so many friends and helps in the world. It is thou, Lord, (who hast the hearts of all in thy hands), that turnest the hearts of any to show me favour, and to do me good. They are but the instruments and means of conveyance; but thou art the blessed author and source of all the kindness. To thee, therefore, where alone it is due, I give the glory, and offer the sacrifice of praise. But for them, whom thou hast enabled, and inclined to benefit me, I am bound in duty to offer up the sacrifice of my prayers. O be thou kind to them, Lord, as they have been kind to me: refresh their bowels, as they have refreshed mine; and requite their love, and all their endearing offices of friendship, sevenfold into their bosoms. Make me studious ever to approve myself grateful, and ready to make all suitable returns in my power. And be thou pleased, O blessed God, to reward them in a better way than I can do, and to turn all the advantages I have received from them, to their own best and greatest advantage. And for all their goodness and their kind favours to me, give them, O Lord, not only temporal, but spiritual blessings, and everlasting consolations. O give them that unspeakably rich gift, the knowledge of thy dear Son, and all the good things of thy Spirit that accompany salvation: yea, give them thine own self, O Lord, (who art ALL in all), to be their blessed, their glorious portion for evermore. *Amen.*

A PRAYER FOR OUR PIOUS FRIENDS.

GLORY be to thee, O Lord, for thy grace discovered upon any of my friends. O how great is thy goodness, which thou hast laid up for them that fear thee, which thou hast wrought for them that trust in thee, before the sons of men! Save thy people, and bless thine inheritance: feed them also, and lift them up for ever. Let none that wait on thee, O Lord, be ashamed; but let all that seek thee, rejoice and be glad in thee, and ever have cause to say, the Lord be magnified, who has pleasure in the prosperity of his servants. O do good to them that are good; and to them that are upright in their heart. And continue thy loving-kindness, Lord, to all those who have chosen the better part, and who desire to know and love thee more, and to serve and please thee better. O answer them in the wishes of their hearts, whose hearts thou knowest to be set upon the increase of thy grace, and the perfecting of holiness in thy fear. Lead them on from strength to strength, from one degree of saving knowledge and grace to another, till (from shining here as lights in the world) they come to shine as the stars, and as the brightness of the firmament, in the kingdom of their Father, for ever and ever. And while they are in the world, O do thou keep them, good Lord, from the evil of it: and prosper all their endeavours to do good in it: that all about them may be the better for them; and that themselves, when come to the end of their pilgrimage here, may depart in peace, and hope, and joy; and find their grace exchanged for a crown of glory, that fadeth not away. *Amen.*

A PRAYER FOR OUR FRIEND,

WHOSE SOUL WE FEAR TO BE IN A DANGEROUS CONDITION.

O LORD! it was from a deep concern for the souls of men, that thy holy apostle declared, he had great heaviness and continual sorrow in his heart, and could wish himself accursed from Christ for his brethren, his kinsmen according to the flesh. Such a concern, though far inferior in degree, I feel in myself, with reference to some of my relations, especially my poor friend ———, who seems to be even in the gall of bitterness, and the bond of iniquity; setting himself in a way that is far from good; and lying under the most imminent danger of eternal misery. O what shall I do for him? and how shall I apply myself to be helpful to him? I would be taught of God; and I desire to learn wisdom of thee, my Lord, and to be enabled by thy grace to use the methods and expedients that shall be most successful to work upon him, and to do him good. O instruct me in the way that I shall take; and assist and bless me in the means and endeavours I shall use to attain this desirable end.

Yea, thou great Almighty God, who workest all in all, and canst do whatever thou pleasest, to enlighten the darkest minds, to soften the hardest hearts, to conquer the most stubborn will, and to turn even the most hopeless sinners to thyself; O be thou pleased to show the almighty efficacy of thy grace in the case that is so deplorable, and so worthy of thyself to relieve. Be pleased, O Lord, to break in powerfully upon him, and discover to him what is amiss with his soul; and make him to know in what an awful condition he stands. Open, Lord, his eyes, and renew his heart, and turn his course, and break the force of his temptations; and make a way for him to escape out of the hands of his great adversary. Let his dead soul hear the voice of the Son of God, and live. Let him be awakened from his presumptuous security, and, though far gone, be yet recovered. Let the lost sheep be brought home: yea, make him so to repent and be converted, that his sins may be blotted out, and his soul be thoroughly healed, and mercifully accepted, and eternally saved.

O gracious God! thou hast no pleasure in the death of the wicked, but art reconcileable, in the

Son of thy love, to the very worst of thy enemies; and not willing that any should perish. O what profit is there in his blood? how shall the dead and damned praise thee? Lord of all power and mercy, get thyself glory in his recovery. O speak the word, and thy sinful creature shall live, and for ever bless thy name. Dear Father! forgive him all the evil thoughts and devices of his heart, and all the offensive and wicked carriage of his life; forgive him all his sins of omission and commission; and bring him out of all the ways of wickedness and ruin, into which he hath turned aside: O bring him at last, with full purpose of heart, to resign and devote himself to the Lord. And make him so diligent and conscientious in all the practices of piety, and charity, and sobriety, that he may approve himself to be truly changed; and show in the whole of his conduct what manner of person he ought to be in all holy conversation and godliness.

O grant him an inheritance among them that are sanctified, through faith in Christ Jesus: and send down that renewing grace into his heart, which may be there as a well of water, springing up to everlasting life. Thus comfort and rejoice the soul of thy servant, O Lord, who waits upon thee. Let me not implore thy help in vain: but hear my feeble intercessions for my poor perishing friend; and grant him mercy for thine own mercy's sake, in the great lover and Saviour of souls, who came to seek the lost, and to call sinners to repentance, even thy dearly beloved Son, our Lord and Saviour Jesus Christ. *Amen.*

A PRAYER FOR OUR CHILDREN.

BEHOLD, O Lord, the children which thou hast graciously vouchsafed to give me, I humbly dedicate and devote to thee. O that they may know thee, and be owned by thee, as thy children, every one of them, from the greatest to the least. Pour out thy spirit upon my seed, and thy blessing upon my offspring. Make them, Lord, thy children by adoption and spiritual regeneration. O take possession of their hearts; and enrich them now, even in their early years, with thy heavenly grace. And teach those whose office it is to instruct them, how to guide them aright; that they may be brought up in the nurture and admonition of the Lord, and trained up in the way that they should go. I have helped to bring them into the world, children of wrath; O that thou wouldst make me instrumental to bring them also into thy church, as children of grace. Lord, have mercy upon them, and speak life to their souls: and, whatsoever else they want, O let them not want thy grace, and the portion of thy children. My God! be thou a gracious Father to them, and a merciful provider for them in all estates and events of their lives. Dispose of them, and whatever concerns them, in such a manner as may most tend to thy glory, and to their salvation.

Shouldst thou see fit to take them from hence before me, O prepare them for thy presence; and make me willing to resign them to thee. Or if thou remove me from them, O my Lord, take them up, and be thou a Father to them when I am gone. O keep them from the evil of this world; and conduct them through it in safety to a better. Take thou care even of their temporal concerns, and choose their inheritance for them; and let all good things be added unto them in this present life: but especially, O my God, take care of their souls; and give them the blessed treasure in heaven; that, when they shall be deprived of all things here below, they may be taken into thy glorious kingdom above; there to live with thee, and all the heavenly host, world without end. *Amen.*

A PRAYER FOR OUR PARENTS.

O LORD God, my heavenly Father, I here prostrate myself before thee, to beg thy blessing, grace, and mercy, upon my earthly parents. Cast them not away in the time of their old age, forsake them not when their strength fails them; but have compassion, Lord, on their infirmities, and help them in all their weakness. O remember not against them any of their former iniquities; but according to thy mercy remember them, for thy goodness' sake in Christ Jesus. O that the true wisdom may be in them, and abundant grace upon them; that their hoary heads may be found in the way of righteousness, and their souls be ever precious in thy sight. Let goodness and mercy follow them all the days of their life. Let their last days be their best days; and the longer they live in this world, make them the fitter to die, and to dwell with thy blessed self, in life everlasting. O be thou their guide until death, and in death their support and comfort; and, when heart and flesh, and all here shall fail them, O do thou never fail them; but be the strength of their hearts, and their portion for evermore. *Amen.*

A PRAYER FOR OUR ENEMIES.

O LORD of love, and Prince of peace, who hast told us, that thou camest to send a sword and fire upon earth, and that through much tribulation we must enter into thy kingdom; what am I, vile, sinful creature, that I should hope to be exempted from the common portion of all thy followers? If I have raised up enemies to myself by my own misconduct, Lord, incline and enable me to appease and gain them: and so direct my ways to please thee, that my enemies may be constrained to be at peace with me. As for such as are my enemies wrongfully, Lord, lay not this sin to their charge: but forgive them, and open their eyes, and pacify their minds, and turn their hearts, that they may see their error; and, being first reconciled unto thee, may learn to dwell with their brethren in unity and godly love. If, while I study, as much as lieth in me, to live peaceably with them, they still render evil for good, enable me to requite them with nothing but good; and evermore to love my enemies, according to thy command, and according to thy example which thou hast showed us in dying for thine enemies. Let me, in all that I suffer from them, consider them as thy rod, and the staff of thine indignation: that, instead of striving to avenge myself, I may humbly submit to thy fatherly corrections.

O good Lord! mortify in all of us the carnal mind, that is enmity against God, and those lusts that war in our members, from whence come wars and fightings amongst us. Turn all our enmity against the common enemies of our souls. And unite all our hearts to thee, in thy true fear and love; that we may not meditate revenge, but study to be quiet; nor foment and pursue our quarrels, but follow after the things that make for peace; and with one mouth, glorify our God, through Jesus Christ. *Amen.*

A PRAYER FOR THE UNCONVERTED.

O LORD God, gracious and merciful! thou art good to all; and thy tender mercies are over all thy works. And thou hast assured us, that thou hast no pleasure in the death of the wicked; but that he should turn from his way and live. Yea, thou that didst convert Zaccheus the publican, and Saul the persecutor, hast power over all hearts to fashion them as thou wilt; and canst, even out of stones, raise up children to Abraham; and make eminent saints out of the very vilest sinners. O Father of mercies! have pity on those who have no pity on themselves: open their eyes to see the error of their ways, and the danger of their state. Soften their hearts into a penitent concernment for their sins; and awaken them to a timely care for their souls. O let thy Spirit convince them what is the wages of sin, and how dreadful is the portion of ungodly men: and make them to know where their help lies, and what they must do to be saved. And the Lord make them faithful to their convictions; that they may not hold the truth in unrighteousness, but may quickly do what they are convinced is necessary to be done for their souls, before it be too late.

O merciful God! give to such as have opposed themselves, repentance to the acknowledgment of the truth; and recover out of the snare of the devil those who have been taken captive by him at his will. Let thy mercy be glorified in their conversion and salvation, and not thy justice in their abandonment and destruction.

Behold, O Lord, how many there are who contradict and blaspheme thy truth, and hate and abuse the followers of Jesus; and not only resist the means used for their salvation, but turn again and rend thy servants, who seek their welfare! O God, our heavenly Father, forgive them; for they know not what they do. Let them no longer stumble at thy word: but do thou stop and turn them, as thou didst the persecuting Saul, when he was mad against the saints, and verily thought with himself, that he ought to do many things contrary to the name of Jesus. Put them in fear, O Lord, that they may know themselves to be but chaff and stubble before thee, who art a consuming fire. And bring down their high looks, subdue their stiff necks, and break their hardened hearts, that they may submit themselves to thee, before thou hast sworn that they shall never enter into thy rest.

And such as think they are rich, and increased with goods, and have need of nothing; and know not that they are wretched, and miserable, and poor, and blind, and naked, O Lord, discover them to themselves, and show them the perilous condition of their souls: that they may be truly penitent for their sins, and thoroughly concerned to flee from the wrath to come.

Such as are ignorant, and out of the way, and to do good unto their souls have no knowledge, Lord, have compassion on them; and call them out of darkness into thy marvellous light; that they may not perish for lack of knowledge. O let them be taught of God to know thee and themselves, and the things belonging to their peace, before they be hid from their eyes. O thou that commandest the light to shine out of darkness, be pleased to shine into their hearts: show them thy ways and lead them in thy truth: that they may not be unwise, but understand what the will of the Lord is.

Such as are in pernicious errors, and damnable heresies, departed from the faith once delivered to the saints, having their minds corrupted from the simplicity that is in Christ; perverting the truth, as it is in Jesus; and not only swerving from the pure doctrine of the gospel themselves, but also lying in wait to seduce and deceive others; O Father of lights, take away the veil which is upon their hearts; that they may see wherein they have erred, and come to receive the truth in the love of it, and earnestly contend for the faith, which they once destroyed.

The prosperous worldlings and secure sinners, who are settled upon their lees, and at ease in their possessions, and admire and dote upon their worldly good, as if it were the chief and only good, applauding themselves in their portion that they have in this life, as if they had no need of

God, or of heaven: O dear Father, show them how base is their choice, so to go a whoring from the Lord; and how sandy the foundation, on which at present they stand. O make them to know, that the friendship of the world is enmity with God; and that all this world can never either satisfy the desire, or compensate for the loss, of an immortal soul. Yea, open their eyes, O Lord, to see how the fashion of this world passeth away; and how soon all that, wherein they trust and delight, will be utterly gone, as if it had never been. Show them what multitudes, by forsaking God and cleaving unto mammon, miscarry and are lost for ever; drowned in that destruction and perdition, from whence there is no redemption. Discover to them whatever may damp their ardour in the pursuit of this world: that they may learn to flee from its snares, as for the life of their souls; and so leave all for Christ, that they may not be condemned with the world, but be saved in the great day of the Lord Jesus.

And such as are loose, and profane, and scandalous in their lives, rebelling against heaven, and committing all uncleanness with greediness, scoffing at the followers of Jesus, and deriding all that is serious and holy, refusing to be ashamed, and hating to be reformed; (how dangerous and desperate soever their case may be,) O Lord our God, interpose with thine almighty power to rescue them from destruction, and to pluck them as brands out of the fire. They are not past thy help and cure; for thou callest those things that are not, as if they were; and canst change the leopard's spots, and the Ethiopian's skin; and canst bring not only something out of nothing, but the greatest good even out of the worst evil. O! where sin has abounded, let thy grace much more abound. Lord God Almighty, make bare thine arm, and let signs and wonders be done in the name of thy holy child, Jesus. Work effectually, we pray thee, to heal the diseases of their souls; make them sensible of their guilt and misery; that, as prodigals coming to themselves, they may arise, and go to their Father; and, from being dead, become alive again; from being lost, may be found. O make them yet to turn so thoroughly from their evil ways, that they may come to see the beauties of holiness, and delight to do thy blessed will, O God, and obtain an inheritance among them that are sanctified, through faith in Christ Jesus. *Amen.*

A PRAYER FOR INSENSIBLE SINNERS.

O LORD, the great Almighty God, who quickenest the dead, and callest those things that are not, as if they were! there is nothing impossible with thee: but the things that resist all the skill and power of man, are (with the greatest facility) brought to pass by thine almighty arm. Thou, the living God, canst speak life to souls that are dead in trespasses and sins; and canst make even such as lie in the grave of their habitual corruptions, to hear the voice of the Son of God, and live. It is the great work of thy eternal Spirit, O Lord, to convince the world of sin; and to make inconsiderate careless sinners to know themselves, and be concerned, as they ought, about the welfare of their souls. O that these poor insensible creatures, who have sinned till their consciences are seared and past feeling, may find mercy from the Lord, and may yet come to feel in themselves the irresistible power of thy grace! O that thou wouldst open their eyes, to see their case; and soften their hearts, to bewail their sins; and turn their course, that they may flee from the wrath to come! Blessed Lord, awaken them with thy terrors, before they be overtaken by thy judgments! O break in upon their souls by thy mighty convictions, to bring them into bitterness for their sins; and let thy quick and powerful word pierce their hearts, to make them inquire in earnest, what they must do to be saved.

O that they did but apprehend their case, and know their transgressions! that, instead of continuing unconcerned, (as if nothing were amiss with them,) and indulging themselves in pleasures, (as if they were in the happiest condition,) they were struck down into the deepest heaviness and consternation, refusing to be comforted! O that they might go mourning all the day long, yea, even roar for the disquietness of their hearts! O God of all grace! be thou pleased in mercy to show such seeming severity; to write bitter things against them, and make them confess their former iniquities; make them to feel now the weight of all their sins, that they may not feel it eternally, when past a remedy. Direct and empower thy messengers, O Lord, to speak to the conviction of their minds: enable them to cry aloud, and not spare, and to show thy rebellious creatures their transgressions and their sins. Yea, make thy word in the mouth of thy servants as fire, to inflame and rouse the consciences of such drowsy sinners, that they may come to perceive what a lost condition they are in; and be restless in themselves, till, coming unto Christ, they find rest unto their souls. O thou almighty God! do marvellous things, worthy of thyself, in taking away that which blinds the minds, and hardens the hearts, of such stupid creatures; and bring them out of the worst lethargy and deadness: that they may understand themselves, and seek after God, and follow the things which make for their peace, through our Lord Jesus Christ. *Amen.*

A PRAYER FOR ALL THAT DESIRE OUR PRAYERS.

O LORD God of the spirits of all flesh! thy word requires us to pray for others, as well as for ourselves; and to call upon thee as our common Father in Christ Jesus. And though I am unworthy to address thy heavenly Majesty either for myself or others, yet, in the hope of thy mercy, and under a sense of my duty, I take upon me to become a humble petitioner to thee, my Lord, in behalf of all such as desire to be partakers of my prayers. O that all of them might share in thy rich mercies, according to their several wants and necessities! They are known to thee by name; O let them be known of thee in the number of thy children. Thou knowest what they most need, and chiefly desire: O thou gracious giver of all good, answer them in the desires of their hearts, as far as they desire the things that are right and good. And, where they desire what is unfitting and hurtful, convince them of their error, that they may not persist in it: and, where they see not the things of their peace, or are indifferent towards that which is most for their good, O Lord, show them the saving way, and grant them an unfeigned love for it, and true zeal to follow it. Bless them, gracious Father, with so much of the world's good, as thou knowest to be good for them: but especially remember them with the favour which thou bearest to thy people. Instruct them, Lord, in the knowledge of thy will; and show them what they must do to be saved. And make them faithful to practise according to the light which thou art pleased to give them: yea, incline their hearts to take pleasure in the performance of their duty. Bless them, O God of all grace, with that favour of thine, in which is life, and with all spiritual blessings in heavenly things in Christ Jesus. *Amen.*

A PRAYER FOR A WOMAN IN TRAVAIL.

O ALMIGHTY Lord God, who bringest to the birth, and givest strength to bring forth, show favour, we beseech thee, to thy servant, in the time of her need and distress; and be not far from her, when trouble is nigh to her, and lies sore and heavy upon her: but let her experience thy help, at hand, according to the necessity of her case. O mitigate her pangs, and support her under the pain and pressure that are so grievous to be borne. And grant her, Lord, a timely, safe, and happy deliverance; and let her see the fruit of her womb, with such comfort and joy, as may make her forget her past anguish, and with a truly thankful heart give glory to thee for all the rich mercies vouchsafed unto her. But if, in thine unsearchable wisdom, thou hast ordained otherwise, and hast decreed that the event should not correspond with the desires which we have presumed to express before thee; if thou hast willed that this expected birth should prove an occasion of thine handmaid's death, O hear us, good Lord, (we most earnestly beseech thee), for her precious soul. Let that be safe in thy blessed hands: let it be fitted for its appearance before thy tribunal: and let her experience that best of all deliverances, a deliverance from all sin and misery, into the perfection of holiness, and the fulness of joy; there to live in thy love, and to sing thy praise for evermore. *Amen.*

A PRAYER FOR A SICK CHILD.

O GOD of the spirits of all flesh, the only giver and preserver of life; the smallest, as well as the greatest, are thy work and thy care: though thou art so great, yet thou despisest not any. O dear Lord, let thy thoughts be full of pity and tender mercy to this poor sick child, for whose affliction we are now concerned; and send him that relief and comfort from above, which none of us are able to give. Either lighten the load, or increase the strength to bear it; and deal gently and graciously with him, good Lord, beyond what we are worthy to ask at thy hands, even for thy own goodness and mercy's sake. Spare him, O Father of mercies, and grant him ease and release from his trouble: yea, make haste to deliver him, we beseech thee: and, in submission to thy will, we beg the recovery of his health, and the continuance of his life, that he may do thee service, and bring thee glory, in this present world. But, forasmuch as children are shapen in iniquity, and conceived in sin, and are therefore subject to death; (which reigns even over them that have not sinned after the similitude of Adam's transgression;) if thou art pleased, Lord, to take him away thus early, O let it be in mercy: and prepare him for thyself, that it may be to him the greatest gain to die: that he may not only be delivered from the miseries and dangers of this world, and of that which is to come, but, by the quickest improvement, may be perfected in knowledge and grace; and be made ripe and ready for heaven and eternal glory. Hear us, O merciful God and Father, through the merits and mediation of thy beloved Son, our compassionate Saviour: who, in infinite condescension, embraced and blessed young children; and who ever lives at thy right hand to intercede for young and old; the only prevailing advocate for us all. And to thy mercy in him, O most gracious God, we commend this afflicted child, beseeching thee to deal well by him, and be good and kind to him; and out of the riches of thy grace, provide for him as thou seest best, in life, and death, and for evermore. *Amen.*

A PRAYER FOR THE MELANCHOLY AND DEJECTED.

O MOST good and gracious Lord! thou knowest our frame, and art a God full of compassion, ready at all times to pity and relieve thy servants under all their troubles. Look down, we humbly pray thee, with thy wonted pity, and remember, in tender mercy, our disconsolate friend who is even distracted in suffering thy terrors. Behold, thy wrath lies hard upon him, and all thy waves and billows are gone over him; so that his mind is grievously oppressed, and he is altogether unfitted for the regular and comfortable discharge of his duty. O thou that speakest to the winds and waves, and they obey thee, compose and settle his troubled breast; speak peace to his soul, that it may no longer be so disquieted within him; and give him comfort and repose under a sense of thy pardoning love. Lord, help his unbelief, and increase his faith, that he may not be faithless, but believing. Though he now walks in darkness and has no light, let him trust in the name of the Lord, and stay upon his God. And in the multitude of the thoughts and sorrows that he has in his heart, O let thy comforts come in to refresh his soul. Be thou pleased, Lord, to ease him of the load that lies upon his spirit : and cause the beams of thy heavenly light to scatter all the clouds and darkness in which his mind is involved. O direct to the means most proper for his help : and so bless and prosper them, that they may be efficacious to promote his recovery, and to raise him from this low estate. Incline his ears to wholesome counsels; and fashion his heart to receive due impressions. O gracious Father! pity his frailties and forgive his sins: and heal him, Lord, both in soul and body; and so rebuke his disorder, that his spirits may revive, and his soul return unto its rest. O raise him up, and make him whole; yea, make haste, O Lord, to deliver him; even for thy own mercy's sake in Jesus Christ, our blessed Saviour and Redeemer. *Amen.*

A PRAYER FOR THE TROUBLED SOUL.

O GOD of the spirits of all flesh! thou knowest the grievous torment of a wounded spirit; and hast promised not to break the bruised reed, or quench the smoking flax: have pity, therefore, upon thy disconsolate servant, whose spirit is sore broken and overwhelmed within him: relieve and heal him, O thou gracious God: comfort him with thy peace; and show unto his soul, that thou hast thoughts of love and mercy towards him. O blessed Jesus, who callest to thee the labouring and heavy laden sinners, and promisest them rest for their souls, give some glimpse of thy mercy, some faith in thy promises, to this poor troubled soul, that is so cast down with a sense of his sin, and with a fear of thy wrath. The sacrifices of God are a broken spirit: a broken and a contrite heart, O God, thou wilt not despise. O hide not thy face from thy servant; nor cast him away from thy presence in displeasure; but speak peace to him, and cause thy grace to shine upon him.

O God of consolation, be thou pleased to cheer him up with the hope of pardon and acceptance with thee: give him a comfortable affiance in thee: give him the witness of thy Spirit with his spirit, to persuade him that he is thy child, whom thou lovest though thou chastenest, and whom by thy terrors thou art preparing for thy consolations. O that he may see love in the rod, and take it as the chastisement of a kind father, and not the vengeance of an incensed judge; and that he may find this humiliation working for his everlasting happiness! Let him find that they who mourn are blessed, and shall be comforted; and that all who sow in tears shall reap in joy. O that his sorrow may be the godly sorrow which works repentance, not to be repented of! Let it, we pray thee, have this happy issue, and end in unspeakable and glorious joy. Let him not sorrow as one without hope: let him see that trouble for sin is a preservative from hell; and that thousands who are now in glory, went this very way to heaven, working out their salvation with fear and trembling; and groaning under the burden of sin here, that they might not lie under it for ever. Let him, in the view of thy dealings with others, learn to commit himself to thee: and when he walketh in darkness, and hath no light, let him trust in the name of the Lord, and stay upon his God.

FOR THE LUNATIC.

O Lord, rebuke him not in thine anger, neither chasten him in thy sore displeasure; but return and set him free from the heavy pressure now upon him. Be pleased, O Lord, to deliver him for thy name's sake; and for thy righteousness' sake, bring his soul out of trouble. Thou hast showed him great and sore troubles: be thou pleased to revive him again, that he may rejoice in thee. Show him thy mercy, O Lord, and grant him thy salvation: O refresh him early with thy mercy, that he may be glad and rejoice in thee all his days. Let him see that thou considerest his trouble, and knowest his soul in adversity; so shall thy name have the glory, and his soul the comfort of thy seasonable relief; nor shall he ever cease to praise thee for thy sweet abundant mercies to him in thy Son, Jesus Christ. *Amen.*

A PRAYER FOR THE LUNATIC AND DISTRACTED.

O LORD, the only wise God, thou givest understanding, and takest it away as thou pleasest; and thou art holy and righteous in all that thou ever doest. Though the reason and meaning of thy works is in many instances unknown to us, yet thou knowest well what thou hast to do; and we must be dumb, and not open our mouths, assured that it is thy doing. The stroke which thou hast laid upon thy poor creature, would be just, if inflicted upon any of us: and we must acknowledge it as owing to thy mercy alone, that we are not all reduced to similar or greater misery. But, O merciful Father, suffer us to address thee in his behalf, and to implore thy mercy for him in this his pitiable condition. Thou madest him out of nothing; and gavest to him that measure of sense and discretion, which he once enjoyed: thou canst with equal ease renew him in the spirit of his mind, and restore to him the faculties which are now so awfully impaired.

O dispel the clouds in which now his soul is wrapped up; that he may come to himself, and exercise a sound understanding, and seek the things belonging to his peace. Have pity on him, O Lord, we beseech thee, and impute not unto him anything that is now said or done amiss by him; but in mercy pass it by, as if it had not been said or done at all.

O that thou wouldst direct to some means for his recovery; and make him tractable in the use of remedies, and willing to comply with the advice of his friends, till he shall be in a capacity to think and act for himself. And where no means will effect a cure, do thou (who never art at a loss, but knowest how to deliver out of the most desperate condition) reveal thine arm, and bring salvation from above. Do a work that shall be worthy of thy glorious Majesty; and command

FOR THE LIGHT-HEADED. 325

such a deliverance as nothing but the knowledge of thine infinite power and unbounded mercy could warrant us to hope for. Interpose for us, O Lord our God, in this great extremity; and we will for ever glorify thy name for this, and all other thy mercies to us in Jesus Christ. *Amen.*

A PRAYER FOR ONE THAT IS STUPIFIED
OR LIGHT-HEADED.

O THOU great Maker and Preserver of men, who knowest how soon our senses may fail us, and our understanding depart from us: and to what accidents, distempers, and decays our weak nature is liable, even such as may make the most acute and judicious to become as a child or idiot, and turn all our wisdom and ingenuity into folly or frenzy; we are every one of us in thy hands, O Lord, to be used as thou wilt; to have our speech and sense, yea, our very breath and life, taken away, when thou pleasest. Thou art righteous in all that comes upon us; and who shall say unto thee, What doest thou? Yet, even in chastening and correcting, thou dost not forget thy mercy and compassion; but biddest us to call upon thee in our troubles; and art still attentive to the prayers of thy servants: yea, waitest to be gracious, and wilt not let them seek thy face in vain. Hear us, O Father of mercies, we beseech thee: and let thy mercy now be showed to thy poor weak distempered servant, according to the exigence of his case, in this time of his need. Thou, O God, who hast created men's faculties, canst as easily restore them, and give light and understanding to the simple; and supply and rectify everything that is defective and amiss. O that thou wouldst be pleased graciously and powerfully to interpose in the present case! Repair the breaches made upon thy servant; and give him sense and apprehension sufficient to discern the state of his soul, and to see the things belonging to his peace.

Thou, Lord Almighty, (who didst command the light to shine out of darkness, and often bringest order and beauty even out of confusion and deformity;) thou canst lighten the darkest mind, and regulate the wildest imagination; yea, thou canst speak immediately to the heart, and canst convey all suitable relief, where all avenues of instruction are shut against us. O God of all power and love, wilt thou speak to the soul of thy servant, so that it may observe thy voice: and seize that precious jewel for thine own, that it may be safe in thy hands. Lord, help and assist him, where we cannot; and accomplish in him the great work of thy grace, which is necessary for his everlasting salvation. O have pity upon his infirmities; and be merciful to his mistakes and failings, his rovings and follies. Give him, gracious God, a broken penitent heart, and a believing, willing mind: and then accept him in thy

beloved Son, according to what he hath: and, of
thy rich grace, give him an entrance into thine
everlasting kingdom, where he may see light in
thy light, and joyfully give thee praise and glory
to all eternity. Be gracious, O good Lord, and
indulgent to him: and do all that thou knowest
to be needful and good for him, through the
merits of thy dear Son, who took part of our flesh
and blood, that he might be touched with the
feeling of our infirmities. And to thy mercy, in
that our merciful and faithful High Priest, we
commit this infirm member of his mystical body;
beseeching thee, O blessed Lord our God, to
show thyself unto him a compassionate and tender
Father, in the same Jesus Christ our only Saviour.
Amen.

A PRAYER FOR A BLIND MAN.

O LORD our God, thou art light, and in thee
is no darkness at all. Thou hast created
the light, and the sun: and givest both the power
of seeing, and objects to be seen. It is a pleasant
thing to behold the light: but of that sweet
benefit thou hast thought fit to deprive thy servant. O blessed be thy name, even when thou
takest away, as well as when thou givest: for
thou art wise, and just, and good in all. Every
thing that happens to us is of thine appointment,
O Lord, who hast made us, and mayst do what
thou wilt with thy own. There is no unright-

eousness with thee: but whatever thou dost, is meet and right to be done. And though thy providential ways are in the great deep, and thy footsteps are often hid from our view, (even as thy visible works are from the sight of thy servant,) yet, Lord, thou art gracious in all that thou bringest upon us; and canst bring the greatest good even out of the worst evil that befalls us. And one glimpse of thee by faith will be infinitely better to thy servants than their eyes, and all the things that ever eyes beheld.

Thy servant here desires, with meekness and patience to submit to thy heavy stroke; and confesses, that thou art just, in quenching that light of his eyes, which he did not use, as he ought, to thy glory.

But wilt thou, O gracious Lord, in judgment remember mercy: and bless to him this deep affliction; that it may promote his repentance and peace with God, and may cut off all those occasions of stumbling and falling, which our bodily sight too often lays before us, and which would be infinitely more injurious than any to which his present darkness may expose him. O that, being freed from the temptations which enter in at the eyes, he may be the better able to attend upon the Lord without distraction; and be more careful in inspecting the state of his soul. Lord, as thou hast showed thy sovereignty and thy justice in taking away his sight, so let thy power and mercy be displayed in ministering comforts to his soul, and supporting him with cheerfulness and contentment under his heavy loss; that so he may be a gainer by it in his spiritual affairs, and in the things that belong to his everlasting bliss. Bring him out of darkness into thy marvellous light: and then, however he may want the light of this world, his soul shall be light in the Lord.

O thou Father of lights, enlighten the eyes of his understanding, that he may see what is the hope of thy calling, and what the riches of the glory of thy inheritance in the saints, and what the mighty power of thy Spirit, which works in them that believe. Now that he cannot behold the things which are visible and temporal, O that he may be more earnest in looking after the things which are unseen and eternal. Enable him to be looking unto Jesus, and studying the mysteries of salvation, the wonders of thy love, and the glories of thy kingdom. O thou giver of all grace! give him the eye of faith, to see him that is invisible, whom no mortal eye hath seen, or can see. Discover thyself to him still more and more, and reveal thy Son in him. And let thy good Spirit, as a Counsellor and Comforter, still abide in him; and bring to his mind all things that shall make for his edification and encouragement in thy holy ways. Have compassion upon him, O Lord, and be gracious and merciful unto him; and do all that thou knowest to be needful and good for him. Lead him, and help him on, continually; till in thy light he shall see light; and his eyes be opened to see the splendour of thy kingdom, and the joy of thy salvation; yea, to see thee as thou art, in that heavenly presence of thine, where is fulness of joy for evermore. *Amen.*

A PRAYER UNDER GRIEVOUS PAINS.

O LORD, thou art a merciful God, and dost not afflict willingly, nor grieve the children of men: but when the necessity of our case requires it, thou chastisest us for our profit, that we may be partakers of thy holiness. Blessed is the man whom thou chastenest, O Lord, and teachest him out of thy law! O let thy servant find that this affliction is sent in mercy to his soul! and now that thy hand is so hard upon him, and that thou hast cast him into so severe a furnace, O that it may be the means of purging out his dross, and of fitting him for thy service. O that he may learn such things in the school of affliction, as may promote thy work within him, and do him good for ever.

But thou, O God of consolation, who knowest our frame, and how litt'e we can endure, even though we deserve so much, be pleased to remember him in mercy; and either lighten his sufferings, or increase his spiritual strength; and, if thou do not see fit entirely to remove his burthen, O enable him to bear what thou art pleased to lay upon him. Lord, all his desire is before thee, and his groaning is not hid from thee: O regard his affliction when thou hearest his cry: and enter not into judgment with him, according to his desert; but according to thy mercy remember thou him, for thy goodness' sake in Christ Jesus. O gracious Father, sanctify to him what thou hast laid upon him: that the present sore evil may have a comfortable issue, and work for his spiritual and eternal good. Lord of all power and might, support and bear him up under it; and bring him safely and happily out of it, to the rejoicing of thy servant, and to the glory of thy name. And however thou shalt deal with him, O good Lord, suppress every murmuring or repining thought that may arise in his mind: and let him never so sin, as to charge God foolishly: make him to see that thou dost nothing but what is most righteous and fit to be done; yea, nothing but what thy servant himself shall see cause to bless thee for at a future period. Teach and help him to glorify thee at the time of his visitation; teach him to honour thee by an humble submission to thy will, a patient abiding of thy rod, and a faithful reformation of his heart and life; that so thou mayst return to him with the visitations of thy love, and show him the joy of thy salvation, for thy own mercy's sake in Christ Jesus. *Amen.*

A PRAYER UNDER LINGERING SICKNESS.

O GOOD God, thou hast long kept thy servant under thy chastening hand; thou hast made him acquainted with grief, and his sickness is become even as his familiar companion. Yet, O blessed Lord, grant that he may not think it long to wait thy leisure, when thou art pleased to wait so long for the return of sinners, and art ever pitiful and of tender mercy; having the kindest intentions even in thy bitterest dispensations. Teach him, O gracious Father, to see love, as well as justice, in all thy dealings: that he may humble himself under thy mighty hand, and confess that it is good for him to be afflicted. Convince him, O Lord, that whom thou lovest thou chastenest, and scourgest every son whom thou receivest: and enable him patiently to wait for thee, in an assured expectation that he shall one day see cause to number his afflictions amongst his richest mercies.

Blessed be thy name, O Father of mercies, that thou dost not pour out all thy wrath, but in judgment rememberest mercy: we bless thee for giving him some ease and relaxation from torturing pains; and for mingling many sweet ingredients with this bitter cup. O make him so sensible of thy kindness and love, that he may be not only contented, but thankful under thy hand.

Yet, that his faith may not fail, nor his patience be wearied out, return, O Lord of love, at the last, and give thy servant a discharge from this warfare; and say to the affliction, It is enough. Make him glad, according to the time wherein thou hast afflicted him, and wherein he has suffered adversity. And till thou hast been pleased to remember him in such mercy, O grant that he may neither despise thy chastening, nor faint under thy rebukes; but take all as he ought: employing the time which thou lendest, and improving the affliction which thou continuest, as a gracious opportunity for his soul's advantage. Under the decays of his outer man, let his inner man be renewed day by day! and let all that is wanting in his spiritual concerns be filled up, and whatever pertains to his everlasting salvation be promoted and perfected through the riches of thy grace, and the multitude of thy mercies in Jesus Christ. *Amen.*

A PRAYER UNDER DANGEROUS SICKNESS.

O LORD God, almighty and ever blessed, in whom we ever live, and move, and are! we acknowledge it to be of thy mercies that we are not consumed, even because thy compassions fail not. If thou hadst long since cut us off in our sins, and shut us up under final despair of mercy, yet righteous hadst thou been, O Lord, and just, and good. Yea, justly mightst thou at this time cast out our prayers, and refuse to hear thy rebellious creatures, who have so long turned a deaf ear to thee. But thou art God, and not man; and thy thoughts are not as our thoughts, nor thy ways as our ways; but as the heavens are higher than the earth, so are thy thoughts and ways above ours. Thou art our refuge and strength, and present help in every time of need: and thou hast commanded us to call upon thee in our troubles; and hast promised to hear us, and to give us cause to praise and glorify thee for thy goodness and mercy to us.

And now we come to thee, O Lord our God, in behalf of this thy servant, that lies here in a low and distressed state under thy chastising hand. Look down, we beseech thee, mercifully upon him: and be gracious and favourable to him, according to the necessity of his case, and according to the multitude of thy tender mercies in Christ Jesus. Great as his danger is, if thou wilt, O Lord, thou canst set him up, and make him whole; if thou but speak the word, it shall be done. In submission to thy most wise and righteous disposal of all things, we would beg this mercy at thy hands; that thou wouldst be pleased to rebuke his distemper, to remove thy stroke, and cause the bitter cup which thou hast given to pass away from him. To this end do thou direct us to the means proper for his help; and command a blessing upon them. Spare him, good Lord, and restore him, (if it be thy will,) that he may have a longer time to work out his salvation, and be more useful in his place, and do more good in his generation. Or, however thou shalt be pleased to deal with him as to the concerns of his body, (which we pray may be in a way of gentleness and tender mercy,) yet, Lord, let his soul be ever precious in thy sight. And may this sickness of his body be for the health of his better and immortal part, and be instrumental to advance his everlasting salvation.

O give him a right discerning of the things belonging to his peace, before they be hid from his eyes. Show him what he has to do, and enable him for the doing of it, that he may have peace with God, through Christ Jesus. Give him repentance towards God, and faith in the only Saviour of the world. Wash and cleanse his soul with the blood of thy Son, and the graces of thy Spirit: that it may be delivered from all the defilements which it has contracted in this present evil world; and be found safe and happy in the hour of death, and in the great day of our Lord Jesus Christ. Fit him, O Lord, for living or dying, or whatever, in thy wise and righteous providence, thou hast designed for him; that it may be unto him, Christ to live, and gain to die: and that in all things he may find cause to glorify thy name. If thou shalt be pleased to release him from his bed of languishing, and to add to him a yet further term of life, O that he may live to thee, and to do thee better service, and bring thee greater glory! Or, if thou hast determined that this sickness shall be unto death, prepare him, O merciful God, by thy grace, for thy blessed self: and grant him a safe and comfortable passage out of this wretched life to an infinitely better; through the merits and mediation of thy beloved Son, our only Saviour, Jesus Christ. *Amen.*

A PRAYER FOR A DYING MAN PAST HOPE OF RECOVERY.

O THE hope of Israel, the Saviour thereof in time of trouble! when all other hope and help fails, it is not in vain to seek unto thee for succour, who canst bring back from the mouth of the grave, and quicken the very dead: and where thou art not pleased any further to prolong the temporal life, yet canst deliver from eternal death, and bring safe to blessedness and glory. We think it too late to beg the recovery of thy servant, O Lord, now that he seems to us going the way of all flesh, and just launching forth into his everlasting condition. But though the time of his departure appears to be at hand, yet we cannot think it too late to beg thy mercy for him, as long as his life is in him. And as we cannot but be greatly concerned for him, so we know not how better to express this our concern for him, than in beseeching thee to be good and gracious unto him.

O Lord our God, leave him not, nor forsake him: but support and assist him now in his sorest extremities, in his last agonies, when he is to conflict with the king of terrors: let him find the most sweet and seasonable aids from thee, the God of his salvation: and take him not out of this life, till thou hast fitted him for a better. O thou ever-living God, stand by him in the dying hour; and secure him in thy hands from the enemies of his soul: and finish all that is wanting of the work of thy grace upon his heart. Freely and fully pardon, and deliver him from all his sins: and fit him to appear with comfort and rejoicing in thy blessed presence. O make his departure easy, and full of peace and hope. Carry him safe through the valley of the shadow of death, and let him find a joyful admission into the everlasting kingdom of his Lord. Into thy hands, O Lord, we commend his spirit: O thou Father of mercies, be merciful to him, and receive his departing soul; and when he is numbered among the dead, let him be also numbered among the redeemed and blessed of the Lord; for his sake, who (himself) died for sinners, and rose again, and lives, and is alive for evermore, and has the keys of death and of hell. To thy mercy, in that blessed Saviour of the world, O most merciful Father, we now humbly recommend him; beseeching thee to be all in all to him, and infinitely better than we are worthy or able to ask for him. And let him be thine in life, and death, and for evermore, through the all-sufficient merits and mediation of thy dear Son, our most prevailing Advocate and Redeemer, Jesus Christ. *Amen.*

THANKSGIVINGS FOR TEMPORAL BLESSINGS.

GRACIOUS God, the bountiful Provider of all good things! the eyes of all wait upon thee; and thou givest them their meat in due season. Thou openest thy hand, and satisfiest the desire of every living thing. Every year thou renewest the face of the earth; and givest rain from heaven, and fruitful seasons, filling our hearts with food and gladness. O how many of thy creatures have bestowed their labours, and lost their lives, and been consumed, to clothe and sustain and gratify us! At what vast expense art thou continually, to maintain the whole world of creatures, that everywhere hang upon thee for life and breath and all things! yet thou art not weary of doing us good; but still showerest down blessings plentifully upon us, to provide, not only necessaries, (to keep us alive,) but also a variety of comforts, to make our lives happy and desirable. Yea, thou delightest in mercy, and hast pleasure in the prosperity of thy servants; and makest us now to find, by our own happy experience, how abundantly good and kind thou art.

FOR RAIN.

O LORD, thou hast sent a gracious rain upon thine inheritance, to refresh the dry and thirsty land, that it might bring forth fruit, and yield to us the desired increase. O that men would praise thee for thy goodness, and for such thy wonderful works to the children of men! O bounteous and ever-blessed God, to thy name be all the glory, now and for evermore.

FOR FAIR WEATHER.

LORD, thou hast in mercy shut the windows of heaven, and put a stop to the overflowing showers, that threatened to destroy the fruits of the earth: and hast caused this sweet and comfortable change, to refresh thy unworthy servants, and to make all the creatures rejoice in thy goodness. Blessed be our God, that deals so graciously with us: and glory be to thy name, thou merciful deliverer from all evil and giver of all good. Let the people praise thee, O God; let all the people praise thee. Then shall the earth yield her increase: and God, even our own God, shall give us his blessing

FOR THE CESSATION OF INFECTION.

O THOU great Preserver of men! thou hast delivered our souls from the hand of the grave; and kept us alive, that we should not go down to the pit. The jaws of death were open upon us, and we went with our lives in our hands; our hearts failing us for fear of the destruction that raged amongst us, when the very air, which we drew in to give us life, was to so many the sad messenger of death. Yet when thousands fell on every side of us, we have dwelt in the secret place of the Most High, and (under the shadow of the Almighty) have been kept in safety. O what shall we say, and what shall we give unto thee, who art our present help, and only Saviour in times of trouble! we are every way thine, O Lord; and to thee only be all the glory. We bless thee, our God, as those that are made alive from the dead. And O that the lives which have been given us at our request, may be devoted wholly unto thee, and be spent in thy service; O that we may love, and serve, and praise our God, while we have our being.

FOR THE RESTORATION OF PLENTY

O GOD, the fountain of all goodness! thou didst threaten to destroy the fruits of the earth, which we have so wickedly abused: but, for thine own mercy's sake, thou hast raised at last for us a new and plentiful supply, and hast crowned the year with thy goodness. O make us more sensible of the obligation which thy love has laid upon us. And as thou fillest us with thy good things, so fill our hearts with thy grace,

that we may use every gift aright to thy glory:
and that in the use and strength of what we are
continually receiving from thee, we may devote
ourselves altogether unto thee; and serve thee
with gladness and joyfulness of heart for the
abundance thou hast given us, and for all thy
rich mercies to us in Jesus Christ.

FOR VICTORY OVER OUR ENEMIES.

O ALMIGHTY Lord, the most high God, who rulest in the kingdoms of men, and dost whatsoever thou pleasest in heaven and in earth! In thy hand is power and might, so that none is able to withstand thee. It is thou that givest salvation unto kings, that deliverest thy servants from the sword. Thou hast saved us from our enemies, and put them to shame that hated us. It was not by our own power or conduct, that we have been so prosperous; nor did our own sword or arm save us; but thy right hand, and thine arm, and the light of thy countenance, because thou hadst a favour unto us Thine, O Lord, is the greatness, and the power and the glory, and the victory. The Lord is our strength and our song, and is become our salvation. Now, therefore, our God, we thank thee, and praise thy glorious name. And O what cause of thankfulness have we, that we were not delivered into the hand of our enemies, and given over for a prey unto their teeth! Great indeed has been thy mercy to us, O blessed Lord: and to thee alone be the whole praise and glory. O make us more sensible of thy goodness to us in this time of our need: and give us grace still to keep the memory of it in our minds, and abundantly to utter it in songs of praise. O thou Lord of hosts, who hast given us such safety and good success teach us, we pray thee, rightly to improve these undeserved mercies; that being delivered from the hands of our enemies, we may serve thee, in holiness and righteousness before thee, all the days of our life. Suffer us not to act as if we were delivered to commit abominations; but, demeaning ourselves as the redeemed of the Lord, O let us love, and trust, and bless, and praise thee, the only giver of all victory, for ever and ever.

FOR PEACE.

O GOD of peace, that makest wars to cease to the ends of the earth; that breakest the bow, and cuttest the spear asunder, and burnest the chariot in the fire! thou hast in mercy put a stop to the effusion of blood, and made peace in our borders: thou hast rebuked the nations; and caused them to beat their swords into ploughshares, and their spears into pruning-hooks; that every man might sit under his own vine and figtree, none making him afraid. O how sweet is thy mercy, and reviving, even as life from the dead! And thou, Lord, who hast given us peace, O give us also grace, to use it to thy glory, and to walk the more freely and cheerfully in thy holy ways. And let us not only have peace with men, but also with thee, our God: even that peace which passeth all understanding, which shall keep our hearts and minds through Christ Jesus.

O that we may be sensible of the kindness and love of God our Saviour, and ever give thee thanks with all our souls! Dear Father of mercies! rather take all our good things from us, than leave us in a state of base ingratitude and stupid indifference. O let our hearts be enlarged in thy love, and be lifted up in the celebration of thy praises! and may all thy works and all thy servants bless thee, and praise thee for ever! And may we have grace to express the thankfulness of our hearts, in the whole conduct of our lives; devoting ourselves to thee in faithfulness, as long as we have any being. *Amen,* and *Amen.*

PRAYER AND PRAISE FOR A PUBLIC THANKSGIVING DAY.

BLESSED Lord, the only living and true God, the Creator and Preserver of all things! We live by thee; and our whole dependance is upon thee, for all the good that we either have or hope for. We now desire to bless thy name for those mercies, which in so large a measure thou hast been pleased to vouchsafe unto us. We desire to pay unto thee that tribute o. homage and service, of prayer and praise, which thou hast made us capable of, and so many ways obliged us to: and we would perform the same in such a manner, that thou mayst mercifully accept both our persons and our services, at the hands of Jesus Christ.

Worthy art thou, O Lord our God, to receive all honour and glory, all thanks and praise, and love and obedience, as in the courts of heaven, so in all the assemblies of thy servants upon earth: for thou art great, and dost wondrous things; thou art God alone. Thou hast been favourable to thy land, and dealt exceedingly graciously with us. Thou hast not suffered all the evils that threatened us, to come upon us; nor those which have come upon us, utterly to destroy us. Instead of giving us over to all the calamities that we feared, thou hast multiplied thy mercies towards us, for which we are now called to solemnize a day of thanksgiving. Of a truth, O Lord, thy compassions fail not; and thy mercy endureth for ever. Thou art gracious and merciful, slow to anger, and of great kindness.

O how much have we to say of the goodness of the Lord by our own experience; and of the succour thou hast afforded us in every time of need! How sweet and wonderful is it to recount all the instances of thy patience with us, and thy

FOR A THANKSGIVING DAY.

bounty to us! How from time to time thou hast signalized us with thy mercy, and enriched us with thy favours! Thou hast cast our lot in a land of light: where we live under the influences of thy gospel, and are called to obtain the glory of our Lord Jesus Christ. Thou hast bestowed on us and our land so many advantages, that thou hast made us the envy of surrounding nations, and distinguished us in a peculiar manner as the objects of thy favour. Though many times we have provoked thee to stretch forth thy hand, and shake thy rod over us, yet in judgment, thou hast still remembered mercy; and after the clouds and darkness that have gathered about us, and the distress and terror that were on every side, thou hast caused the heavens again to clear up, and smile upon us; and returned with the visitations of thy love, and the joy of thy salvation.

In the late dangers, thou hast been to us a tower of defence; and in the time of our need and perplexity, thou hast shown thyself graciously and powerfully on our side. Thou hast helped us for the glory of thy name, and redeemed us for thy mercy's sake; not because we were worthy, but because thou hadst a favour unto us: and therefore to thy name alone be all the praise. O what shall we render to the Lord for all his benefits! O let not our hearts be straitened towards thee, whose hand has been so open and bounteous unto us. But do thou enlarge these hearts of ours, and fill them with more love and thankfulness to the gracious giver of all our good things. And make us more sensible of thy goodness and love bestowed upon us: that we may give thee thanks from the ground of the heart: and have our mouths filled as with marrow and fatness, while we praise thee with joyful lips.

O make us a truly thankful, as we are a highly indebted, people. And let us not only speak of thy loving-kindness, O Lord, but glorify thy name in bearing much fruit: fruit answerable to the mercy and encouragement which we have received at thy hands. We can never enough admire and magnify the riches of thy grace, and the multitude of thy mercies: but, O good Lord, enable us still more to love thee, and better to serve thee; and in so doing for us, thou wilt still further oblige us: because in loving and serving thee, we most effectually serve our own best interests. As our minds cannot but muse, and our tongues speak of thy works, so let our lives be spent in thy service: that thou, the great and blessed God, mayst in all things be glorified by us, through Jesus Christ. *Amen.*

THANKSGIVING AFTER A SAFE AND GOOD JOURNEY.

ALL thanks and praise that I am able to render, is a debt that I owe unto thee, O Lord, my God: and I desire with all my soul to pay it, for that goodness of thine, which I have experienced throughout my journey. Thou hast not only been nigh to me, and watchful to secure me from the perils of the way, and the many evil accidents that might have befallen me, but hast surrounded me with blessings and comforts on every side. At every turn and every step, I have been exposed to evils. I might now have been groaning under broken bones, or bruised limbs: yea, I might have been cut off, and have perished in the way; I might have lost not only health and strength, but life itself: but thou, Lord, hast in mercy preserved and kept me in safety; and brought me to see my habitation in peace, and to find all things according to my heart's desire.

A horse is a vain thing for safety; and nothing upon earth can we confide in, to defend us: if thou, O blessed Keeper of Israel, dost not cover us under the shadow of thy wings, and give thine angels charge over us, to keep us in all our ways, no other power whatever can preserve us. But such invisible guards have I had; and such favour have I found from thee, O Lord. Thy mercy and thy goodness which have followed me all the days of my life, have been renewed afresh, and further manifested to me, in these my travels. And, O how inexhaustible is the kindness and bounty of my Lord, who is never weary of doing me good! To thee, O God of my life, and safety, and comfort, to thee be all the glory. O fill me with a most grateful sense of thy continued mercies. And give me a heart abounding with thankfulness, and with thy love and praises: yea, give me also grace to express the unfeigned thanks of my heart, in all the ways that are pleasing to thy holy will, through the beloved of thy soul, my blessed Saviour and Redeemer, Jesus Christ.

THANKSGIVING FOR PRESERVATION

AND DELIVERANCE FROM DANGERS AND TROUBLES.

MANY, O Lord my God, are thy wonderful works which thou hast done, and thy thoughts which are to usward for good; they cannot be reckoned up in order unto thee: if I should declare and speak of them, they are more than can be numbered. According to thy name, so is thy praise, to the ends of the earth. The dead praise thee not, nor any that go down into silence: the living, the living, he shall praise thee, as I desire with all my soul to do this day. My heart is fixed, O God, my heart is fixed: I will sing and give praise. I will be glad and rejoice in thee, and sing praise to thy name, O thou Most High. I will praise thee, O Lord, for thou hast heard me, and art become my salvation. I found trouble and sorrow: then I called upon thee; and thou wast attentive to my cry, and nigh to my help. And though thou mightst have made me an example of thy judgments to others, as others have been to me, thou didst not consult my deserts, but my distress; doing great things, and working strange deliverance for me, not because I was worthy, but because thou aboundest in mercy.

I was in woful perplexity: fear was on every side, all my hope was ready to expire, and I thought there was no help for me; but that I must sink and perish. Then didst thou, O Lord, interpose between me and the threatening mischief; and didst reveal thy glorious arm, to pluck me out of the jaws of destruction: and didst set me at liberty from my fears, and in safety from my dangers. Thou hast kept me alive, and restored my comforts; not taking me away in the midst of my days, nor cutting me off untimely from the land of the living; but sparing me in mercy, and giving me, as it were, a new life from the dead. Thou hast chastened me, but not given me over unto death. When my foot slipped, thy mercy, O Lord, held me up. Thou art the God that dost wonders; wonders of power, and wonders of mercy. Yea, thy kindness and thy help at hand, in the time of my need, has been greater than I am able to express.

Thou, Lord, hast made me glad through thy work: I will triumph in the works of thy hands. I will sing of thy power; yea, I will sing aloud of thy mercy. For thou hast been my support and my refuge in the day of my trouble. Unto thee, O my strength, I will sing; for thou art my defence, and the God of my mercy. O Lord God, merciful and gracious; I will extol thee, who hast not suffered the trouble and danger to overwhelm and ruin me. In my distress I cried unto thee, and thou hast enlarged me. O blessed be my God, who hast not cast out my prayer, nor taken his mercy from me. But, dearest Lord! I cannot, without amazement, look back upon the perilous state that I was in, and the brink of ruin to which I was brought. And that I should escape, as I have done, O how marvellous is it in my eyes! What cause have I for thy praise, that I am here alive to praise thee! O my God, it is thy good hand that hath wrought so wonderfully for me, and thy fatherly kindness that has shown such extraordinary favour to me. O! if I had been snatched away unprepared, how dreadful a change should I have found! But in mercy and love to my soul (I give thee glory), thou hast made a way for my escape: and I am preserved a living monument of thy unspeakable goodness.

O what shall I say unto thee, whose name is exalted far above all blessing and praise! and what shall I render unto thee, to whom my goodness will not extend! I can never answer the obligations which thy love, dear Lord, has laid upon me: but let me admire and love, and bless and praise thee, with all the faculties and powers which thou hast given me. And O that thou wouldst imprint so deeply on my heart a sense of thy mercy, that I may never forget, never slight, never abuse the great goodness that thou hast shown me, and the signal deliverance which thou hast wrought for me; but may ever give thee thanks with all my heart; and walk, as becomes me, all the days of my lfe; not secure and careless, because I have so escaped; but the more watchful and diligent, in proportion to the mercies vouchsafed unto me: approving my thankfulness in such a manner, as that thou mayst graciously accept me through my blessed Lord and Saviour Jesus Christ.

A THANKSGIVING AFTER A SAFE DELIVERY.

BLESSED for ever be thy name, O Lord, our gracious God, who rememberest us in our low estate, and dost not abhor the affliction of the afflicted; but hearest thy servants crying to thee in their distress, and sendest relief and help in time of need! O that we may praise thee, Lord, as we ought, for such thy goodness and wonderful works to the children of men! Thou bringest down and raisest up; thou givest trouble and sendest help from trouble; thou afflictest us with fears and griefs, and again revivest us with hopes and joys. Thou, O God, art good in all, and worthy to be admired and praised in every dispensation of thy providence. But chiefly we are affected with thy seasonable aids in time of trial; when thou givest us beauty for ashes, the oil of joy for mourning, and the garments of praise for the spirit of heaviness. Thou hast now (for ever blessed be thy name!) refreshed thine afflicted handmaid, and rejoiced the souls of thy servants. We desire therefore to offer unto thee, O gracious Lord, our devoutest acknowledgments, and present unto thee the sacrifice of our unfeigned thanks and praise. O that thine handmaid, and all of us, may be duly sensible of this favour, which has been to us as life from the dead. May thy great goodness lead us to repentance: and may this fresh instance of thy love constrain us to love thee with all our hearts, and to render to thee the services of our lives, and to give thee all possible glory, both now and evermore. *Amen.*

THANKSGIVING AND PRAYER
AFTER RECOVERY OUT OF A DANGEROUS SICKNESS.

O GOD of my life, in whose hand my breath is, and by whom all men do live, and have their days prolonged or shortened, I was brought low, and ready to think that thou wouldst now cut me off, and make an end of my days upon earth: I counted myself so nigh unto death, that I expected every day, when that last enemy which lay in wait for me, would come and seize upon me. But thou, Lord, hast graciously disappointed my fears, and rescued me from his

AFTER RECOVERY FROM SICKNESS.

hands, and raised me up to walk again before thee in the land of the living. Though thou broughtest me even to the mouth of the grave, yet hast thou brought me back; that the pit of corruption should not swallow me up. And thou that gavest me life at first, hast now given it to me afresh. To thee therefore, O my God, I desire with all my soul to give thee praise. O blessed be my great Preserver, the dear and only Saviour of my body as well as soul, the God of my health, my heavenly Physician, my life, and the length of my days! O that I may live to declare the works of the Lord, and set forth the honour of his name! Let me never look upon my extended life as an occasion to the flesh, to enjoy my liberty and pleasure upon earth; but as an engagement on my heart, to abound in gratitude, and love, and praise, and all faithful duty, and cheerful obedience to my gracious God.

In mercy to my soul, O Lord, thou hast prolonged my life, and given me space to repent; that by correcting what was amiss, and filling up what was wanting, in my spiritual estate, I might be more ready for the arrival of the bridegroom, more ready to give up my account to thee. O that my life being now renewed, I may henceforth live as one restored from the dead; and retain such an abiding sense of eternity upon my mind, as may keep me unwearied in my preparations for it.

It is only a reprieve that is now granted to me:

my death is a debt to nature which I must pay, I cannot avoid it: death will yet certainly take hold of me; and I know not how soon: the grave is my house, where, after all, I must make my habitation, and go to rottenness and dust: yea, when I least think of it, how suddenly may I be cut off!

O then let me not live as if I should never see death; nor put it far from me, as if it should never arrive; nor reckon upon any sure standing, or long abiding, in such a changeable transitory world, that is but the house of our pilgrimage, and not the place of our rest. But, since dust I am, and to dust I must return, O help me, Lord, so to remember and consider my death, that I may be the better for it in all the course and conduct of my life! Enable me to walk with such wise and holy circumspection, and so to order all my conversation in the world, that when I close my eyes upon this present scene of things I may depart hence full of peace, and hope, and joy. And for my recovery, and such health as I enjoy at present, O let me pay my vows to the Lord; and from the ground of my heart, ascribe to thee, the God of my salvation, all glory, thanks, and love and service throughout the whole remainder of my life, and for evermore. *Amen.*

A PRAYER AND PRAISE FOR A CONVERTED SINNER.

I WILL praise thee, O Lord my God, with all my heart: and I will glorify thy name for evermore. So great is thy mercy towards me, that thou hast delivered my soul from the lowest hell. My lips therefore shall greatly rejoice, when I sing unto thee; and my soul, which thou hast redeemed, shall make her boast in the Lord. For I was in darkness, but now am light in the Lord; I was dead, and am alive again; I was lost, and am found. When no eye pitied me, and when I had not a heart to pity myself, then didst thou, O most merciful and ever-blessed God, look upon me in my blood, and bid me live. O sinful wretch! that I should be taken, and others left! I stand amazed at thy kindness, O God my Saviour! The great things, which thou hast done for my soul, are incomparably more in my estimation than if thou hadst set me up with the princes of the earth, and blessed me with all the fulness and glory of the world. For how soon do all these things pass away and perish! but the word of God, by which I am born again, lives and abides for ever. The grace of God, which brings salvation to my soul, is in me a well of water springing up to everlasting life. O God of all grace, who had such thoughts of mercy towards me even when I was in enmity against thee, and did nothing but forget and provoke thee, thou wilt not despise the day of small things: thou wilt not be extreme to mark what is done amiss, or cast me off for the failings of my services, now that thou hast wrought in me some good thing towards thee, and brought my soul from the gates of hell, within prospect of thy heavenly glory.

O what great and sore troubles hast thou showed me! yet didst thou turn again and refresh me, and comfort me on every side, with the most reviving and richest of all mercy. I must for ever have perished, if thou, Lord, hadst not brought me from my state of death in trespasses and sins to newness of life: and better had it been that I had never been born, if I had not been born again. O blessed change! and mighty work, worthy of God! O the riches of grace, and the wonders of divine power and love! What shall I render to the Lord for these greatest of all benefits, which I am not able so much as worthily to express; I can never enough admire and bless thee, O my God, for thy love to my soul, which thou hast brought to see the joy of thy salvation. How hast thou borne with me in all my dulness and perverseness; and what exertions hast thou been forced to use, in order to overcome my reluctance, and make me willing to be saved! But thou wouldst not suffer me to undo myself; thou gavest me checks in the way of my sins; till thou hadst overcome my heart by thine almighty grace, and brought me home to thy blessed self.

Bless the Lord, O my soul: and all that is within me, bless his holy name. My God and Saviour! I was helpless and hopeless; yet at the lowest, thou hast remembered me; and at the worst, thou hast holpen and comforted me. The fear of hell was upon me; and thou hast raised me above it, and made me to rejoice in hope of thy glory. I thank thee, O Father, Lord of heaven and earth, that thou hast hid these things from the wise and prudent, and hast revealed them unto babes. O who am I, unworthy wretch, that I should be made so happily to differ from others, and from my former self! O what have I done, that I should be thus distinguished with thy saving mercy, when so great a part of the world is still in darkness, and in the shadow of death! I am unworthy, O Lord; I am utterly unworthy: but thou art the God infinitely good, and abundant in mercy.

O blessed God of my salvation! accept the oblation of myself, and of all my services, together with my thanks and praise, for this thy love to me in Christ Jesus. O what abundant cause hast thou given me to love and serve thee! Grant, I pray thee, that my life may henceforth be entirely devoted to thee; and that, as I have received such mercy at thy hands, I may be ever active and unwearied in showing forth thy praise. Let me bless thee, O Lord, at all times; and have thy praise continually in my mouth, as long as I have any being. Accept, O gracious Father, and continue me for thine own: and make me still fitter for thy blessed and everlasting acceptance in Jesus Christ my Saviour. *Amen.*

THANKSGIVING FOR RECOVERY AFTER A FALL INTO SIN.

I BLESS thy name, O Lord my God, infinitely good, that thou hast kept me alive to this day; and after all my ill carriage towards thee, my presumptuous boldness with thee, and manifold rebellions against thee, thou hast not given me over as a prey to the deadly enemy of my soul, that seeks to devour me : but dost yet give me room to hope, that it is not in vain to seek thy face, and to wait for mercy at thy hands. O my God! how wonderful is thy patience, that thou hast not left me to perish in my sins! It is through thy grace that I have begun to consider my danger, and to inquire after a way to escape. Yes, Lord, thou hast spared me thus in all my sins, tna., by the long-suffering which thou hast exercised towards me, thou mightst show forth all the wonders of thy grace.

O Father of mercies ! hast thou yet a blessing for such a rebellious wretch ! and may I yet presume to look for thy blessed favour, after I have done thee such infinite wrong? O the inconceivable depths of goodness that are in thy gracious nature, in that thou dealest with me as a dear friend, notwithstanding I have behaved myself towards thee as the vilest enemy; and that thou givest me hopes of heaven, when I deserve nothing but the torments of hell! And hast thou, Lord, kept me to this day, and brought me thus far, to be avenged on me, and to destroy me at last? O my gracious Father, the God of all my mercies! I cannot think that thou delightest in my death. I have wronged thee too much with all my sins already; let me not increase the heavy score, by distrusting such tried mercy, or doubting its continuance. Lord, I believe, help thou my unbelief: I know that thou art not willing I should perish; but that by repentance I should come to salvation. And O what a gracious God have I, to deal so bountifully with me! and what a stony heart, to be no more affected with such stupendous mercy! O what a life of sins, and what a life of mercies, has mine been! With amazement I reflect on both; to think how vile I have been towards thee, my Lord; and yet how good thou hast been to my soul. O that these wonders of love may constrain me to cast down the weapons of my rebellion, and bring me nearer to my God, and make me more to abound in thy love, and more to delight in thy service, than ever I have yet done! O that I may no more offend so gracious a God: but being warned by these escapes, and won by these mercies, let me be more watchful and faithful in keeping myself from my iniquity, and in striving continually to please thee in all things, through Jesus Christ. *Amen.*

THANKSGIVING FOR SPIRITUAL VICTORY.

O ALMIGHTY and most merciful Father, who givest strength and power to thy people, and, with their temptations, makest them a way to escape, it is by thy grace that I am what I am : and thy grace bestowed on me has not been in vain. Thou hast helped me in time of need, to withstand and overcome the temptation wherewith I was assaulted. My own strength, Lord, thou knowest, is but weakness; and my heart is not to be trusted. But thy hand held me up : and by the help of my God, I have preserved my integrity; and so resisted the devil, as to make him flee from me. I find, O Lord, by sweet and joyful experience, that thy ways are ways of pleasantness and peace; and that in observing thy laws there is great reward. O how much are the heavenly raptures of victory to be preferred before the filthy pleasures of sin ! I now see, that shame and sorrow are the cursed consequences of yielding to the tempter; but glorying, and confidence, and the peace of God, and joy in the Holy Ghost, are the portion of those that overcome.

I will greatly rejoice in the Lord; my soul shall be joyful in my God; who has lifted me up, and not suffered my foes to triumph over me. They have thrust sore at me, that I might fall; but the Lord was my help. The Lord is my strength and my song, and is become my salvation. The voice of rejoicing and salvation is in the dwellings of the righteous. The right hand of the Lord doth valiantly, and brings mighty things to pass. I shall not die, but live, and declare the works of the Lord, and tell what he has done for my soul. Blessed be God, who has not turned away my prayer, nor his mercy from me. O Lord my God! thou hast been watchful over me for good; thou wast nigh to me; and hast showed thy fatherly care of me; and, in love to my soul, hast preserved me, because thou hadst a favour unto me. I am thine; and I will be thine; and will love thee, and bless thy name, and give thee thanks for ever. *Amen.*

A FAMILY PRAYER IN THE ORDER OF OUR LORD'S PRAYER.

O GOD, the Father of our Lord Jesus Christ, by eternal generation, the Father of all things by temporal creation; and the Father of thy people, by adoption and spiritual regeneration! What manner of love is this, that we who have been rebels against heaven, slaves of Satan, and children of wrath, should be made the children of the Most High, and heirs of everlasting glory! We are thine, O Lord, for thou hast made us out of nothing; yea, thou hast created us anew, after that we had destroyed ourselves: thou hast looked upon us in our blood and hast bid us live. Thou art in heaven. O that we may, in heart and mind, thither ascend; and, with all lowliness, worship at the footstool of thy glorious Majesty! Thou art our Father: O that we may with confidence and delight draw nigh unto thee as dear children! And may we also love as brethren, and be united to each other as children of the same heavenly Father!

And, O that all the world may give thee the glory due to thy great name; that thou mayst be more known, and feared, and loved, and honoured by us, and by all men, as our supreme Lord, and as our chief good; and that we may glorify thee as we ought, in our thoughts and desires, and in our words and ways!

O that the kingdom of sin and Satan may be still more and more weakened, till they be utterly destroyed! that all the powers on earth may use for thee the authority which they have received from thee! that all the kingdoms of the world may become the kingdoms of our Lord, and of his Christ, and Jerusalem be made the joy and praise of the whole earth! O that Christ may dwell and rule in our hearts by his Spirit and grace; and make us a willing people, the faithful subjects of his holy kingdom; and still reign over us here, till we are made fit to reign with him in glory for evermore! O thou blessed and only Potentate¹ let thy kingdom come so powerfully into us, that thy will may be done by us faithfully and without reserve.

And may thy will and word, O Lord, and the way of salvation, be everywhere known upon earth. Let the light of thy gospel shine and prevail, and win more proselytes daily throughout the world. O send the means of grace, where they are not; and make them prosperous and successful where they are. Let not the will of the flesh, nor the ways of the world govern us; but let the word and will of our God be the rule of our lives, to guide and sway us in all our conduct. Make us more conformable to thy will, in all that thou requirest of us; and more submissive to thy will, in all that thou layest upon us. Yea, make us pleased with whatever is thy pleasure; that loving thy word, and delighting to do thy will, we may joyfully and cheerfully serve thee as thy glorious angels and saints above, whose heaven it is to please and enjoy the Lord.

And, till we are fitted for the life to come, give us, O Father, (of thy gracious bounty,) all things needful and convenient for us. Preserve us from all the snares and dangers that attend both the prosperous and the afflicted state. When we have this world's good, O that we may use it wisely and piously, to thy glory : and, whenever thou takest it from us, make us contented, and patient, and thankful; and the more intent upon that good, which shall never be taken away. O thou all-wise and merciful God! we beg, that we may ever be in that state of body which thou knowest to be best for our souls. and that all which we have in this life may help to fit us for the life to come.

We are ashamed and grieved, that we have so much and so long dishonoured thy blessed name, disobeyed thy holy word, and abused thy rich mercy. We desire to return, and to be reconciled to our God; to be humbled and penitent for our sins, and to intreat thy gracious favour, in Christ Jesus, for the pardon of them. Forgive us, we beseech thee, O Father of mercies, for his sake, all the sins that ever we have committed against thee; especially we beg to be discharged from those wasting and presumptuous sins, which we have at any time committed against the strivings of thy Spirit, and the checks of our own consciences; and which have filled our souls with the dread of thy wrath. O give us tokens for good, to persuade and assure our hearts, that thou hast mercy in store for us. And incline our hearts, O Lord, to forgive as we need to be forgiven, and to be merciful as we desire to obtain mercy.

And, that iniquities may not prevail against us

to spoil us for the future, subdue them, O God of all grace, by the power of thy Holy Spirit: and never suffer us to be tempted above the strength wherewith thy grace shall supply us. Make us careful to avoid all the temptations we can, and strong in the Lord to overcome what we must encounter. We are poor frail creatures: but thou art the Lord Almighty. O do thou protect us (we beseech thee) by thy powerful aids: and so keep us from falling, that we may never be made a prey to the cruel murderer of souls; nor be delivered into those bitter pains of eternal death, which are the sad wages of our sins: but may we find a way to escape every snare, and be preserved safe to thy heavenly kingdom.

Thine is the kingdom, O Lord most high! thou art the King of all the world: and happy are they who are under the conduct of thy good Spirit, as the willing subjects of thy spiritual kingdom. We desire and beg that we may all be found of that number. Save, Lord, and let the King of heaven hear us when we call.

We ask great things at thy hands, but not too great for the Almighty God to grant: for thine is the power; and thou art able to do for us exceeding abundantly, even above all that we can ask or think. O reveal thy glorious arm, to do things worthy of God, which none but thy blessed self can do; in forgiving, and healing, and helping us, who are helpless and hopeless in ourselves.

Thine is the glory, O God, and such are the wonders of thy grace, whereby thou gettest glory to thyself in the salvation of those that were lost.

Therefore, though we are exceeding guilty, and utterly unworthy; yet we pray and hope, that thou wilt glorify thy mercy, remembering us in our low estate, and relieving us in all our wants and straits. We would forsake every other refuge, to come to thee: our expectation is from thee; and our whole dependence is placed on thee alone. In thy gracious goodness do we trust through the merits and mediation of our blessed Redeemer; looking for the mercy of our Lord Jesus Christ unto eternal life.

And to thee, O great and glorious Lord God, whose kingdom ruleth over all; to thee who dost whatever thou pleasest in heaven and in earth; to thee who showest forth all thy glory to the blessed saints and angels in thy presence; to thee be glory in the highest, and all thanks and praise ascribed, by us, and by all the world, for ever and ever. *Amen.*

A SOLILOQUY

FOR THE PIOUS SOUL'S SOLACE, BY WAY OF PARAPHRASE ON THE CREED.

Let not your heart be troubled, (saith the Lord of love, our dear compassionate Redeemer:) ye believe in God, believe also in me; (the messenger of his love, sent to be the Saviour of the world.)

Why art thou cast down then, O my soul! and why art thou disquieted within me! when

I BELIEVE IN GOD,

And am not exposed (as one forlorn) to shift for myself, and to make me a happiness out of my own stock; but I have a God to repair unto, and depend upon; and to expect all that ever I can desire from him. And this God is

THE FATHER,

Not only of our Lord Jesus Christ, by eternal generation, but my Father, by a late creation, which has brought me out of nothing to what I am; not only to being, and life, and sense, but to the use of reason, and to the enjoyment of all that ever I have in the world. Yea, I am bold to father myself upon him also by a spiritual adoption; and am persuaded that a woman may sooner forget her sucking child, than the Lord will forsake that work of his hands, which he has new created in Christ Jesus: nor is he less able than willing to do me good, being

ALMIGHTY

And what is too hard for Omnipotence? or who can pluck me out of his hands, to whom the very powers of hell are but weakness? though I am weak as a shaken reed myself, yet my help stands in the name of the Lord, who is the

MAKER OF HEAVEN AND EARTH,

And what can any of his creatures do against me, when God himself is for me? he that made all, will he see his child want a competency in the world? or should I be turned out of the earth, yet all heaven is the Lord's. And when he is my portion, I am sure of that which is infinitely better than all the world's good; the whole sum of which is but a poor drop from the eternal fountain of all goodness. And what can be better than him that made it, and gave it all that goodness which it has? Myself, and whatever I see in the world, was once nothing. And the great Lord, who was most blessed before all worlds, and would have been nevertheless blessed, though we had never been at all; he has brought us into being; not for any need he had of us, but to communicate of his goodness to us,

IN JESUS CHRIST,

And what so sweet as Jesus in my mouth! no such

A SOLILOQUY UPON THE CREED.

music in my ears; no such gladness in my heart. I was lost, and Jesus is my Saviour. I was dead, and Jesus is my life. I was an enemy, and Jesus is my peace. Still I sin, and Jesus is my advocate with the Father. Christ is my prophet to direct me; my priest to atone for me; my king to defend me, and to watch over me for good. He is all that I want, and all that I can wish. I am worse than nothing without him : but I have all things given me together with him, who is the beloved of the Father,

HIS ONLY SON,

The only one, by nature, that is co-equal with the Father: and, having such a friend in the court of heaven, I will come boldly to the throne of grace. For if the Son make us free, we shall be free indeed. The Father will deny us nothing, that we ask in his name. And the Son himself upbraids us that we make no more use of this our blessed privilege. Hitherto ye have asked nothing in my name (saith he:) ask and ye shall receive, that your joy may be full. Such pleasure has he in the prosperity of his servants, who is

OUR LORD,

Our heavenly Sovereign; at whose feet kings do cast their crowns; and all the angels of God worship him. O happy the servants that have such a Lord ! and blessed be the Lord, that will admit me among the number of his servants ! Is not he my Lord, that has bought me? In one sacrament I was enlisted into his service: and in the other, how often have I sworn allegiance to him! This is the crown of all my glorying, that Jesus is my Lord;

WHO WAS CONCEIVED BY THE HOLY GHOST,

In a miraculous manner, above all the power of nature; and without any the least spot of sin; that he might be a suitable propitiation for our sins. He is fairer than the children of men, who are (all of them) shapen in iniquity, and conceived in sin. But he is free from every blemish, and altogether lovely; being

BORN OF THE VIRGIN MARY;

And so he has done the highest honour to our poor nature, by uniting it to the divine: taking part of our flesh and blood, that he might not only be touched with the feeling of our infirmities, but also taste death for our offences: coming down to earth, to raise us up to heaven; and manifested in our flesh, to bring salvation home to our very doors. O how can I ever now be at a loss, when the Lord, in whom lies our help, is become God with us; and, to embolden our addresses to him, has vouchsafed even to set up his dwelling among us? May all the glory of salvation be to thee, O Lord, who hast brought such glorious salvation to a ruined world.

HE SUFFERED UNDER PONTIUS PILATE:

And, having no need at all to suffer for any sins of his own, he was wounded for our transgressions, and bruised for our iniquities. O wicked wretch! that I should be one of those, who put the Son of God himself upon suffering! But, O how happy is it for me, that he was pleased to suffer once, to save me from suffering for ever!

HE WAS CRUCIFIED:

Love, that was strong as death, fastened my Saviour to the accursed tree, with his arms extended to receive me: and his side was opened to make me a passage to his very heart. O my dearest Lord! forbid it that I should glory, save in thy cross. On that let me rest my weary soul: to that let me cling, though menaced by all the powers of hell: and by that let me ultimately rise to thine everlasting glory in heaven. He was

DEAD:

Not only Abraham, the friend of God, gave up the ghost; but he that was before Abraham, our blessed Saviour himself, the well-beloved Son of God, when he took upon him the seed of Abraham, was not excused from dying. Shall I then conclude, that my God has no kindness for me, because I must follow such forerunners, and go the way of all flesh? No, though he slay me, yet will I trust in him; and have hope even in my death. For the death of Christ is my life, since he has taken out the sting of death temporal, and made it the very entrance to life eternal. He has led us the way, through that gloomy vale, to the glorious region of immortality. And shall death separate me from my Saviour, or divorce my soul from the heavenly bridegroom? No, I depart hence, that I may be with Christ, and that I may get nearer to him whom my soul loveth. He is gone before; and, Lord, I will follow thee whithersoever thou goest. Thou wast laid in the grave,

AND BURIED,

To make that desolate place inviting by thy presence; to perfume the chambers of death, and turn the horrible pit into a happy cemetery, where the poor, weak, perishing flesh is sown, to come up again, powerful, glorious, and incorruptible. And shall I shrink from the bed, where my Lord himself lay? Would I lie better than he did? No, the grave itself is become a goodly lodging since Christ was there. And I will not go down in sorrow to my grave, seeing that I am going but to sleep with Jesus, the life of my soul, and the source of all my joy.

HE DESCENDED INTO HELL;

Three days he continued in the state of the dead, that none might question the truth of his death, upon which depends all our hope of pardon and life; that I might not dread the parting of soul and body, which befell my Lord himself; and that none belonging to him might be out of heart, even at the lowest ebb, when our Redeemer himself lay so long under the power of death.

THE THIRD DAY HE ROSE AGAIN FROM THE DEAD.

And shall I be in bondage all my life, through fear of death, when under the conduct of such a victorious Captain of salvation, who has triumphed over all the powers of the grave? No, he liveth and was dead. And though I know I must die, yet I know that my Redeemer liveth, and is alive for evermore: and because he lives, I shall live also: for he has no life, but what every member of his shall share in. Now therefore, O death, I can triumph over thee, since my Lord has routed all thy forces. It is true, thou yet canst kill me; but thou canst not hurt me. For, when thou takest down this crazy cottage, a better fabric shall succeed, to stand for eternal ages. But could not all the bonds of death hold my Almighty Saviour? Dearest Lord! thou wast arrested for our debt; and laid up in the prison of the grave on our account. But thy release gives me a cheerful assurance, that thou hast satisfied divine justice to the uttermost. Since thou art come so gloriously forth, I am sure that all is discharged. Then blessed be the God and Father of our Lord Jesus Christ, who, according to his abundant mercy, has begotten us again to a lively hope, by the resurrection of Jesus Christ from the dead.

HE ASCENDED INTO HEAVEN,

And O with what joyful acclamations was he welcomed home into those high regions of the blessed after all his wondrous achievements, to effect eternal redemption for us! He led captivity captive, and dragged the infernal powers after his triumphant chariot; to show that hell, as well as death, is subject unto him. And now he has cleared us a way to glory, and opened the kingdom of heaven to all believers; being gone to prepare a place for us, that where he is, there we may be also. Even where

HE SITTETH AT THE RIGHT HAND OF GOD THE FATHER ALMIGHTY.

Far above all principalities and powers, a glorious King for evermore, with all power and authority in his hands, and all the crowns and mansions of glory at his disposal. He is not only the Prince of the kings of the earth, by whom they all do reign; but all the angels in heaven fly to do his pleasure. In heaven he has cast off the veil, under which he once concealed the brightness of his majesty: and now he shows himself in all the splendour of the King of glory. To him I look as the great author and finisher of our faith; and the blessed object of my daily worship and devotion; who, in all the height of his glory, does not forget his poor servants here; but has still bowels of compassion to intercede for us, as well as fulness of power to prevail on our behalf. And God forbid that I should forget this absent friend: or be unmindful of all that he has done and suffered for me. O where should be my heart, but with the great lover and beloved of my soul; who not only humbled himself on earth, but even now in heaven so humbles himself, as to remember me in my low estate. And when I am in a strait, so that I know not what to do, I will commit the matter into his hands, and cast my care on him who careth for me. For, what enemies have I, which he cannot speedily make his footstool? Or what blessing is so great, but he can, in a moment, obtain it for me? Whenever then I am afraid or troubled, I will look unto Jesus, sitting at the right hand of God: I will remember him as my all-prevailing Advocate and Intercessor; and will intreat his gracious favour, who is ever worthy to be heard for me, though I am most unworthy to speak for myself.

FROM THENCE HE SHALL COME TO JUDGE THE QUICK AND THE DEAD,

And shall appear in greater power and glory than ever he was seen here in weakness and poverty. Then shall his stubborn enemies, who would not that he should reign over them, be brought forth, and slain before him. Then too shall all his sheep, that heard his voice, and followed him, and waited for his coming, and loved his appearing, hold up their head with joy, and receive their complete redemption. That day, so replete with horror to the ungodly, will be to them a day of discharge, and jubilee, and coronation; the sweetest and most joyful day they ever saw. Then shall I behold him seated on his throne, who once, for my sake, died upon the cross. My Advocate, my Life, my Saviour, will be alone exalted in that day. And will my Advocate accuse me? Will my Life destroy me? Will my Saviour condemn me? No, though my iniquities have been great, and my best actions very imperfect, yet, assured that he who is my Judge has made satisfaction for my sins, and procured acceptance for my poor imperfect services, I will pray, Come, Lord Jesus, come quickly.

I BELIEVE IN THE HOLY GHOST,

The Lord and Giver of life, the heavenly Counsellor and Comforter of our souls, by whom I call Jesus Lord, and cry, Abba, Father, unto my God. And having such a blessed Guardian, and divine Inhabitant; why do I drag on heavily, as if I were left comfortless? Why do I not overflow with joy in the Holy Ghost? Am I weak? he is the power of the Most High, to help my infirmities. Am I forgetful? he is the kind Monitor, to bring all things to my remembrance. Am I afraid lest I should fail of God's acceptance and salvation? this blessed Spirit witnesseth with my spirit, that I am a child of God; and seals me to the day of redemption. Away then, thou foul accuser of the brethren! Peace, thou clamorous conscience! and stand aside, all ye pitiful creature-comforts! I have affiance in the Holy Ghost, the Comforter. For I belong to

THE HOLY CATHOLIC CHURCH,

I am a member of that most blessed society, some of which (already entered into the joy of their Lord) have got possession of their crowns, and are passed from their warfare to everlasting triumph. And the rest here (yet on our pilgrimage and warfare) are reaching forth to the glorious prize of the high calling of God in Christ Jesus. The lines are fallen to me in pleasant places, where the Sun of Righteousness is risen upon us, and causes the heavenly day-spring from on high to shine upon us; even in that church, against which the gates of hell shall not prevail. I believe

THE COMMUNION OF SAINTS,

The same life and spirit pervades the multitude of believers everywhere; and like so many rivulets, they run all to the same sea, though not in the same channel. Or like divers strings of a musical instrument, though they have several notes, yet they make up one song of praise and glory to their common Lord; from whom they receive influence, as all the bodily parts do from the head; and are knit together as fellow-members of Christ's body. They are the household of faith; of that corporation and family of heaven, for the sake of which they forget their own people, and their father's house. Yea, as all the parts of the body (how mean soever) share in the same life as is in the head and heart; and the noblest members despise not the vilest; but the lowest are of use to the highest; and all conspire for the joint interest of the whole : so I, as a part of this great body, (whilst I wander not by myself, but keep to the flock of Christ, and join with them in the worship and service of my Lord, and love them in my heart,) am one of their happy number, and do share in the prayers of every faithful Christian throughout the world. And communicating now with the saints in all offices of love, I shall be advanced, with them, to the possession of their heavenly inheritance in eternal life.

THE FORGIVENESS OF SINS.

This is the article that strikes at the very root of bitterness, and removes the ground of all my fears and griefs. O how numerous are my sins! and what a heavy load upon my soul! But it lightens my heart to hear of God manifested in the flesh; to undergo all the penalties of sin, in the very nature that sinned: to bear our sins in his own body on the tree. And when our all-sufficient Surety has finished the atonement, will the justice of God require a second payment? No, God is not only merciful, but just also, in justifying the believers in Jesus; who was made sin for us who knew no sin; that we might be made the righteousness of God in him. And now all the frightful guilt is swallowed up in that fountain opened for sin and uncleanness, as a drop of ink is lost in a mighty river; so that my spirit rejoices in God my Saviour: and I thank God through Jesus Christ our Lord, whose blood cleanses us from all our sin. O that I could love him yet more, who forgiveth me so much.

THE RESURRECTION OF THE BODY.

This is the Christian's stronghold, that although we fall into the grave, we shall not be utterly cast down; but have a Lord, that will be the plague of death, and the destruction of the grave; to redeem us out of the hands of both. My flesh is perishing as the grass that is green and withered in a day. But this mortal shall put on immortality; yea, mortality itself shall be swallowed up of life. This heavy log, though sown a natural, shall rise a spiritual body, swifter than the light, to follow the Lamb whithersoever he goes. Even this vile body shall (in the great morning of the resurrection) come gloriously forth, as a bridegroom out of his chamber; and, (like the trees new apparelled in the spring,) shall be more orient and beautiful of itself, than all the robes and jewels in the world can now make it: it shall shine as the stars in the firmament, yea, above the brightness of the meridian sun. Is then my body now reduced to hardships? be it so: I do not expect my rest in this world; but I look for it in the world to come. In the mean time, I must not think it strange to be tossed on tempestuous waves, till I arrive at the haven, where I would be. Am I tempted to excesses, or any lusts of the flesh? I will not surfeit on the meat that perishes; nor sink the vessel that is carrying me over to the land of promise. I do not so hate thee, my own flesh; but desire thee to keep thy appetite for entertainments infinitely better; seeing that I believe the resurrection of the body,

AND THE LIFE EVERLASTING, AMEN.

This is the centre of our desires, and the crown of our joys; the drift of our whole religion; and the height of all perfection. That which eases all our labours, and makes our heaviest troubles to be of little or no account. Wretched relief is the heathen's antidote against the dread of death; only to think that die we must. But Christians have a consolation strong indeed; that, after death, we shall live for ever. Our present lives are (for the most part) spent in providing a support for the body. And, though God has graciously made it pleasant to repair the decays of our nature, yet he would not have us mistake that poor pleasure for our heaven: the soul that knows itself, is rather weary of this attendance on the corruptible flesh; and aspires after that state, where the body shall feel no weariness, and suffer no decays; where shall be nothing vexatious or troublesome; nothing to hinder or abate the perfection of our bliss. Every faculty of the soul shall there imbibe that fulness of satisfaction which so long it had sought, but never found before. And neither shall the body want an agreeable entertainment for its feast and solace. But it is not for a human tongue to utter, what

A SOLILOQUY UPON THE CREED.

no eye has ever seen, nor ear has ever heard. It is enough to know, that the blessedness of heaven is above our knowledge; being a life sweetened with goodness no less than divine, and measured with a duration no shorter than eternity.

All this I believe. And more than all this I believe, in believing the life everlasting. My life is hid with Christ in God: and the life which I now live, I live by the faith of the Son of God, who loved me, and gave himself for me. And when Christ, who is our life, shall appear, then shall I also appear with him in glory. O let me now begin the life of heaven; and hereafter I shall never know its end. While I am here alive, may I so die to the flesh, and to the world, that when I depart from hence, I may live to God with Christ; which is the life incomparably best of all. *Amen, Amen.*

THE END.

www.ingramcontent.com/pod-product-compliance
Lightning Source LLC
Chambersburg PA
CBHW031417230426
43668CB00007B/342